T5-BPY-435

Political Development in Micronesia

Political Development in Micronesia

Edited by
Daniel T. Hughes
and
Sherwood G. Lingenfelter

Ohio State University Press
Columbus

Library of Congress Cataloging in Publication Data

Hughes, Daniel T
Political development in Micronesia

Bibliography: p.
1. Pacific Islands (Ter.)—Politics and government.
2. Micronesia—Social conditions. I. Lingenfelter, Sherwood G., joint author. II. Title.
JQ6451.A2H83 320.9'96'5 74-8161
ISBN 0-8142-0197-0

Manufactured in the United States of America

Contents

Illustrations

Political Development in Micronesia

1

General Introduction

The phenomenon of political change, though not new in the history of mankind, has assumed a fundamentally different nature in the nineteenth and twentieth centuries. David Easton (1959) has observed that before this time the vast majority of political changes were in the composition of the government with its leaders and administrative organization. With the advent of colonialism, however, the colonizers began to alter the basic rules by which power was organized and distributed among the colonized. These latter changes were much more fundamental in nature and had profound effects on other aspects of the colonized societies. This type of planned political change, often called "political development," is the subject of this book.

Political development is a concept that provokes many meanings and emotions among those who hear and use it. To the colonial administrator, development is a positive, "progressive" program for change. Such change is directed toward filling a perceived power vacuum, revitalizing a shattered sociopolitical system, or reorganizing to meet newly introduced needs and goals. To the indigenous people subject to development, such changes rarely provoke the positive aura and optimism found in their rulers. Frequently such changes are seen as the redistribution of power. Authority is taken from those who have it and given to those who will serve the ends of the developers. Such redistribution is obviously advantageous to some members of the society and disadvantageous to others, but the critical issue for indigenous people is the confusion in the distribution of authority and the rules for obtaining decision and action within the political field.

Among those who study politics, government, and political change, the concept of development stirs similar conflicts and emotions. Some political theorists not only have proposed certain directions for "development" change but have become actively engaged as agents of colonial governments working to bring about such changes in the administered societies. Others vigorously oppose the whole idea of development, arguing that such programs are culture "tinkering" at its worst, and see nothing but ill for the subjects of the programs. Development is seen as a phenomenon to be fought at every turn because its end result is the ultimate destruction of the traditional societies being changed. The contributors to this volume fall somewhere on a continuum between these two poles. Some express deep concern over the destructive nature of planned change in Micronesia. Others propose directions that planned change might take, and some explore the resilience and adaptability of the traditional societies as they adjust to the demands of over one hundred years of colonial rule. All of them, regardless of position, have done extensive investigation on "developmental" programs and policies of the past, and, from these critical evaluations, have drawn their own conclusions with regard to future political change in Micronesia.

The objective of this volume is not to present position papers for or against political change, but rather to investigate "political development" as a phenomenon of planned, directed political change in traditional societies, with particular reference to the U.S. Trust Territory of the Pacific Islands. Whether such planned change is "progressive," "regressive," "beneficial," or "destructive" is certainly a critical question, but one that defies simple analysis or solution. The goals of this work are to explore the complex interaction of colonial government, agents and policies, and the traditional sociopolitical structure, elites, and values making up the situation of change, and to identify areas of conflict, noncommunication, failure, and success that are part of the process of cultural adaptation and change.

It is our ultimate hope that our research will contribute to a greater understanding of the processes of political change and to the consequences of such change. By this critical look at the benefits, pitfalls, and problems of "development," we hope this work will be of use both to administrators and administered as they work to plan the political future of Micronesia.

Since the end of World War II, the United States has administered, under the auspices of the United Nations, the Trust Territory of the Pacific Islands (Micronesia).[1] This territory includes the Carolines, the Marshalls, and the Mariana Islands (exclusive of Guam). During the past twenty-seven years, the United States administration has introduced into Micronesia a democratic political system that in many ways parallels our own political system and that is quite unlike any of the traditional political systems of the area and also quite different from the system introduced by any of the preceding colonial powers.

From the very beginning, the U.S. administration of Micronesia as a U.N. Trust Territory was intended to be a temporary arrangement. In the last few years, both U.N. Visiting Missions and Micronesian leaders have pressed for a change in the political status of the Territory. In October 1969, a delegation of Micronesian congressmen met in Washington with members of the U.S. Congress and the Departments of Interior, State, and Defense to begin negotiations concerning the future political status of Micronesia. The talks reached a stalemate, with U.S. representatives proposing a permanent commonwealth status and the Micronesian delegation countering with a proposal of either "free association" or independence. Free association would be a looser partnership than commonwealth status. It could be terminated by either side, and it would give the Micronesian government greater control over Micronesian land.

Negotiations were resumed on Saipan in May 1970, and then continued in Hawaii in October 1971 and on Palau in April 1972. In Washington during the fifth round of negotiations in July 1972, the two sides drew up a preliminary draft for a free-association compact containing those terms thus far agreed upon. According to the terms: (1) the people of Micronesia would write their own constitution; (2) the Micronesian government would have authority over all internal affairs in Micronesia and the U.S. government would have responsibility for foreign affairs and defense of Micronesia; and (3) the United States would have the right to maintain military bases in certain specified areas in the Marshall Islands and the Palau Islands but would have to negotiate with the government of Micronesia if in the future it should wish to use additional land for military bases. Other terms of the compact were to be negotiated at future meetings, including termination procedures of the compact.

In August 1972, the Congress of Micronesia met in special session on Ponape to consider the preliminary draft of the free-association compact. The Congress refused to endorse the draft, but directed its negotiating team to begin negotiating for possible independence while still continuing to negotiate for free association. The following month at the sixth round of negotiations in Hawaii, the U.S. negotiating team asked for a "pause" in the negotiations so that they could consult with their own government and with the U..S Congress to determine what the U.S. position would be concerning possible Micronesian independence.

As this introduction is being written, the future of the negotiations and the future political status of Micronesia are uncertain. It does seem clear, however, that Micronesia's status as a United Nations Trusteeship will soon end and a new era of political change will begin. At this particular point in time, when Micronesia is moving toward a new stage of political development, it is most appropriate to review the political change that has taken place in Micronesia under the American and other colonial administrations and to see what effects this change has had upon the lives of the Micronesians.

The major significance of this book is that it brings together the work of twelve anthropologists and political scientists who have studied various problems associated with the introduction of a new political system in the same general culture area, Micronesia.

The chapters that follow originated at two symposia on political development in Micronesia held at the New York meetings of the American Anthropological Association in November 1971 and at the Seattle meetings of the Association for Social Anthropology of Oceania (ASAO) in March 1972. A group of cultural anthropologists and political scientists who have all worked in Micronesia at various times since World War II gathered together to discuss this topic in the light of their own studies and experiences. Comparing the findings of these various studies at the two symposia proved a stimulating and profitable experience for the participants. We hope this book will illustrate the values of cross-disciplinary analysis within a general culture area.

Despite the acknowledged value of comparing findings from separate individual studies, there are obvious limitations to such an approach. Even though all the studies reported in the contributing chapters focused on political development in Micronesia, many of them employed different analytical frameworks, different methods of operationalizing research problems, different sampling techniques, and different amounts of quantification. Results from such varied studies are comparable, but only on a very general level of analysis.

To improve the quality of comparative analysis of political development in Micronesia, greater uniformity is required among research projects. The ASAO newsletter and annual conferences have already helped toward this goal by facilitating communication among interested professionals and increasing consultation on proposed research projects. But we believe that further initiatives are still required. Research in Micronesia has reached a stage where team studies are necessary to yield the type of data required for more specific comparisons. We strongly advocate research projects on political development in Micronesia in which specialists of several disciplines determine significant research problems, formulate an applicable analytical framework, and draw up a research design designating the same variables to be investigated and the same methodology to be applied to individual studies in various parts of Micronesia. If such studies are carried out simultaneously or at least in the space of a few years, the resulting data will be such as to greatly facilitate comparative analysis of political development.

Traditional Political Systems

Before proceeding to the reports of our contributing authors, it will be helpful to review briefly the traditional political systems of Micronesia and also the major changes made by the various colonial administrations in that area.[2]

The traditional political systems of Micronesia are so varied that very few generalizations are valid for all of the societies there. Two elements that do seem important in all systems are lineage membership and the control of land. The very name "Micronesia" ("the tiny islands") indicates the limited quantity and therefore the valuable nature of land in these societies. Land is usually owned by an extended kinship group, frequently a lineage. Birth in a particular lineage determines an individual's social, economic, and political position within his society. But what is actually determined is generally the limits within which an individual can maneuver for power. Thus, there is a good deal of flexibility and competition within most Micronesian societies despite the ascriptive nature of leadership.

Other important traits found throughout Micronesia are ranking and stratification, although they are much less developed in some societies than in others. On Ponape, Yap, Palau, and other island groups where ranking and stratification are highly developed, some dyadic principle divides and balances authority on all levels of the sociopolitical system.

Marianas

When the Spanish took control of the Marianas, they were determined to Christianize the native Chamorro population. In part because of the bloody wars that followed and in part because of introduced diseases and several devastating typhoons, the Chamorro population shrank from an estimated 50,000 to 4,000 in the last thirty years of the seventeenth century. Today there are about 10,000 "Chamorros" living in the Marianas (excluding Guam), but many of them are part Spanish, Filipino, American, or Japanese. The colonization of the Marianas has so devastated and transformed the precontact society there that our knowledge of traditional Chamorro culture is quite limited.

Before the arrival of the Spanish, the Chamorros lived mostly along the coasts in villages of as many as 600 people. Households consisted of extended families. The extended family was part of a lineage, which itself was a unit of a matrilineal clan. The lineage functioned as a kind of corporation in which the lineage members shared.

The whole society was divided into three classes: the *matua* 'nobles', the *atchoat* 'high-ranking commoners', and the *mangatchang* 'low-ranking commoners'. Rank and class were associated with land ownership and clan membership. The nobles and high-ranking commoners owned the land, and the low-ranking commoners worked the land belonging to the other classes. The nobles controlled the economy of the islands, and prestigious specialists such as canoe-builders, navigators, and warriors were drawn from their ranks.

The islands were not united under a single rule. Rather, there were a number of autonomous districts, each ruled by a *maga* 'paramount chief' who had ultimate control over most of the district land. The paramount chief was probably the leader of the strongest or highest-ranking clan of the district. Fighting took place among the districts, and the relative status of the districts probably changed at times as a result of this warfare (Alkire 1972:10–14).

Palau

The Palau Islands span 100 miles from northeast to southwest along the westernmost border of Micronesia. In contrast to the Marianas, the Spanish exercised only nominal control over Palau and the rest of Micronesia. Consequently, far more of the traditional systems have endured in this area.

In the traditional Palauan sociopolitical system, there were two major confederations vying for power. Both confederations were highly stratified into strictly ranked districts, villages, clans, and lineages. The hallmark of this system was competition for higher positions within the constantly shifting ranking of the individual segments at every level of the system. This competition involved manipulation of kinship ties, land ownership, and native goods—especially bead money.

Even today, competition in Palau is ordinarily a group endeavor involving members of a lineage, clan, or village. However, the indivividual is not submerged by the group. Though Palauans stress maternal kinship ties, paternal ties are also acknowledged as important. A child can elect to join his father's matrilineage rather than his mother's. Thus competition between the paternal and maternal relations for the allegiance of a person encourages individual flexibility.

Stability and continuity in this highly competitive society is provided by the dualistic organization in force at every level of the system. Every level is divided into two counterbalancing groups. A lineage, clan, or village is never in competition with all other parallel units, but only with those within its own group or division. Consequently, when any lineage, clan, or village shifts its rank, the larger unit of clan, village, or district continues to be ruled as before. On the village level, for example, the ruling body is a council composed of the heads of all village clans. The clans of the village are always divided into two alliances, and each clan competes for relative position within its own alliance. When a clan does change position, it affects only the relative position of the other clans in its own division and does not alter the structure of the council itself.

In Palauan society, members of the two highest-ranking lineages of each village formed the *meteet* 'elite', and members of the remaining clan were *chebuuch* 'commoners'. There is a further stratification among the elite, the elite of the capital village of a district outranking those of the outlying villages. The elite of these capital villages are respected in all districts.

Yap

Although Yapese society, like other societies in Micronesia, has been modified by extensive foreign contact and domination, Yap seems to have retained more elements of its traditional system than the other regions of Micronesia. All political authority in the traditional culture of Yap is vested in land estates that serve as household sites and provide headquarters and resources for small patriclans (following Murdock 1949). Leadership within the clan is exercised by the oldest male member, who "speaks for the land."

People of a village share land resources divided among the various clan-estates. The clan-estates confer upon their members titles or responsibilities, or both, for the organization and functioning of villages. Within each village, three important statuses divide the authority and powers of leadership. The *pilung ni pilbithir* 'sitting-chief' speaks for the ritual and sacred places in the village; the *pilung ko binaw* 'talking-chief' speaks for the land and its care, protection, and development; and the *pilung ko pagel* 'walking-chief' speaks for the young men and acts as executive officer for the council of chiefs. Each village is divided into two or more ranked sections, and the sections are divided into several subsections. Other titled clan-estates distribute administrative authority and responsibility within the subdivision of the village.

Decision-making and government within the village is a function of a council of the heads of titled estates. All important issues must be brought before the council for their consideration. Decisions are made by consensus of the group, and matters are discussed until consensus is reached. Decisions made outside the council are frequently denied support, and in some cases punitive action is taken against the leader.

The village furnishes the basic political unit in regional and Yap-wide politics. Villages are linked into two major alliances called *banpilung* 'side-of-chiefs' and *banpagael* 'side-of-young-men.' Within each alliance, villages are ranked into regional hierarchies of leaders and followers, supplying channels of communication and support for any member of the alliance. The lowest-ranking villagers are grouped into a "caste" of landless serfs who supply men and labor for alliance leaders. The ranking system is as follows:

Yapese Ranks		*English Equivalents*	
1. Bulce'	2. Ulun	Chiefs	High "caste"
3. Methaban	4. Tethaban	Nobility	
5. Daworcig		Commoner	
6. Milngay ni arow		Chief's servants	Low "caste"
7. Pimilngay		General serfs	
8. Yagug, Milngay ni Kan, etc.		General serfs	

Leadership for the two alliances emanates from three paramount centers in Gagil, Tamil, and Rull. Each center includes a paramount sitting-chief and two villages representing each of the two alliances. Each village has its council of chiefs, with one member as its spokesman. The talking-chiefs of both villages and the paramount sitting-chief provide a triad of leadership. Although each center has representation in both alliances, Gagil is recognized as leader of one and Rull leader of the other. The third center at Tamil acts in the role of the village sitting-chief, supplying a third force to balance the power between "chiefs" and "young men." These themes of dual opposition and triadic resolution appear throughout Yapese political thought. Yapese describe Yap as a pot sitting upon three supports, and if one of those supports falls, the whole system collapses.

The traditional political system, then, emphasized balanced power vested in clan-estates and villages. In the past, individual leaders occupying leadership statuses engaged in intense competition and rivalry for prestige and rank for themselves and their village within the alliance system. Warfare provided the dynamic for the system, furnishing mobility in rank and means of redress for betrayal or withdrawal of support. The *mitmit* 'ceremonial gift exchanges' recognized publicly the rank and relationships of villages. Rival leaders attempted to increase their prestige and rank by outgiving their opponents. Among the important items of exchange were the famous stone disks or "stone money" quarried in Palau and brought to Yap. Because any presentation of such a gift called for a return of an equally valuable item at some future date, these exchanges became self-perpetuating. In summary, competition, status rivalry, opposition, and a triadic balance of power constitute the basic themes in Yapese political thought.

Truk

The islands of the Truk lagoon and the atolls stretching from Yap to Truk (the central atolls of Micronesia) have far less stratification than many other Micronesian societies, such as Palau, Yap, and Ponape. Rank is important here as elsewhere in Micronesia, but social stratification into separate classes is not highly developed.

On Truk, the general postmarital residential pattern is matrilocal. The resulting lineage constitutes a landholding and work group, which is the basic unit of Trukese society. After marriage, a man assumes obligations of labor toward his wife's lineage, while still being obligated to perform similar tasks for his own (his mother's)

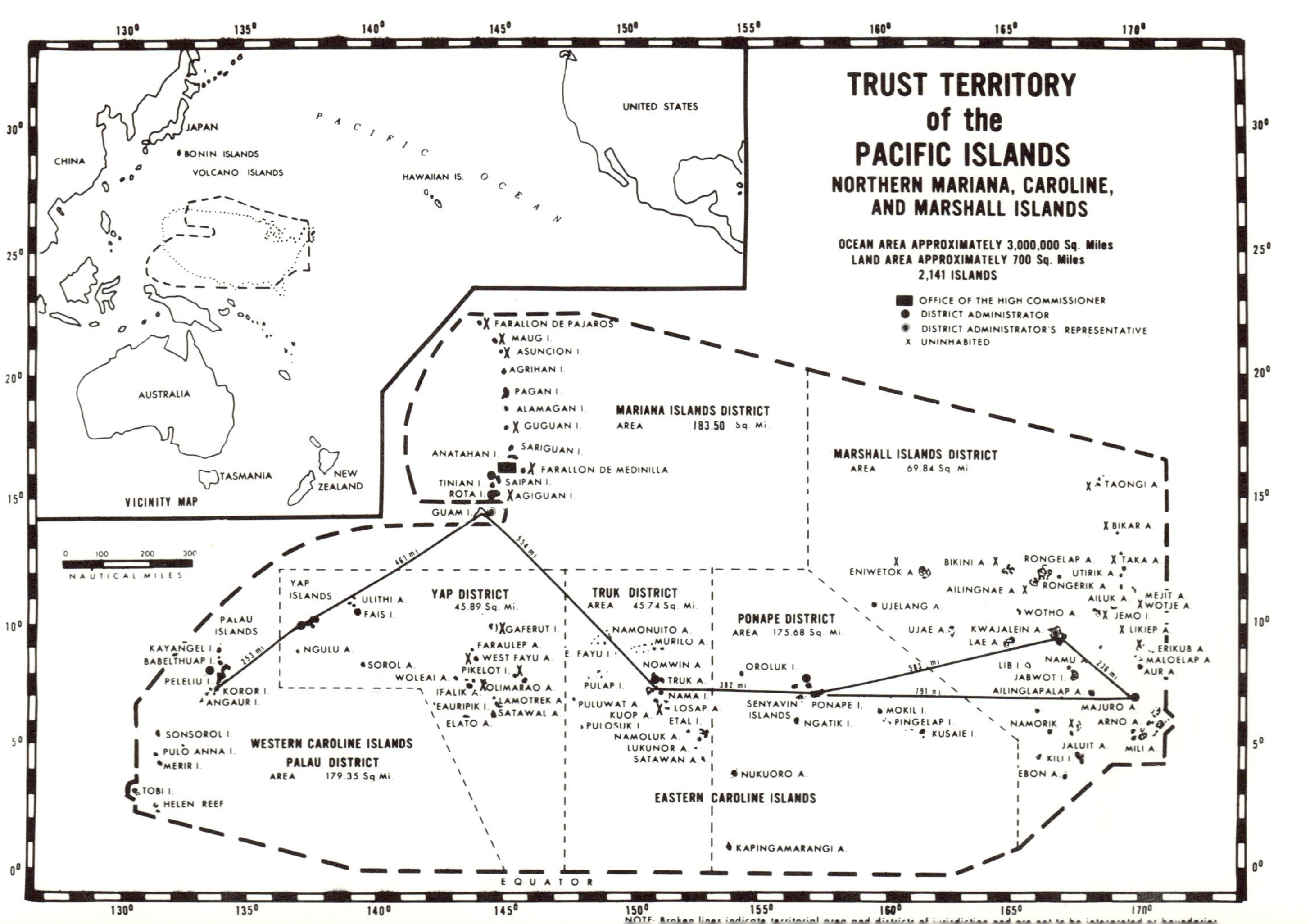

NOTE: Broken lines indicate territorial area and districts of jurisdiction and are not to be interpreted as boundaries

lineage. Pressure from such competing and sometimes conflicting obligations may be partly the cause of the relative instability and impermanence of Trukese marriage that some authors have noted (Alkire 1972:29).

Trukese villages consisting of one or more lineages are grouped into relatively independent districts. In precontact times, as many as eighteen districts were found on one island in the Truk lagoon. The district chief was the leader of the senior lineage of the district. The rank of a lineage of a district was related to time of settlement in the district, size of landholdings, and number of lineage members (Alkire 1972:31).

Traditionally there were two loosely knit confederations of districts in the Truk lagoon, one centered on Moen Island and the other on Fefen Island. The island of Wuman remained unallied with either confederation and constituted a third division in the lagoon. Other districts shifted allegiance back and forth between the Moen Island and the Fefen Island confederations. Thus, neither confederation was ever able to gain control of the whole lagoon, and at the time of first European contact, the highest political organization with any degree of stability and permanence was the district.

Central Caroline Atolls

The sociopolitical systems of the Central atolls are similar to that of the Truk islands, but adapted to limitations in the size of the communities and the availability of resources in the atoll environment. All clans are ranked in these atolls, the chiefs coming only from the highest clan. The same clan, however, can be ranked differently from one island to another.

Most islands comprise two or three districts, the leader of the ranking lineage of each district acting as the chief of the district. Sometimes there is also a paramount chief over the whole island. In any case, chiefs generally make joint decisions, frequently in consultation with the heads of other lineages. The chief's authority is not extensive, but he may organize district activities such as fishing expeditions. The chief also receives some first fruit offerings, although he does not hold the right of eminent domain over the land as is true in some other parts of Micronesia.

Traditionally, the central atolls were all part of an extended Yap-centered empire. Most of these islands acknowledged a dependent relation to two villages in Yap, and once a year they sent an expedition bringing tribute to their Yapese chiefs. Alkire (1965) has shown how this alliance with Yap and the exchange system accompanying it served as a guarantee of assistance in times of devastation from typhoons and other disasters. The formal tribute expeditions were prohibited by the Japanese, who in turn assumed responsibilities for typhoon assistance. Individual Carolinians, however, still maintain a profitable "tribute-trade" relationship with their Yapese overlords. Further, the interisland structure of the empire, with Ulithi at its head, supplies the framework for modern political activity.

Ponape

The traditional political system of Ponape is centered on five autonomous *wehi* 'states' or 'chiefdoms', each governed by a *nahnmwareki* 'paramount chief' and a *nahniken* 'minister'. The paramount chief is the primary ruler, and the minister is his chief adviser. In each state, a graded line of titleholders extends below both rulers, the first twelve in both lines constituting a privileged noble class. Those with lesser titles comprise the commoners.

Traditionally, the paramount chief and the minister owned all the land in the state. Commoners and nobles alike held their farmsteads on a feudal basis as tenants of the paramount chiefs. This ownership of the land was the basis for the chiefs' right to a constant flow of tribute in the form of feasts and first fruit offerings. Besides the land, another strong tie linked the people to the paramount chiefs: only they could confer the coveted "state titles" that were so important in the prestige system of the island. In addition to the noble titles, many other titles of varying prestige were distributed in every state.

Whenever a vacancy arose in any of the twelve positions in either of the noble lines, each person with a lower title in that line was supposed to move up one step. Ideally, all the high titleholders of a state would be members of the two ruling sub-clans, and each one's position in the order of titles would coincide with his seniority in the sub-clan. Because Ponape is a matrilineal society, a man was a member of his mother's clan and sub-clan. His position within that sub-clan depended upon his order of birth. If his mother's sub-clan was the ruling sub-clan of the kingdom, he would be in line for the noble titles. In practice, many factors influenced political advancement, and a noble's career was more often characterized by a number of jumps past other titleholders rather than by an orderly progression step by step up the scale.

The Ponapean states are divided into a number of geographical areas known as *kousapw* 'sections', each of which is ruled by a *kaun en kousapw* 'section chief'. This man holds the first in a series of section titles and in this resembles the paramount chief. There is also a second line of section titles, but its head has no authority in the section comparable to that of the minister in the kingdom. The section itself is subdivided into farmsteads, generally clusters of two or three houses whose inhabitants work the surrounding landholdings.

Traditionally, the section chief was ordinarily the head of the ranking sub-clan or matrilineage within the section. Upon the death of the section chief, the normal procedure was for his title as section chief and the land of the section to be passed on to the next ranking male in the matrilineage. In theory, the paramount chiefs could ignore the norm of matrilineal inheritance and appoint anyone they wanted as section chief, but the pressure of public opinion often gave them little choice.

The section chief held the land of his section as a tenant of the paramount chiefs or of some other high noble, who in turn might have the land in fief from them. In either case, commoners living in the section worked the land as his tenants. Like the higher rulers, then, the section chief had a right to tribute from his tenants. The people gave him feasts of tribute and first fruit offerings just as they did for the paramount chiefs. The section chief also controlled the titles of his section; only he could award or revoke a section title. He could also influence an individual's chances of receiving a higher state title by reporting to the paramount chiefs about the individual's contributions to feasts and first fruit offerings for these paramount chiefs.

One interesting feature of Ponapean society was that although, in theory, all authority was centered in the paramount chief, ordinarily he did not directly rule the state. He was considered too sacred to be bothered with mundane affairs of state, so the minister ruled in his name. At times, of course, a strong minister would take advantage of this privileged position to assume control of the state. Actually, such a reversal of positions did not occur very often, thanks to various mechanisms in the system designed to maintain balance and harmony between the paramount chiefs. One such mechanism was a fictive relationship according to which the minister was always considered to be the son of the reigning paramount chief. Because of a custom of the men of the paramount chief's line marrying the women of the minister's line and vice versa, the paramount chiefs were frequently related, sometimes one actually being the son of the other.

There was also a practice of the paramount chief and the minister each choosing his attendants from the other's line. The practice meant that both leaders were constantly surrounded by relatives of the other. Such pressures for cooperation appear to have been generally successful. Many wars between different clans and between different sub-clans of the same clans have been reported. But there is no record of any war between the paramount chief's clan and the minister's clan in the same state.

Marshall Islands

The Marshalls are the easternmost district of Micronesia, with a contemporary population of 20,000. The low coral islands composing seventy square miles of land area are scattered in two parallel chains running southeast to northwest across 375,000 square miles of ocean. The western chain includes fifteen atolls and three single coral islands; the eastern chain has fourteen atolls and two islands.

The resources of these atolls and islands are meager by world standards. Minerals are lacking, commercial agriculture near impossible, and commercial fishing not yet probable. However, the Marshallese perceive their land and lagoons with their flora and fauna as sufficient resources for island life. The resources that are available are not evenly distributed in the Marshalls. The southern atolls, from Kwajalein and Wotje south, are relatively rich. Rainfall is plentiful, vegetation lush, and population relatively dense (200–300 people per square mile). In the north, there are droughts, some plants do not grow well or at all, and populations are less dense (50–100 per square mile). These differences in subsistence base have been influential on the type of polity characteristic of the northern and southern atolls.

European contact with the Marshall Islanders was not intense or important until the late 1800s, and thus traditional Marshallese polities persisted through 1900. European trading in the Marshalls was begun by Germans and others in the 1870s. When the Germans declared a protectorate over the Marshalls in 1885, they gave their own traders such a competitive advantage that the others were put out of business. The Germans established their headquarters at Jaluit. The Japanese followed them there in 1914 and expanded the economic exploitation of the islands. The United States succeeded

Japan during World War II and moved the administrative center to Majuro. The Marshalls have seen nearly 100 years of colonial administration at the hands of three different countries.

The structure of traditional Marshallese politics is based on two cultural premises. First, the Marshallese divide their population into an aristocratic class and a class of commoners. Aristocrats are perceived as inherently different people because of their membership in aristocratic lineages (Mason 1947:52–61). The second premise is that the control of land rights is the major resource for developing political power. The confiscation and reallocation of commoner land rights by aristocrats was part of the political process of building support among commoners.

Rights in land were shared by commoner and aristocratic matrilineages. A commoner matrilineage controlled several plots of land as its estate. Within the matrilineage, a lineage head presided over the use of the land and represented the lineage to other lineages. The right to work lineage land was held first by all other lineage members, but could also be granted to nonlineal kinsmen. An aristocratic matrilineage controlled other rights over several commoner estates. They had the right to expect that commoners keep their land in production and that part of the produce be given to them. The head of an aristocratic lineage was also paramount chief over the commoners whose estates he controlled. His younger lineage mates were lesser chiefs with general rights in the lineage's estates. The paramount chief could appoint some of them, or even nonlineal kinsmen, to representative posts throughout the chiefdom. Through this hierarchy, the commoners were organized to give tribute to the aristocrats and to serve them in warfare.

The traditional Marshallese redistributive chiefdom is described well by Tobin:

> The chiefs were surrounded by an entourage or court which included such functionaries as a steward who assisted him in redistributing foodstuffs, and in stockpiling non-perishable foods and other surplus consumer goods against periods of shortages, and executioner, navigators, bodyguards and watchmen, seers, who fortold the favorable times to go to war, to sail, to go on fishing expeditions, and the like; magicians, who protected the chief and his family against evil spirits and the black magic of his enemies, and who directed black magic against the enemies of the chief when necessary; war leaders and administrators of land, and other specialists of achieved status who supported the chiefly position in society. They were compensated for their services in land, material goods, including food, and the high prestige which accompanied these positions. Members of the chiefly class

> also served as administrators and assistants to the ruling class (Tobin 1967: 77–78; Marshallese terms deleted).

The economic base for the chiefdom was derived from the surplus produced on commoner lineage estates, and the defense of the chiefdom depended on warriors recruited from commoner lineages. In both bases, aristocratic and commoner leaders were used to organize and expedite the necessary actions.

What is known of actual traditional political organization is valid only for the nineteenth century. The entire Marshalls were never united under one chief or one aristocratic dynasty. Instead, there were always several warring chiefdoms that fluctuated in size and fortune. Chiefdoms sometimes encompassed single atolls, sometimes several atolls, and sometimes, especially in cases of intradynastic warfare, only part of an atoll. Some strong chiefs had an area of influence larger than their actual chiefdom. There are cases in the oral history of raids from one chain to the other in the Marshalls, and even raids into the eastern Carolines, especially on Mokil and Pingelap.

The more powerful chiefdoms in the 1800s were located in the southern Marshalls. Political organization of the northern atolls was never as hierarchically structured or elaborate as those in the south (Tobin 1967:13–18; Kiste 1967:99–109).

The entire west chain was probably subjugated by a pair of brothers in the early 1800s (Mason 1947:164–69). Their bases of operation were Jaluit and Ailinglapalap Atolls, in the south. Their sister's son succeeded them for a long reign. When he died, the chiefdom was split between the sons of his two half-sisters. Each of these chiefdoms was split a second time between nonlineal heirs in the absence of lineal heirs. Thus, the western chain eventually came to have four paramount chiefs, and their domains were scattered among the atolls so that any given atoll might have lands and commoners under all four chiefs.

In the beginning of the nineteenth century, a single dynasty also subjugated the whole eastern chain. Various traditions place its base at Majuro, Arno, or the Aur-Maloelap area (Mason 1947:153–64; Spoehr 1949:82–91; Rynkiewich 1972:79–98). The dynasty first split into a northern chiefdom, from Aur and Maloelap north, which persists to this date, and a southern chiefdom including Majuro, Arno, and Mili. The southern chiefdom then split by atoll into three chiefdoms, and later each atoll chiefdom split again. Eventually, there were as many as ten paramount chiefs in the eastern chain.

The pattern of traditional Marshallese politics of the nineteenth century is clear. It is one of consolidation of a large chiefdom under a single matrilineage as an aristocratic dynasty. Then, through competition for power, each chiefdom was broken up several times, often through warfare at the death of the former chief. The Europeans came at a time when the chiefdoms were highly fragmented.

Pre-American Administrations

According to the Treaty of Tordesillas in 1494, Spain was responsible for all the islands of the Pacific. Actually, Spanish attention quickly focused on the Marianas, particularly on Guam, which served as a station in the lucrative galleon trade between Mexico and the Philippines. The rest of Micronesia received little attention from the Spanish administration.

Eventually, Germany moved into the power vacuum in Micronesia. In 1885, she declared a protectorate over the Marshalls, took possession of Yap, and laid claim to Truk, Ponape, and Kusaie. In arbitrating the dispute between the two powers, Leo XIII confirmed Spain's claim to the Carolines as well as to the Marianas, but he awarded the Marshalls to Germany. Despite the edict of Leo XIII, Germany's economic interest in the Carolines and the Marianas remained strong, and her trading companies continued to operate in these areas. With the United States defeat of the Spanish in 1899, Germany purchased the Carolines and the Marianas except for Guam, which became a United States possession at the time.

Spain's efforts at economic development in the Carolines and the Marianas were never very effective. Even in the Marianas, aside from the use of Guam as a station in the galleon trade, her only concerns were to Christianize the indigenous population and to maintain her own administration of the area with a minimum of effort and expense to herself.

The German administration of Micronesia was quite a different affair from that of the Spanish. They continued the pattern of indirect rule established by the Spanish, but they gave much stronger and more detailed directions to the indigenous leaders than the Spanish had given. Health measures were instituted and public schools erected on most of the inhabited islands. On the larger, more populated islands, roads were constructed or extended. In a drive to establish a monetary economy and an economic stability in their colony, the German administration instituted various political reforms concerning land ownership and required landowners to plant larger numbers of coconut trees. This move marked the beginning of the large-scale copra industry throughout Micronesia.

The Japanese took possession of Germany's Micronesian colony during World War I and remained in control of the area until they were displaced by the Americans in 1945 after World War II. The Japanese administered the islands under the auspices of the League of Nations, just as the United States later administered them under the auspices of the United Nations. From the beginning, the Japanese followed a policy of economic exploitation and rapid colonialization. Great numbers of Japanese migrated to Micronesia, particularly to the larger district centers. In governing Micronesia, the Japanese followed a policy of much more direct rule than either the Spanish or the Germans had followed. They continued to use indigenous leaders as their spokesmen with the Micronesians, but they were quick to replace those who were not compliant enough with their directives.

American Administration

In 1945, the latest colonial power moved into Micronesia. The United States took control of the former Japanese possessions in this area and established the United States Trust Territory of the Pacific Islands. The United States Navy administered this Territory until the United States Department of the Interior took charge in 1951. From the beginning, all executive, legislative, and administrative functions of the territorial government have been assigned to the high commissioner, an official appointed by the president of the United States and, since 1951, responsible directly to the secretary of the interior. The Office of the High Commissioner has been successively located at Truk, Honolulu, Guam, and Saipan. The Trust Territory itself is divided into six administrative regions or districts: the Mariana Islands (exclusive of Guam), Palau, Yap, Truk, Ponape, and the Marshalls. In each district, an appointed district administrator represents the high commissioner on the territorial level.

Under article six of the trusteeship agreement, the United States and the Trust Territory administration are committed to fostering political development toward self-government in the Territory. In 1948, the naval administration stated that its official policy was that the Micronesians should be granted the highest degree of self-government they could assimilate (forgetting that Micronesian societies had self-government for centuries before colonial rule was imposed), and that the administration would assist them to conduct their government and manage their affairs within the framework of their own sociopolitical institutions and traditions. Commenting on this policy statement, Richard says that the naval administration never considered the term "self-government" to imply democracy specifically, and she quotes Admiral Fiske, the deputy high commissioner, as saying: "We advocate self-government—not necessarily democracy" (Richard 1957, III:385). However, in a short time this policy was revised to one of actively inculcating American-style democratic processes and institutions on every level of government. Self-government thus became equated with American-style democracy.

The first step in the democratization of Micronesia was the formation of 118 municipalities throughout the Territory in 1948. These municipalities were to be the basic political units of the territorial government. As far as possible, they corresponded to the traditional Micronesian sociopolitical units. The chief executive official in each municipality was called the municipal magistrate. At first, these officials could be either chosen by popular election or appointed by the district administrator. Although elections were preferred by the administration, in many cases the district administrator followed the simpler course of appointing traditional chiefs as magistrates. Later, the administration instituted a program of chartering the municipalities, and the election of magistrates was specified in each charter. The charters also established a legislative council of elected members in each municipality. Thus, the executive and legislative powers were split between the magistrate and the council.

On the district level, advisory groups of Micronesian leaders were established to assist the district administrator. These gradually evolved into district legislatures, which are elected bodies with lawmaking authority over each of the six districts in Micronesia. They are the legislative bodies that parallel the district administrator's position. Finally, in 1965, the Congress of Micronesia was formed, with elected representatives from all six districts and with legislative jurisdiction over the entire Territory. Thus, the Congress of Micronesia is the legislative counterpart to the high commissioner. The executive and legislative officials in the introduced political system on all three levels of government in Micronesia are discussed by Hughes (this volume, p. 95).

In recent years, the U.S. administration has greatly expanded educational and health services in Micronesia, far surpassing the accomplishments of previous administrations in this regard. The record of the present administration in economic development has been far less impressive. The overall economy of the islands is still based on subsistence farming and fishing. Cash flow into the Micronesian economy is mainly employment in various capacities with the U.S. administration. Outside of the district centers, the major source of cash income is still through copra production.

In the following chapters, we shall examine the interaction of various colonial agents with the Micronesian people and report on the effects of some colonial policies on the different societies in Micronesia. Our hope is that a critical review of both the successes and failures of colonial programs will be of some use to both Micronesian and American administrators in planning future political programs in Micronesia.

1. Although geographically Micronesia actually extends beyond the U.S. Trust Territory to include Guam, Nauru, and the Gilbert Islands, in our introduction and through the remaining chapters the words "Micronesia" and "Micronesian" are used to refer only to those islands encompassed by the U.S. Trust Territory.

2. Excellent summaries and syntheses of the ethnographic literature on Micronesia are provided by Mason (1968) and Alkire (1972). Both of these sources have been used extensively in preparing this section of the introduction.

PART ONE
Colonial Inputs: Policy and Problems

2

Introduction to Part One

During the symposium in which the chapters in this volume were first presented, an observer from the Office of Territories of the U.S. Department of the Interior questioned the use of the word *colonialism* in reference to the U.S. Trust Territory of the Pacific Islands. Defining colonialism in the classical economic sense in which European nations extended their political sovereignty over undeveloped territories for the specific purpose of economic exploitation, he failed to see any relationship between colonialism and the U.S. administration of Micronesia. The problem with this particular perspective, however, is that it does not identify the broader facets of colonialism. Brookfield (1972:1–2) defines colonialism as "a thoroughgoing, comprehensive and deliberate penetration of a local or 'residentiary' system by the agents of an external system, who aim to restructure the patterns of organization, resource use, circulation and outlook so as to bring these into linked relationship with their own system." Applying this definition, any observer of historical and recent events in Micronesia must immediately conclude that the United States' interests in Micronesia are colonial in design, if not in public dogma, and that the objectives of the United States' policies are to achieve a "linked relationship" between Micronesia and the United States. This volume is almost wholly dedicated to the investigation and analysis of the Trust Territory government's efforts to restructure Micronesian political organization according to an American design. Other volumes might well be written on the restructuring of resource use for strategic military or administrative purposes, or the restructuring of outlook through education. It is not then improper to speak of "colonial inputs" when discussing U.S. political development in the Trust Territory. Furthermore, by identifying these efforts for directed change as part of a colonial context, it becomes possible to draw valid comparisons with similar colonial systems elsewhere.

The chapters in Part I of this volume address themselves primarily to the inputs and impact of the planners as they attempt to achieve political change in Micronesia. In the chapter to follow, McKnight challenges the rigidity of models applied by both planners and researchers in their programs and interpretation of development. In chapter 4, Lingenfelter examines the role of administrators and other colonial agents in translating and interpreting new forms of government to an indigenous leadership. In chapter 5, Singleton views education as a tool employed by the government to indoctrinate the populace with its political ideology and to identify and recruit new leaders to fill the roles introduced in the new political system. In the concluding chapter of this section, Hughes investigates the possible causes of the failure of a newly introduced institution to take hold in a traditional Micronesian society.

The Structure of Colonial Administration, 1952-1968

The organization of the government of the Trust Territory may be considered from a number of perspectives. The first and most obvious is that portrayed in the various organizational charts of the government itself.[1] The secretary of the U.S. Department of the Interior is the chief executive of the colonial government and answers only to the president of the United States and the U.S. Congress. Under the secretary, the Office of Territories supplies the executive staff that serves as the channel of communication to and from U.S. territories and proposes policies, programs, and legislation in reference to their problems. Below the secretary of the interior and his staff, each major territory has its own governing hierarchy consisting largely of Americans appointed to, or selected by, civil service for their positions. The government of the Trust Territory includes an executive branch, headed by a high commissioner appointed by the president; a judicial branch, appointed and directed by the secretary of the Department of the Interior; and a legislative branch, the Congress of Micronesia, elected by the Micronesian people. The territory is then divided into six districts and the districts into municipalities, all of which have their own executive, legislative, and judicial branches. (See figures 2-4.)

If one examines the distribution of power and influence within this system of organization, a slightly different picture emerges. At the highest levels of the organization, groups, such as the United Nations, the U.S. Department of State, and the U.S. Department of Defense, are not found on the charts, but are very much part of the power and influence structure. The Trusteeship Council of the U.N. reviews the status of the territory each year, and the reports of these inspections have provoked new policy and action on several occasions. The Departments of State and Defense are also very much interested in the status of the Territory. The Department of State attempts to influence policies that affect the international relations of the United States. The Department of Defense seeks greater security and permanent strategic rights in the area. Each of these interest groups has direct access to the president of the United States, who has the final word on territorial policy, and they have used this access to influence the directions of territorial administration.

At the territorial level of organization, another view of power emerges. Although the charts show the legislative branches on an equal standing with the executive branch, the fact of the matter is that the former is subject to the veto of the latter. The Congress and legislatures may override executive veto, but the decision is made by the next higher executive in the hierarchy, with the secretary of the interior the final authority. It would be false to say that the legislative bodies are not influential, but their powers are circumscribed by the administration.

Parallel to the district legislatures are the American executive officials, appointed by the high commissioner. These officials do not, however, have the same degree of contact and interaction with the people. In most districts, the officials of the administration enjoy special quarters set apart from the local people and have restricted facilities for their own relaxation and entertainment. Therefore, though officials and legislators reside in the same district, their customary life styles create a cultural and social distance between them.

The significance of distance in looking at a governmental structure lies in its relevance for communication and feedback between the

ORGANIZATION CHART OF THE GOVERNMENT OF THE TRUST TERRITORY

SHOWING THE THREE BRANCHES OF GOVERNMENT

DEPARTMENT OF INTERIOR

Secretary

VOTERS
OF
MICRONESIA

JUDICIARY

Chief Justice *

EXECUTIVE

High Commissioner *

LEGISLATURE **

* As established by Secretarial Order 2876, dated January 30, 1964, superseding Orders 2658 of August 29, 1951, and 2812 of April 6, 1956.

** As established by Secretarial Order 2882 dated September 28, 1964.

August 3, 1966

OFFICE OF THE HIGH COMMISSIONER
High Commissioner
Deputy High Commissioner
Assistant Commissioner for Community Services
Assistant Commissioner for Public Affairs
Attorney General
Assistant Commissioner for Resources & Development
Assistant Commissioner for Administration
Public Health
Department of Education
Community Development
Political Affairs
Information
Publications
Office of Attorney General
Economic Development
Agriculture
Budget and Finance
Property and Supply
Personnel
Communica-tions
Land Management
Transportation
Engineering and Construction
Public Works
Administrative Services
LNO Guam
District Administrator Mariana Islands
District Administrator Marshall Islands
District Administrator Palau
District Administrator Ponape
District Administrator Truk
District Administrator Yap

August 3, 1966

ORGANIZATION CHART - OFFICE OF THE HIGH COMMISSIONER

TRUST TERRITORY GOVERNMENT ORGANIZATIONAL PLAN TYPICAL DISTRICT

governors and the governed. When dealing with the processes of planned political change, communication distance becomes a very important variable. In Micronesia, the territorial level of government is of necessity confined to one location, in earlier years in Guam and currently in Saipan. In this center, administrative officials live, work, and relax apart from the local inhabitants, except for those Micronesians who are employed on the staff. Although regular contacts by radio, plane, and ship are maintained with the districts outside of the administrative center, the officials are not significantly closer to the problems of the Territory than if they lived in Hawaii or even California.

Perhaps most significant for understanding the directions that development took in Micronesia is the location of final policy determination in Washington, D.C. The president, the Congress, and the Office of Territories frame the major policies for the Trust Territory, yet are farthest removed from the subjects affected by these policies. This is, of course, a truism, stemming from the very nature of colonial rule.

Process of Directed Change

Pressures for restructuring a traditional system administered by colonial government largely originate in the "home office." The Trust Territory is no exception. Demands for change in the political systems of Micronesia originated with the United Nations, the U.S. Congress, and the Departments of State and Defense. The framing of policies to satisfy these demands occurred in the Office of Territories at a time when Micronesians had no influence. The planners formulated a model for government borrowed directly from the structure of the U.S. federal government and adapted slightly to the administrative hierarchy already established in the Territory. This model was then transmitted to the territorial government with the charge of interpreting and implementing it among the local Micronesian populations.

The implementation of these goals and plans for change was passed through two levels of administrative officials or "brokers." The Office of the High Commissioner served as the voice of the U.S. government, transmitting decisions made in Washington to lower-level officials in Micronesia. District officials transmitted directives from the high commissioner to their subjects and feedback from their subjects to the high commissioner. Because the high commissioner's task was to execute policy, rather than to define it, the feedback was used primarily to aid in implementation, rather than in definition, of policy. The chartering of the Congress of Micronesia in 1964 furnished an organized legislative structure that could demand reconsideration of policy decisions by the secretary of the interior, but by this time, the major program for political change had been largely accomplished across the Territory. The previous Council of Micronesia, which had met as early as 1956, was no more successful than the district administrators in interjecting Micronesian designs into the program for change.

The significance of the interrelationship among these four levels of decision-making and policy should not be underestimated. The ultimate plan and policy for each local area was determined outside of that area in a distant and impenetrable locus of power, buffered by two levels of brokers. The execution of plan and the implementation of policy, however, occurred on the local level between protagonists who had to work together, yet who lacked the authority to determine precisely what form of organization or what rules for allocating power would serve to expedite their mutual desires or mediate their conflicting interests. To understand the implications of this administrative system for directed change, it is useful to look at the nature of the models for change employed at both levels of the system.

In the 1950s, the general model for political development in Micronesia, defined in the Office of Territories but emerging from a broader climate of opinion among government leaders and political scientists of that period, was evolutionary in perspective and proceeded in a direct line from "primitive" types of organization to democracy. Democracy, however, was very narrowly defined. In chapter 5, Singleton notes that the model prescribed for change in Micronesia was founded on the "holy trichotomy of administrative, legislative, and judicial functions." The new leaders required to effect such a system were assigned single-function roles, assuring that no overlap would occur between separate areas of authority. The organizations designed to flesh out the model included unicameral district legislatures and local municipal governments. The executive and judicial structures of the territorial government completed the requirements of the trichotomy. At the local levels of each district, the municipality system followed a generalized model of small-town American government. A magistrate was chief executive officer and sometimes judge. The municipal council formed his legislative counterpart. The role assignments of magistrate, legislator, councilman, and even traditional chief were set in the general policy for development emerging from the territorial government.

In each of the separate districts, then, a rigid plan for change had to be translated, interpreted, and applied by an American official to an indigenous people and leadership. The product of this task was a series of trial organizations in which administrators and local leaders maneuvered to accomplish their own objectives and at the same time to accommodate to the demands or wishes of the higher echelons of the hierarchy. Various organizational alternatives were introduced to achieve the broad general goal. A unicameral congress including traditional chiefs was chartered in Palau. A unicameral congress excluding chiefs was chartered in Yap, and a bicarmeral congress was formed in Ponape. None of these structures satisfied the general goal, and they were periodically revised to force the direction of change toward the general model. Part of the variation was due to the separate administrators, whose definitions and methods of implementation differed, and part was created by the need for strategic compromise to overcome perceived resistance to administrative plans. After each compromise, a new stage of negotiations was initiated to meet the territorial government's demand to push on.

The ultimate consequences of this program were a series of district legislatures and municipal governments, the forms of which satisfied the demands from Washington and the U.N., but which left much to be desired by the Micronesian people. Along with the sometimes dysfunctional legislatures, the changes perpetuated confusion between traditional and elected leaders over the rules for decision-making and allocations of power. In most cases, administrative officials carefully manipulated changes to push traditional leaders farther and farther into the background.

Problems of Directed Change

In the chapters that follow, the authors identify a number of problems arising from planned political development. Perhaps one of the most common themes running throughout is that of the pitfalls of noncommunication. The onus for much of the noncommunication falls on the administration. All too often the channels are open only one way, from top to bottom. Without feedback, the administration fails to recognize that they have educated Micronesians in forms and symbols, without supplying their essential function and content. They have failed to recognize that the only effective change is that in which the elite and the people are taught the content, power, and functions of the new political institutions.

Among the key objectives of directed change in Micronesia has been that of training and selecting a new elite. Singleton, in chapter 5, suggests that the schools have provided the channel for identifying and recruiting these leaders. At the same time, education has set them apart from their peers, and drawn them together as a new stratum in Micronesian society. They are people outside of Micronesian traditions, well traveled, skilled in English, and often with long experience in working with colonial officials. These leaders are well equipped to cope with nontraditional problems, but frequently lack the strong local support given to traditional leaders.

In chapter 6, Hughes suggests that the failure of new leaders to gain support lies primarily with inadequate role definition for new political statuses and poor communication between new leaders and their constituents. The problem of role is further complicated when traditional roles overlap with new roles, or when administrators and people accept a status as legitimate but define it in altogether different ways.

Perhaps the most serious issue found in these chapters is the refusal of Trust Territory planners to recognize the existence of fully operative traditional political systems. A number of assumptions made by American planners appear consistently in the history of political change in Micronesia. Among these are: (1) traditional governments are unrepresentative and therefore bad; (2) the traditional political structures are unable to cope with the present demands or needs of the current administration; (3) traditional leaders oppose planned change and create a stumbling block to development; and (4) the superior knowledge and political skills of the administering government must necessarily be transferred to the colonized in order for them to adapt effectively to the modern world. Such a transfer requires extensive political education and new indigenous leadership.

The tragedy of these assumptions is that they preclude a serious study of existing political structures that might have supplied alternative models for a viable plan of development and change. In chapter 3, McKnight decries the insistence upon development without careful consideration of possible in-cultural modernization. The crushing impact of the direction taken was that it forced change at the expense of traditional systems and leaders that in many ways were more responsive to, and representative of, the people than those introduced.

For those who may have some influence over plans for directing political change, the contributors to Part I offer the following suggestions for consideration.

1. *Procedures.* Genuine political modernization will not occur without effective participation of the indigenous people in defining both the goals and the directions that development will take.

2. *Planning.* In colonial systems, political development is most often changed to forms native to the colonial officials rather than to forms most compatible with modernization of existing structures. In order to modernize existing structures rather than to destroy them, it is necessary to identify multiple alternatives from among Western, Eastern, and traditional societies. Artificially maintained foreign institutions should be abandoned, and a new formal government constructed, founded as far as possible upon tradition and designed to meet the needs of contemporary society.

3. *Implementation.* First, models selected for implementation should be flexible, adjusting to the conditions present. The more rigid a system, the more rapidly it becomes dysfunctional. Uniformity, created by rigidity, is in itself of little value. Second, indigenous leaders should be educated in the skills of political process as well as in the formal attributes of the new system. Forms, like buildings, may look good to observers; but without significant functions, they are worthless. Third, new roles should be explicitly defined and their importance conveyed to the people. Successful innovation must be based upon local support, which is impossible to obtain without such clear definition of both position and function.

4. *Maintenance.* Successful continuation of political innovations requires consistent, open channels of communication between leaders and the people. Planning and education should include definition of such channels and instruction in their use. Finally, any political system must have a strong economic base to support it. Economic development should be the first step in the creation of a new indigenous polity. Without such an economic base, the system will collapse soon after colonial supports are withdrawn.

Political Development in Micronesia

1. The year 1966 has been selected for describing the structure of the Trust Territory government because this year reflects the pattern of administration characteristic of the 1952-68 period. Recent changes, particularly in assigning Micronesians to leadership positions in the administration, have altered this picture somewhat. These changes will be discussed in a later chapter.

3

Rigid Models and Ridiculous Boundaries: Political Development and Practice in Palau, circa 1955-1964

Robert K. McKnight

American and Micronesian narratives about what has happened during the era of American political development in Micronesia are likely to be at some variance with one another. There will, no doubt, be general agreement regarding dates and the formal characteristics of innovations undertaken by the American administration: the municipalities, the district legislatures, and the congress. Beyond this, however, the two perspectives will tend to diverge. The American perspective, on the one hand, will tend to accentuate the Micronesian achievement, or lack of it, of the particular political model being introduced or will focus attention on factors such as increased scale in political integration gained through the new institutions. The model itself is accepted as a proper one, and increased political integration is viewed, with little or no debate, as proper growth. The Micronesian perspective, on the other hand, will tend to be comparative in approach, emphasizing the displacement of authority and loss of symbolic meanings attributable to the new institutions and the decreased sense or actuality of local autonomy inherent in the new political structures.

Because the bulk of commentary on political development in Micronesia is made by American observers, governmental or otherwise, the American perspective, with its particular perspectival distortions, will tend to dominate the documentation of what has taken place. To the extent that this is so and that the source of these distortions is unclear, we will have learned little from the experience, and Micronesia's understanding of her own political identity will have been little advanced.

This chapter and several of those that follow adhere, insofar as it is possible for an outsider to do so, to a Micronesian perspective—adopting, as possible, an anthropologist's-Micronesian bias as an alternative, at least, to the more widely documented history of the past couple of developmental decades in Micronesia.

The bulk of commentary that I hope to bring to bear on a discussion of political development in Micronesia can be summed up under two sources of distortion that most clearly adhere to American narratives: (1) the simplistic use of a single, lineal model of political progress; (2) the ineptness of cross-cultural studies of political behavior resulting from academic compartmentalization in the Western world.

1. Although some social scientists have adopted a wider perspective, our applications of social science in developmental programs adhere closely to a nineteenth-century lineal model of progress and evolution. There is no such thing as cultural modernization (e.g., building upon existing cultural prototypes); development becomes merely Westernization. Deviations from the Western model, in the context of changing institutions, become incidents to be expected but not evaluated beyond the observation that they deter from the full achievement of the model. For example, a bicameral Congress of Micronesia, recognized as only a moderate deviation from the approved unicameral model, is not spoken of as functionally adaptive to the needs of a rapidly changing Micronesian polity, but is labeled a "compromise" or, in our meaning of this term, a setback, a deviation from the proposed and supported ideal. Transitional or original models of political organization, other than the unicameral or bicameral Congress, go unmentioned or are unknown at least in part because no effort is made to discover whether a suitable pan-Micronesian polity could emerge from behavioral potentials germane to the cultures of Micronesia. This is not a relevant question as long as we adhere to a nineteenth-century lineal model of cultural evolution with European traditions as the end product of progress.

2. Additionally, though many social scientists have reached beyond the boundaries imposed on their discipline by classical academia, many others have not; and in the administration of planned cultural change, tightly drawn departmental boundaries (e.g., De-

partment of Education, Department of Public Health, and so on) typically reflect or even magnify their academic counterparts. Hence, when an analyst with only the tools and models of a particular social science discipline attempts to cross cultural boundaries to understand cultural change as administered by a twin governmental agency, for example, a Department of Political Affairs, the results are likely to be meaningful only to another like analyst with the same perspectival bias. The results are largely the same for any of the social sciences as they are for Christian mission work, but for those disciplines that are distinctly "European" in conceptual commitment, rather than cross-cultural in scope, the results can be dramatically disheartening.

The situation is pandemic in the social sciences: economists debate the existence of economic institutions in societies without mediating markets; psychologists question the existence of institutionalized techniques for managing the mentally deviant in societies that have shamans but lack Freud; political scientists question the existence of "government" when the demarcation of political and familial institutions is ambiguous; sociologists question the objectivity of anthropologists who present information in the bias of a non-Western perspective—the bias of "my people," and so on. Until the first or second decade of this century, students of theology questioned the existence of religious institutions in societies lacking the familiar ritual trappings and belief systems of Christianity. The differentiation between "science" and the advocacy of particular "belief systems" in the social sciences is still far from resolved—nor is it in the purview of this chapter to offer much relief. It is not simply optimistic, however, to point out that the situation is rapidly changing with the expansion of the social sciences to a score of non-Western societies (or to societies classed as technologically underdeveloped). The study of economic behavior, for example, has its "formalists" and its "substantivists," and parallel debate exists among students studying legal institutions cross-culturally. But it will be some time, I suspect, before debates of the formalist-substantivist variety ramify themselves in terms of programs of administered development.

Much the same criticisms, then, can be leveled (with appropriate word changes) at each of the social sciences. I do not feel, therefore, that I am being biased in any specific sense. This chapter is undertaken from the perspective of an anthropologist—a few comments on the ramifications of perspectival bias in anthropology would seem, then, to be in order.

In the administration of developmental programs, there is a curious or tragic analogy to the process of organ transplants in the field of medicine. Traditional or "cold" cultures, as they are sometimes called, are perceived to be nonadaptive—to lack what may be termed persistability or the capability for sustained identific continuity. In general, the more a society appears to be "non-Western," the more likely it is to be labeled "cold." Few societies in Micronesia would not qualify for this chilling stereotype.

When such societies become targets for planned change under the management of Western social practitioners, they are subjected to "organ transplants" and an accompanying process that is closely analogous to that of "antibody inhibition"—limiting the capability of the system to exercise normal maintenance functions in reaction to foreign antigens (read "institutions"). Good medical practice would seemingly oppose the idea of inhibiting antibody formation in order to introduce a foreign organ without first assessing fully the patient's capability to accommodate the new organ—to exhibit metabolic persistence. Yet this would often seem to be the accepted procedure in developmental programs of "planned" change.

For the past forty years or so, anthropological cross-cultural research has been dominantly concerned with the synchronic or structural aspects of culture, with primary focus on the maintenance subsystems of society. Although most anthropologists recognize that this approach is mainly a methodological convenience, a preliminary step toward understanding culture, and that the familiar static models of social anthropology have little bearing on the actualities of the cultures under observation, the models have become the accepted reality for many social scientists peripheral to the field (as well as some orthodox anthropologists), with the consequence that we are told about such supposed realities as "cold" or "traditional" cultures—the maintenance subsystems are mistaken for the totality. The result of this confusion between method, model, and reality is that license is provided to the practitioners of planned change to undertake whatever operations seem justified to accomplish organ or institutional transplants. In the ensuing events, the static model seems to be realistic as documentation upon documentation is compiled describing the resistance of "traditional" cultures to "development." The logical development of the concepts or stereotypes "traditional" and "cold" has taken place largely within anthropology, and the analytical results, when applied to the study of developmental programs, have been satisfactorily self-fulfilling. Most societies, Western or non-Western, do resist change at the institutional level.

Yet all societies do change, and there is some reason to believe that particular approaches to culture change are an institutionalized aspect of all cultures (McKnight 1971). It is this potential for change that is ignored and potentially inhibited by the "transplant" approach to development or the Westernization of institutions in planned change. The term *in-cultural modernization* has been used to designate an alternative approach undertaken in full recognition of a capacity for change in any society with developmental planning undertaken in terms of guidelines provided by the target society itself. However, as long as the principal models of analysis in the social sciences remain tied to Euro-American experience (or, as in anthropology, adhere to stereotypical concepts such as "traditional societies"), there is very little opportunity for the planning of culture change to develop the information and techniques that would apply to an in-cultural approach to modernization.

In what follows, I will adhere to a particular perspective; hopefully it will be one that will help clarify some of the distortions that inhere in Western analyses of cultural development.

Americans found in Micronesia a people, in various cultural forms, who were by and large ready (in Margaret Mead's terms) to exchange "new lives for old."

A glimpse at political change in Palau at the community level, a study of the results of administrative fiat and local adaptation, should illustrate the effect of rigid political models and the impropriety of the conventional boundaries of analysis imposed by academic disciplines when applied to cross-cultural observations of developmental change.

The potential for in-cultural change, cultural modernization rather than culture change dictated by external models, has been rather greater than usual, in my opinion, in Palau. This potential has been consistently difficult to realize because of the nature of developmental programs espoused by the American administration. In Palau, at least, we have tended to stultify in-cultural modernization by our own developmental efforts. Additionally, our simplistic stereotypes of traditional society have inhibited realistic interpretations of the results that our developmental efforts have yielded.

In 1958 when I arrived in Palau to serve as district anthropologist, the program of political development was well under way. The United Nations had recently put pressure on the United States to stress political development generally in Micronesia; and in Palau, particular emphasis may be attributed in part to the fact that the district administrator at the time had served previously as political adviser to the high commissioner. Municipal chartering was nearly complete throughout the fourteen traditional village clusters of Palau, and the Palau Legislature (then Congress), actually formed in name in 1947, had been formally chartered by the high commissioner three years earlier in 1955.

The legislature was composed of voting members, elected in each municipality according to demographic formula, and nonvoting members (the magistrates or elected "mayors" of the municipalities and the hereditary leaders of the village clusters), and was beginning to view its potential role in Palauan affairs with some seriousness. It is relevant to what follows that the hereditary leaders, who had been relegated to a separate table during sessions of the legislature, were becoming more interested in the organization as time passed; and in about 1960, they chose to join the voting legislators of their particular municipality in their seating arrangement. Many Palauans viewed this show of interest on the part of their traditional leadership as progress. From the standpoint of our program in political development, there seemed to be no easy way to evaluate it. There were those in the American administration who expressed concern that the hereditary leaders would interfere with progress.

There was an evident administrative posture against bicameral legislatures at the district level, although in effect this was the informal structure that was evident in the Palau Legislature. The elected, voting members were fairly rigidly bound to any position adopted by the hereditary leaders. The formalization of a bicameral legislature might have made this informal decision-making structure apparent, and, given time, a healthy dialogue between the houses might have promoted greater synthesis and in-cultural modernization in Palau. Administrative theory, however, dictated a unicameral legislature; and with this structure, hereditary leaders exercised control indirectly, with little recognition, and with the result that the posture of the legislature on many issues was difficult for the administration to comprehend. The approach is one that illustrates why some American administrators appear to feel that non-Western cultures constitute mainly stumbling blocks, having no inherent purpose beyond vexation and opposition to "development."

The fact that hereditary leaders seldom gained elected political office in Palau (e.g., as municipal magistrates) was much noted by a variety of Western observers and, as we will observe in more detail later, was given the obvious interpretation that Palauans had come to reject their traditional form of government.

A more reasonable interpretation would have been that both sides, traditional Palauan and administrative American, had chosen, insofar as possible, to ignore one another. The administration adhered to a policy that, in practice, paid as little heed as possible to hereditary leaders. The leaders, for the most part, chose not to participate in the games offered by the administration's program of elected officialdom, at least not to the extent of personal involvement in elections. The legislature met and, in form at least, offered the administration an image of political development. The form, however, was one that for a considerable number of years (to come?) contained the elements of a stalemate. The elected legislators were not those who could easily initiate political action in Palau, and those who could do so viewed their position in the new structure as passive. For a while, particularly between 1961 and 1963, the administration sponsored the vast majority of bills considered by the legislature, thus further contravening in-cultural modernization in favor of imposed culture change.

For many hereditary leaders, the reaction has been one of frustration. They have been confused and peeved by the posture of the administration, and not without some justification.

During the mandate period, the Japanese sought to implement a formula of indirect rule through which hereditary leaders played an important part in carrying out government programs as directed by the Japanese administration. It was in this context that the idiom *ouisae-kaigi* 'yes-meeting' (Palauan-Japanese) came into usage in reference to the lack of authority vested in hereditary leaders. Their function was to respond in agreement with any program sponsored by the administration. As one observer stated it, if hereditary power were viewed on a ten-point scale, ten being an ideal high, it sank to 4 or 5 during this period. In this approach to administration, however, the Japanese administration was keenly interested in who was who and who did what among hereditary leaders. The success of their programs depended largely on cooperation and compliance from such leaders, and when such was not evident, the Japanese, on occasion, deposed a titleholder in favor of another who could be depended upon to cooperate. In short, their position involved little autonomous power, but they were important functionaries.

Such has hardly been the case during the American administration. The same observer noted that, without the restrictions imposed by the Japanese, hereditary power during the American administration had risen on the scale to about 7 or 8. But the context of this revitalization was peculiar. The administration was mildly interested in the ability of a municipality to "display" a chief when rare instances of protocol and ceremony seemed to make his presence relevant. For most purposes, however, the position and potential authority of the hereditary leader, whoever he might be, was ignored. In administrative theory, political authority (beyond its own strong executive authority) resided in two categories of officials: the voting legislators and the elected magistrates of the municipalities. Chiefs were to be accorded courtesy, but little more.

The switch from indirect rule, as applied to Palau by the Japanese, to the narrowly conceived political model imposed by the American administration was not, as should be anticipated, easily accepted by the hereditary leaders, especially those who felt that their position of leadership was relevant to progressive modernization in Palau.

The American administration appeared willing to provide the opportunity for development as a benefit to Palauans (in contrast with the colonial posture of the latter period of Japanese administration), but the definition of progress was clearly to be provided by the Americans.

When necessary, in their judgment, the chiefs did what they could to preserve their image of the proper texture of Palauan society; but given the passive structural position that they occupied, their function in practice became more and more obstructionist and conservative. Ironically, they were the ones, Palauans would say, who could insure the success or failure of any given program sponsored by the administration. Occasionally they would demonstrate this power. The village cluster called Airai, for instance, resisted municipal chartering for about six years. More typically, however, hereditary leaders in Palau were progressive in posture. Concrete structural recognition of their interest in Palau's modernization and effective use of their power would have eased the course of many administrative programs—it is granted that this would have meant the creation of a new kind of political structure, or the sacrifice of a purely Western political model.

The hereditary leaders were given a back seat structurally in the Palau Legislature by virtue of granting them membership but denying them the right to vote. This slight of their traditional authority offended the hereditary leaders. Although they could run for the office of legislator, they seldom did so.

The same situation has held, generally, for the elected office of magistrate, the chief executive official recognized by the administration at the municipal level. It should be made clear that the boundaries of municipalities, as formalized by the chartering program, were based on traditionally recognized boundary zones comprising one politically dominant village and its subordinate hamlets. Such village clusters, generally with populations of from 500 to 800 (Koror, exceptionally large, has about 5,000), were local levels of political authority relevant to the traditional political structure: the highest-ranking chief of the highest-ranking clan of the dominant village was recognized as the political leader of such a cluster (and has been referred to here as the "hereditary leader"). However, the authority of such leaders was hedged about and balanced in a complex system of clan representation and shared or delegated political functions. Additionally, lines of communication between clusters, even between villages viewed traditionally as enemies, were maintained by the leadership for a variety of political and economic purposes. Although there have been dictatorial, arbitrary, and selfish chiefs in Palauan history, the structure probably inhibited this likelihood about as effectively as any structure can. The ideal of a good chief differs from our image of a good political leader mainly in two respects: it is somewhat more embodied with sacred symbolism, and there is more emphasis on craftiness (as opposed to candidness). Granting that our "chiefs" have been comfortably Christian and that craftiness may be a term for diplomacy, the ideal "chief" in American and Palauan ideologies may be exceedingly close. But this, for the moment, is beside the point.

It is relevant to note that the position of magistrate in the municipality was structurally proximal to that of the traditionally recognized political leader of a village cluster. There were fourteen village clusters in the traditional geopolitical structure; there are now fourteen magistrates corresponding to the same geopolitical units.

In Trust Territory reports to the United Nations dated about 1957, it is observed that Palau appears to be the most advanced district politically in Micronesia. In evidence of this statement was the observation that the office of magistrate, often occupied by hereditary leaders elsewhere in Micronesia, was usually held by "commoners" in Palau. I do not know who wrote this report—probably an American administrative official in Palau. The interpretation was probably supported by some Palauans out of a desire to share with Americans a progressive image of Palau. It is true that since the formation of municipalities relatively few hereditary leaders have been elected to the office of magistrate. They have been elected, however, when they have chosen to be nominated. This is not to say that hereditary leaders will automatically be elected if they run for office in Palau, but merely to observe that they probably will and that, in any event, hereditary leaders have not generally sought nomination.

On inquiring why not, none of the answers that I received would lend much credit to the interpretation given in our reports to the United Nations. Perhaps the most frequent reasons given for the lack of magistrate-chiefs were as follows:

1. The office was too lowly to be occupied by one with the sacred authority of a chief.

2. Although a chief *could* be deposed by known traditional processes, the title was granted for life, not for a one- or two-year term.

3. The magistrate was considered, not without reason, as a lowly official of the American administration. Of the sixteen responsibilities listed for magistrates in a guide prepared by the administration, five refer directly to obligations to the administration and seven more refer to duties associated with programs implemented by the administration through its various departments. The popular image of the magistrate as a messenger boy of the administration, in a structure reminiscent of the Japanese mandate formula, was not easily disputed. The problem was not necessarily one of opposition to the administration but rather of incongruity and, potentially, serious conflict of interest, particularly on the part of a lesser-ranking chief with additional obligations to chiefs of higher-ranking village clusters. Congruently, the chief (until 1972) of high-ranking Koror municipality occasionally did a stint as magistrate (not without some criticism).

4. Others observed that a traditional leader once elected to the position of magistrate would be a very difficult incumbent to displace. This could be a disadvantage to a community if, in fact, the incumbent chief turned out to be a poor negotiator with the American administration. If the object of the community was to seek to place in office a man with the right kind of skills, the community would seek to elect an individual with specific and special (not general) abilities in the management of occasional confrontations with the administration. In this view, which was not uncommon, hereditary chiefs remained the ideal general administrators of the community. However, (when they were not present) it was possible to observe that they lacked some specific skills. The same sort of argument may be raised with regard to a chief's participation in economic enterprise, as follows. Suppose that there are two boat-

builders in a community and that the chief backs one of them through financial assistance and such, to the exclusion of the other. Before long, it is reasoned, everyone would buy boats from the builder supported by the chief, not necessarily because he was more skilled but simply to avoid offending, or to curry favor with, the chief. Economic favoritism by a chief may thus be regarded as unethical and damaging to the interplay of competitive skills. The position of magistrate as a skilled specialization may be regarded in like manner. A chief could become magistrate if he wished, and there would be little option except to back him; but he should not because it would be unethical and nonadaptive: it would tend to prevent men of specialized ability (in interaction with the American administration) to demonstrate their skills. Congruently, the chief of one northern municipality became so angered at the lack of ability demonstrated by an incumbent magistrate that he did run for office. He won, of course. Whether his term was more successful, I do not know.

The administrative model applied to a magistrate was a peculiarly illogical one. The often-repeated policy formula was as follows: hereditary leaders would serve largely as social symbols in their communities, conducting their traditional functions in their traditional spheres; the magistrates, in turn, would be the executives of modernization, carrying out the programs sponsored by the administration. The two spheres, traditional and modern, were seemingly presumed to lack overlap. Verbalizations of the model generally ended with a happy image of cooperation between chiefs and magistrates, each going about their individual duties, keeping the other advised but never treading on each other's toes. Overlooked in this policy formula is the fact that both the traditional political sphere and the new programs being introduced by the administration constituted hypothetical total community programs of administration. In theory, at least, one should be able to demonstrate perfect functional duplication (overlap) between the so-called traditional sphere and the sphere of administrative programs. Fortunately, perhaps, neither sphere was perfect in its comprehension of community needs; but neither did the two spheres support one another systematically, supplementing the other's weaknesses. The programs of the administration were dictated by a host of models (agricultural, medical, educational, as well as political) that were supported and promoted mainly because they could be recognized by American observers as goals in the Western world. Needs or program emphases voiced by Palauan communities were, as a generality, not noted unless there was evident correspondence with goals voiced by Western administrators. *Ngkora kaidos* 'like kaldos' (a medical technique), applying the medicine to the wrong foot, was the idiom that Palauans used to describe the result.

Confrontation between traditional government and the administration at the level of the municipality was minimized in large measure because the administration lacked comprehensive programs at the village level. Schools, medical aid stations, and the homesteading program (with some agricultural assistance to the coconut grower) were the main thrusts of administrative programs (other than the municipal chartering program itself) that reached beyond the district center. In the highly compartmentalized "department" structure of the Trust Territory government, these programs were organizationally separate from the political development program and were thus independent of the magistrate, since that position was the creation of the political development program. To add to the confusion, departmental employees involved in programs at the village level (i.e., education, public health, and agriculture) carefully sought out the hereditary leader when local authority or support was felt to be important. At one stage, the Palauan official in charge of political development in the administration found himself at a loss to define the appropriate functions, beyond collecting tax to pay their own salaries, for the magistrates.

In any event, traditional leaders left little to chance. In their model of political behavior, anything that the administration might attempt to do at the village level was within their jurisdiction, and it was their responsibility to ensure that all things remained within manageable bounds in their communities.

Who, then, was elected to the position of magistrate? In a few instances, hereditary leaders sought and got the office; but, as we have seen, this was generally considered inappropriate. The range of community response to the problem of filling the magistrate position was considerable.

At one extreme was the response described by several persons in one municipality who claimed that there was rarely more than one nominee for the position and that would be the one individual who failed to show up to erase his name from the municipal office blackboard. With considerable humor, it was observed that the community aim was to find one individual who was too inept or lazy to get off the nomination list. In the same community, the chief occasionally made it a point to demonstrate to the unfortunate incumbent magistrate that the village would not function as long as he, the chief, remained merely passive.

One stormy day a party from the administration, invited to this community to share its annual municipal charter day celebration, was kept at bay beyond the reef in a small open boat in a rain squall while the magistrate could be observed running up and down the beach searching for someone who would provide canoe or raft transportation to get the party across the fringing reef to shore. Eventually, a Palauan member of the administration party swam ashore and persuaded the chief to relent, and several canoes soon put out to fetch us in.

The fall-guy approach, which was not very common, approximates a more widely expressed rationale for magistrate qualifications, namely, that the nominee be sufficiently subordinate so that there would be no question regarding his subservience to the chief. In this approach, though administrative plans might occasionally be frustrated, there was little likelihood of serious confrontation between the traditional spheres and the new programs.

Perhaps the most functional approach (at least in the short run) was that in which the magistrate's office was viewed primarily as a training or apprentice position for young men in line of inheritance for traditional political office. In earlier traditions, village clubs served as miniature societies with leaders whose functions closely paralleled those of the titled village leaders. The clubs provided training and testing situations for future community leaders. For a variety of reasons, such clubs are largely defunct. In some municipalities, however, the magistrate's position has been used to fulfill this training function. Since the incumbent would be one of the elite and could expect eventually to function as a village chief or elder leader, it was not anticipated that he would consciously undermine the authority or position of chief.

In practice, then, the position of magistrate was only in a highly restricted sense an "elected" office. Nominees were those who were approved by the traditional leadership because they would cooperate, would not interfere with, or might enhance, the position of chief.

A footnote should be added to this sketch noting that in about 1964, when a new school building program was launched with buildings under construction or scheduled for construction in numerous rural communities, a number of municipalities found themselves electing chiefs to the office of magistrate. I was no longer in Palau and could not assess the meaning of this fully, but it would appear that (1) with more attention directed at rural communities, the position of magistrate had become a more interesting one to occupy, and (2) problems of land usage associated with school sites and problems associated with the organization of community labor involved in some communities were too important to risk bungling by an inept or inexperienced hand. The relevant observation would appear to be that when it seems important to do so, Palau regresses from the Western political ideal: traditional leaders can and will step into executive or legislative positions to get a job done. In this instance, traditional leaders, fully in support of better schools, placed their authority where it would count most for modernization.

Though the administration view might often have been otherwise, it appears that Palau is not, and perhaps never has been, lacking in progressive leadership. A study of Palauan folklore strongly suggests that Palauan culture heroes are best viewed as agents of change; few conservators of traditions appear to have survived as such the selective memory of folk history. This seems congruent with recent history in Palau as well as the recall of the distant past. Under German colonial, Japanese mandate, and American Trust administrations, the prominent hereditary leaders in Palau appear to have been committed to culture change and, as variously defined, progress. Earlier chiefs, such as the various prior Ibedul "Chiefs" of Koror municipality, who are recalled in most favorable terms are those who vigorously promoted programs that appeared at the time to enhance Palau's progressive image. The chief of Ngiwal during the Japanese mandate period is proudly remembered for his complete restructuring of Ngiwal village after a visit to Japan. Ngiwal is now laid out in two neat rows of homes facing a wide roadway called the "Ginza." A standing dispute exists among leading communities in Palau as to which chief played the dominant part in changing Palauan dress and hair styles. An effective leader, in the traditional view at least, was a pace-setter in culture change and innovation.

But in the years following the introduction of formal Western political structures in Palau, the chartered municipalities and the unicameral legislature, many hereditary leaders appear to have reversed their political orientation, viewing their chiefly authority mainly as an instrument of conservatism rather than modernization. It would probably be difficult to provide absolute documentation relating to this seeming reversal. I must, however, account somehow for contradictions in my notes relating to some interviews in the municipality of Peleliu in southern Palau. In discussions relating to the past, two elders of Peleliu portrayed their community as the locus of cultural innovation in Palau, tracing to events in Peleliu (for example) the innovation of clan representation in village government and the structure of the economic distribution system. *Kebliil*, the name given the Palauan clan, is spoken of as a woman of Peleliu who devised out of chaos the correct role relationship between brother and sister, and so on. In interviews concerned with the past, Peleliu conveys an image of innovation and progress. In the recent past, shortly before my arrival in Palau, the community of Peleliu had built a large, fine elementary school, putting up community labor against government matching funds. The elder leader of the community was unusual in that he maintained carefully written records of his career as chief, and another elder, a practitioner of traditional medicine, was pleased that a daughter of his clan was a nurse in the Koror hospital (but dejected that Western training in medicine involved a severe rejection of his own interests in the field.) In terms of interviews concerned with the past, and evidence from the recent past, Peleliu conveys an image of innovation and progress. But in terms of the present or the period of my sojourn in Palau, Peleliu seemed often comparable to Boston as a repository of traditional usages.

Traditional correctness was also the line, during the period under discussion, in three major communities central to the 'side-heaven' opposing Koror. This takes a moment of explanation.

Palau was divided into two *bitalianged* 'side-heavens', which were, in the popular image, traditional enemies. Generally, the division between the side-heavens runs down the middle of the large island of Babelthuap, then cuts east, placing most of the western side of Palau in the side-heaven dominated (in recent years) by Koror, and most of the opposite or eastern side-heaven within the current domination of the community of Melekeiok. The chiefs of Koror and Melekeiok are thought of, by Western observers, as parallel ranking high chiefs of Palau, although traditional interpretations would necessarily be more complex. Koror, of course, as the center of administration and as the port town of Palau, has been the focus of developmental (and all other varieties of) change.

During the period under discussion, from the mid-1950s to mid-1960s, three communities of the eastern side-heaven (Ngaraard, Melekiok, and Ngechesar) adopted strongly conservative positions, maintaining that the success of a Palauan community (or lineage or clan) was to be correctly measured in terms of adherence to proper traditional form in political, economic, and social interaction with other social units. In general, during this period, developmental programs clearly attributed to the administration were given a cool reception or were rejected by these communities. However, in years preceding, all three communities had produced young men who have consistently spearheaded progressive development in every major department of the administration. From some perspectives, it would be appropriate to observe that the entire eastern side-heaven and some communities of the western side-heaven (such as Peleliu) have adopted in recent years a conservative position. In large measure, I believe, this has been in response to the administration's political development program, which, in effect, has relegated hereditary leaders to a passive role in which they are practically ignored.

What has been overlooked in planning political development in Palau and other parts of Micronesia is the fact that the traditional societies boasted more or less complex, and in all cases complete, functional political systems. Although it is true that most of the hereditary leaders would have had difficulty managing some of the chores assigned to magistrates and might have experienced some difficulty with some of the technical problems faced by younger men in the legislature (though the major difficulty was the English language and could have been resolved by a simultaneous translation system permitting a closer communication between the American administration and all levels of local leadership), it should be recognized that, except for some periods of frustrated conservatism, the primary drive for cultural modernization in Palau has come from its principle spokesmen, its titled elders.

The actual situation in Palauan culture combined a complex and highly representative form of community government with a positive drive for modernization. The situation as viewed by the administration involved a highly limited view of traditional political behavior (a simplistic opposition between dictatorial, hereditary chiefs and elected representatives) and an inadequate understanding of political behavior in its functional relations with other institutional spheres of community behavior. As a result, cultural adaptation in terms of political development has been dominantly one-sided in Palau. Traditional leadership adapted to the form of political program imposed by the administration.

Palauans would appear to enjoy "playing" with new varieties of social organization and, in most instances, have found both the position of magistrate (as a new political phenomenon) and the legislature (as a rather complex social organization) to be of interest as novel social games. Perhaps hereditary leaders in Palau, in the absence of their traditional right to wage intrigue and war with other communities (but still close to the folk histories of war-lore and war heroes), appreciate the diversion involved in maintaining social control in the context of the new political structures brought as gifts of modernization by the American administration. Hereditary leaders have generally approved of the idea of new political ventures; congruently, many of them have felt deep personal frustration and affront with the simplistic political forms actually imposed on them and with the total lack of comprehension shown by the American administration either for the form of traditional government or its functions at the community level. It is relevant to note here that some of the churches within the Modekngei, a Palauan religious movement that developed during the German period of administration, have attempted general cultural reformulation, seemingly in an effort to manage in-cultural modernization. Adaptation and modernization appear to be goals germane to Palauan society.

The traditional leadership structure in Palau is indeed failing and will, no doubt, eventually collapse. As long as possible, in any event, the transplanted institutions will be maintained artificially by the American administration. The heart will be kept beating, as it were, regardless of the patient's condition. At the local level, it can be observed that the program of political development was salvaged from absurdity because hereditary leaders have been sufficiently adaptive to find ways to control and, in many instances, to foster the aims of their communities while tolerating the pretext of new, imposed forms. Seemingly, however, the eventual success of the transplanted model, the time when model and political practice will be more nearly the same, will depend on the failure of Palauan society. This failure is, and will probably continue to be, largely an economic failure; that is, a failure of the American administration to sponsor or promote effective economic programs. Monetary strength in Micronesia derives almost entirely from government programs as such, and the direction of all developmental programs responds mainly to the source of incoming financial strength. Of course, it will not be the chiefs alone who will suffer this failure; rather, it may be viewed as a comprehensive failure of the texture of Palauan society. This seems to me an unfortunate commentary on the technology of political development.

4

Administrative Officials, Peace Crops Lawyers, and Directed Change on Yap

Sherwood G. Lingenfelter

Anthropologists studying directed political change in both Oceania and Africa have often been so preoccupied with the consequences of these changes for the indigenous people that they have forgotten to examine the causes. Whereas they described traditional structures and systems in great detail, they considered the structure and regimes introduced by the colonial powers to be either synonomous with "given" models "back home" or they described them only superficially. Careful analyses of the inputs of colonial powers for political "development" are practically nonexistent in the anthropological literature. Today researchers have begun to recognize that the substance of the cause is as important as the consequence, if not more so. In the previous chapter, McKnight shows very clearly how the rigidity of the formulas for change is the force for disintegration in Palauan polity, and not change per se. Later chapters identify other aspects of colonial policy critical to the understanding of directed political change.

The primary purpose of this chapter is to examine colonial inputs for political change in the Yap District of the U.S. Trust Territory of the Pacific Islands, with particular reference to the Yap Islands.[1] The major question considered is the role administrators and other colonial "agents" have had in altering rules by which power was organized and distributed in Yap. For the purposes of this chapter, the analysis is limited to the structural models or forms of government present in traditional Yapese society or introduced by colonial powers.

Some of the specific questions considered are as follows: What particular goals have motivated colonial agents to alter the structure of Yapese polity? What models of government are applied in directing change? What strategies are used by the agent to assure compliance from the colonized? What counter goals, models, and strategies are posed by the Yapese in response to those introduced? What outside interests, institutions, and policies intercede in the decisions and programs for change? What kinds of variation occur in inputs from agent to agent? Finally, how are the demands and counter demands of agent and colonized resolved in decision and policy?

The data considered here apply primarily to the Yapese and the Yap Islands, where the Trust Territory government has made its most substantial efforts to introduce new forms of government. Until recently, the Carolinians in the atolls to the east remained on the periphery of these programs, insulated by the difficulties of communication and the lack of resident government officials. The time period ranges from 1945 to 1968, with particular reference to four shorter spans within that period. In each of these four spans, particular "agents" launch and pursue particular plans for political development on Yap. The overall purpose of the chapter is to discover if these different agents within the same colonial system use different models for political development and thereby cause significantly different changes.

Naval Administration

At the close of World War II, the United States Navy landed a small occupational force on the islands of Yap to oversee the surrender of the Japanese and to restore the indigenous people to their normal routines of life. During the war, Yap had been bombed, but not directly invaded. Therefore, although the people had been displaced and were without homes and good food supplies, they had not suffered the devastation found in other areas of the Pacific.

During the first year of naval occupation, the strategy of the administrative office was directed toward the basic postwar problems of resettlement of the local population and restoring roads, health services, and social control. Yapese leaders were as much concerned about these problems as the navy and cooperated as much as possible to accomplish these ends. At the same time, the particular leaders representing the various regions or districts of Yap were concerned about the nature of their leadership role in the "new" regime.

From their experiences with the Japanese, the Yapese were quite familiar with forced labor, a strict hierarchy of command, and the execution of "orders." In the years immediately preceding the war, certain Yapese who were fluent in Japanese and influential, if not leaders, in their own communities were chosen as native *soncho* 'headmen' and acted as intermediaries between local leaders and the Japanese. The Japanese did not attempt to work through the traditional political structure of Yap, but manipulated it through appointed headmen for their own purposes. As a result, the Yapese developed two distinct models of government: one structured by the Japanese for the execution of Japanese programs and policies and one structured on traditional considerations of land and kinship and utilized for local community programs and control. The Japanese prohibited traditional political activities at the regional and Yap-wide level, so though the structure still existed in the minds of Yapese leaders, it had no part in the colonial framework. The native *soncho* were the leaders who first acted for the Yapese in their relations with the U.S. Navy.

The naval officers applied a relatively simple model of government. Viewing Yapese chiefs as powerful leaders presiding over their people as a sergeant does over his platoon, they issued orders and expected them to be carried out. The naval command introduced two structural changes to facilitate administration. They held elections for "chiefs" to verify the legitimacy of the hierarchy of command between the occupation force and the local people, and they requested that each elected chief appoint a representative from his locality to live in the town and act as messenger for the navy to the outlying region. Although these changes were not the only possible solutions to their administrative problems, the young officers in charge followed methods that from their experience were most likely to produce the results desired. This, of course, precluded investigation and utilization of existing Yapese channels of communication or criteria for legitimacy of leaders. The elections did, however, remove Japanese appointees who were not titled chiefs and placed titled men in these positions.

Although the Yapese were familiar with the military custom of giving orders to initiate support and action, they could not apply it to mobilize local support without special coercive sanctions, which were not provided by the military government. Custom circumscribed the authority of a traditional chief to a far greater extent than the Americans realized. The inability of Yapese leaders to execute their policies caused the naval officers to conclude the Yapese were recalcitrant and opposed to change.

In fact, quite the opposite was true. Yapese leaders were placed in the somewhat precarious position of being forced to mediate between two inherently conflicting systems. They were quite eager to gain power and legitimacy in the new government, but at the same time they were acutely aware that to do so required their ability to mobilize local support to meet that government's demands. Therefore, calls for labor by the navy had to be satisfied through traditional authority. The navy assumed that a chief could make such demands, but in fact he could not do so except in very specific traditionally defined cases. As a result, even though he could mobilize a work force of reasonable size on the basis of his prestige and promise of future reward, he could not maintain it over a long period of time without other, more satisfactory long-term inducements. The small wages ultimately paid by the navy were inadequate, and maintenance of a steady labor pool became next to impossible.

Yapese leaders worked to maintain a balance of satisfaction between these conflicting interests. When they could readily comply with naval orders, they did so. In situations of difficulty, they attempted to convince the officers to accept alternative methods or explanations; and when this was not possible, they merely agreed to the policy and then let it die the slow death of inaction.

After the first year of its administration, the navy instituted more direct programs for political change. In a visit to Yap in 1946, naval officer and anthropologist John Useem told the Yapese that though the United States would not force them to change their customs, it desired that the Yapese *develop* self-government and economic self-sufficiency. From this point on, it became quite clear, despite Useem's denial, that the primary goal of the United States was to bring about directed and even forced political change. The fact that the Yapese had governed themselves for centuries without American aid carried no weight at all. It is ironic, although in character, that in the very same meeting Americans attacked the Yapese customs of class and "subjugation of women" and asked the Yapese leaders what they would do to resolve these problems. In addition to this, a few days after the meeting Yapese chiefs were presented with sufficient mess kits to supply one for each member of their families, and thus enable them to break down the traditional segregation in eating customs (Yap District Chief's File, 1945-47).

The Yapese response was consistent with the stimulus. Mess kits were distributed to friends and supporters from their home localities, and the issues of class and women were tabled for further discussion. When the navy issued new directives establishing municipal governments, Yapese leaders accepted the forms and filled them with traditional content. The same traditional chiefs were reelected as magistrates, and both the Yapese and the navy carried on in much the same manner as before.

The Yap Islands Council, 1955-1959

In the early years of civil administration, the relationship between administrator and administered remained much as it had been during the navy period. The administrators looked at Yapese as uneducated, even simple-minded natives who had to be told everything they should do. Meetings of the leaders consisted of an address and instructions from the district administrator (Distad) and frequent lectures about what should be done to improve the lives of the people.

By 1955, a new Distad for Yap began to make significant moves to place greater responsibility and authority on the Yapese leaders. His primary goal was to change the role of the Council of Magistrates from government servants and intermediaries to a functioning organization of leaders, which would both initate and execute programs and policies for the people.

The model of government to which the Yapese had become accustomed included defined municipalities, municipal councils made up of traditional village chiefs, and elected magistrates. The magistrates were charged with the tasks of collecting taxes, submitting financial reports, and creating and enforcing municipal ordinances. They also assisted in the direction and support of such government programs as census, voting, public health, and education. The changes introduced in 1955 were not in the external forms, but in the internal operations of the council. The Distad expanded and revitalized the committee structure of the council and charged it with the task of outlining its organization and duties. The term of office for the magistrate was expanded from one to three years, and an executive committee was formed from the new officers of the council, including the president, the secretary, and the treasurer. The Distad then asked the magistrates to review orders and ordinances, to examine programs in agriculture, education, and health, and to make recommendations for future programs and changes. In short, the Distad loosened the government controls and gave leaders increasing responsibility and decision-making power.

The Yap magistrates welcomed the increase in power and responsibility. Meller (1969:154) notes that the council's "outstanding characteristic was a desire and willingness to initiate and plan its own program of improvements and to support them with labor, material and funds." This desire no doubt stemmed in part from the better knowledge and understanding of the municipal system. But even more, the structure of the council paralleled very closely the traditional framework of Yap-wide alliances. The executive committee with three members met with Yap ideals on the distribution of power, and the programs of improvements were precisely the tasks assigned to leaders in the traditional system. The colonial government had finally delegated the authority to the magistrates that would have been theirs in the traditional political system.

This ideal state of affairs did not, however, last for long. The model of government being propounded by the high commissioner distinctly separated the executive and legislative powers contained in the structure of the council. The high commissioner was anxious that Yap should be brought into line with the other districts where this division of powers had been established, and he directed that the Yap Council take the necessary steps for chartering municipalities and establishing a legislature.

The magistrates were quite satisfied with the structure of the council as it existed at that time and resisted the pressure for change. The Distad applied slight but steady pressure. Several magistrates were sent to Palau to observe the legislature there. A committee was formed to review again the organization of the council with the aim of changing it into an incorporated legislative body. The Yapese delayed any decision, and increased their own legislative productivity in an attempt to demonstrate the effectiveness of the present organization. Although the Distad was convinced of their effectiveness, territorial policy required the formation of a legislature, and he pressed toward that end.

Finally, after over three years of debate, stalemate, and delay, the council proposed the formation of a new legislature, retaining the council as an executive body, which enabled them to maintain their traditional roles. The Yap Islands Congress was chartered in 1959, and the topic of municipal charters set aside until a more convenient date.

The capitulation of the council was one of form, but not of power. The new legislature operated very much under the direction of the council. Winners in legislative elections were predetermined in municipal meetings of traditional chiefs. The council proposed legislation, and the congress enacted it. Although the control of appropriations and legislation resided in the congress, the legislators voted the way the council instructed them.

The pressure of the colonial administration for a legislature is another example of what McKnight in chapter 3 termed "rigid models and ridiculous boundaries." Both the Yapese and the local administration were satisfied with the work of the council, but the colonial hierarchy and policy, far removed from the local scene, would not permit it to continue. Why? Because it did not fit their design for "self-government." One must conclude that the nature of colonial bureaucracy is such that it is frequently impossible for political "development" to produce a viable structure ideally compatible with local interests. Colonial dogma intercedes, demanding unified forms regardless of adaptability.

The Yap Islands Congress, 1962-1966

By 1962, the Yapese political situation had become much more complex. The fledgling congress had exhibited greater confidence and skill, and the council had adjusted to the inconvenience of working through the congress to obtain funds and to form policy and law. With these changes settled, the council sought once again to gain legal status. A new Distad petitioned a new high commissioner to grant a legal charter to the council and to each of the ten municipalities. However, though the personnel had changed, the basic ideology had not. The high commissioner was not only opposed to granting a legal charter to the council but his staff recommended that he phase out the council altogether by forming a single municipal government for the Yap Islands and merging the congress into the municipal council.

The most obvious question is, Why the strong opposition to the Yap Islands Council? The answer appears to be a persistent American design to destroy or at least neutralize the locus of traditional political power, based upon the belief that such power was unjust and inconsistent with the principles of self-government. The high commissioner did not want to grant recognition to a de facto body of traditional leaders. Because of provisions in the legislative charter of the Yap Islands Congress, the administration was prevented from resolving the dilemma by incorporating the traditional leaders into the congress, giving them nominal recognition but divesting them of power, as had been done in Palau. Therefore, recognizing that the council sustained considerable support from the Yapese people, the high commissioner did not follow the advice of his staff. The council persisted as the executive body for the Yap Islands Congress, but without legal charter. In actual fact, testimony of the Yap Distad indicated that, without the council, the work of the administration on Yap would have been much more difficult.

Following what the high commissioner's office viewed as a temporary stalemate in the political development of Yap, the administration shifted its emphasis back to the more flexible unit of Yapese government, the legislature. Later in 1962 the Distad proposed to a conference of Carolinian chiefs from the outer islands of the Yap District that they consider the formation of, and participation in, a district-wide legislature. At the same time, it was proposed that they send observers to the next session of the Yap Islands Congress. The Carolinian leaders rejected both the visit and the proposal on grounds that they were totally ignorant of those things and first needed to be educated in order to understand what they were seeing and what was proposed. Instead, they countered with a proposal that a program of education be initated to prepare them for future consideration of the idea.

The government's strategy for this program reflected two contrasting approaches. The Public Affairs Office of the high commissioner pushed for quick resolution of the problem, first presenting a ready-made charter, and then later employing a professional political scientist to help negotiate a solution. The Yap Distad and his administrative officers proceeded with the much slower educational programs and the formal and informal negotiations.

For the Yapese, a district legislature did not appear as a threat but rather as an advantage. Some magistrates believed that the creation of a legislature would return to the council certain local powers and jurisdiction previously lost to the Yap Islands Congress. On the other hand, members of the congress viewed such a change as extending their own powers and were also favorably inclined. The Yapese, then, supported the administration in its efforts to convince the Carolinian leaders.

The Carolinians strongly resisted the idea of a district legislature. They failed to see a genuine need for such a governing body and suspected it as a Yapese tool for stealing tax money from their people. They responded to the urgings of the administration and the Yapese by flatly refusing the charter sent from Saipan and requesting more education, more time, and equal representation in any proposed legislature. Because of the major effort required to assemble leaders from the various atolls, the delaying tactics were quite effective.

In 1965, the office of the high commissioner introduced a new agent of the government, Professor Norman Meller, a political scientist from the University of Hawaii, whose task was to help resolve the Carolinian objections to a district legislature. Meller writes (1969:160) that his primary method was to "probe into questions so delicate that none of the parties to the negotiations would raise them, . . . this strategy was deliberately adopted to bring into the open all potential major stumbling blocks to the formation and functioning of a legislature for Yap."

Meller succeeded very well with the Carolinians, but was somewhat frustrated by the Yapese. The Carolinians quickly posed a number of significant problems and fears. Meller encouraged them to talk out these fears and to keep them foremost so that a viable structure for a legislature might be worked out with these reservations in mind. The Yapese, however, refused to admit that the proposal contained dangerous implications for themselves or for the Carolinians. They persisted in their support of the proposal and attempted to allay any fears of the outer islanders. They denied any feelings of superiority toward the Carolinians and said that they considered them equal to Yapese.

In the closing meeting of these negotiations, Meller withdrew himself from the mediating role. When the Yapese speaker presented him with the time-honored opportunity to present the administrative solution, he declined, and the Yapese and Carolinians were forced to develop their own views. After some prolonged hesitation and groping, they finally agreed upon a series of proposals that would lead up to the formation of a district legislature. They agreed that such a legislature was needed and that the Carolinian chiefs should be educated to see that need. They decided that the outer island chiefs should observe the next session of the Yap Islands Congress and that a member of the high commissioner's staff be present to assist in that session.

Meller (1969:174–77) notes that extensive preparations were made in the outer islands for the proposed trip to Yap. However, just before the session, word was sent that the high commissioner lacked the funds for transportation. The trip was postponed, first until the next session and then indefinitely. Despite the serious and sensitive efforts of Meller to draw Yapese and Carolinians together, the attempt to form a district-wide legislature succumbed again, but this time from lack of administrative support.

Peace Corps Lawyers and Formation of the Yap District Legislature

The appearance of Peace Corps lawyers in January 1967 initiated political changes far more extensive and significant than any since the emergence of the council in the mid-1950s. In their first monumental effort, they collected into a coherent, ordered code all laws and district orders passed in previous legislative sessions, and established effective systems for recording and filing new legislation. They updated the charter of the Yap Islands Congress and suggested that the name be changed to Yap Islands Legislature. Before they had finished this task, they became deeply involved in the May 1967 session. As legislative counsel, two lawyers worked throughout the session training legislators in the formal procedures of writing, introducing, and pushing bills through the congress. When they were not preoccupied with procedures, they suggested specific acts that extended the authority of the legislature into other branches of the government. By the close of the session, legislators were not only more confident in their work but had also expanded their powers to include subpoena of witnesses and audits and inventories of the local government. For the first time, legislators began to grasp the rules for exercising legislative power.

Training continued for the leaders of the legislature between sessions, and a special presession was scheduled in November to further instruct legislators in the skills and powers of their office. After the opening of the November session, legislative committees held extensive hearings for the first time in their history. The head of each branch of the administration and local government was summoned before an appropriate committee and interrogated as to problems, programs, and plans. The committees criticized, probed, and admonished these leaders, and followed up with appropriate bills and resolutions.

The most significant acts of the November 1967 session were the adoption of the Yap Island Code and the establishment of a commission to study the creation of a district legislature and the chartering of municipal government on Yap. The code confirmed the legislature's legal power and responsibility. By creating the study commission, the legislature assumed leadership for the most important decisions confronting Yapese officials, i.e., the questions of the structure and composition of the district and local governments. Yap was the only district in the Trust Territory without a district legislature at that time, and they experienced increasing pressure from the high commissioner to resolve this matter. With the assistance of the Peace Corps lawyers, the legislators responded to this pressure, initiating procedures leading to their ultimate decision.

Significantly, these same lawyers were included on the municipal government study commission and played a central role in its deliberative processes. One lawyer acted as secretary for the commission, and the other was appointed as a voting member. Even though both cast themselves in the role of advisers, the Yapese placed them in central directing roles. Together they defined the operating procedures of the commission (parliamentary), outlined possible alternatives for decisions on apportionment, boundaries, and forms of government, and then highlighted the advantages and disadvantages of each alternative. The Yapese participated vigorously in the discussions, and both lawyers often abstained from voting, but the parameters of choice were decidedly limited by the perspective of the lawyers. In the case of alternatives for municipal government, models presented were based either on the existing council or on the lawyers' experiences in the United States. None of the alternatives were satisfactory to the Yapese, although one was ultimately selected by a split vote. This choice later proved unsatisfactory to the legislature and was tabled.

Following the deliberations of the commission, the formation of the Yap District Legislature was almost an anticlimax after the many years of negotiation and delay. In early 1968, the legislature invited the Carolinian chiefs to visit their May session. The chiefs asked the district administration if they could hold another conference on Woleai prior to this session. At this time, the Distad, who had deliberately remained aloof from the commission's deliberations, agreed to discuss the commission's recommendations with the outer island chiefs. At the Woleai conference, the Distad, a representative from the high commissioner, and one of the lawyers presented the proposal. The Distad impressed upon them the desire of the high commissioner that Yap have a district legislature. The Carolinian chiefs agreed to the proposed charter on the condition that representation be based upon population distribution. The commission's report had slightly favored Yap in terms of representation. The charter was subsequently passed by the Yap Islands Legislature and approved by the Congress of Micronesia in 1968.

The primary impact of the Peace Corps lawyers came in the vitalization of the legislature.[2] Once legislators recognized how powerful they really were, they stepped out of their dependency relationship with the council and initiated their own legislation and programs. Their independence culminated in a committee to investigate the duties and functions of the magistrates.

The Yap Council was most obvious by its obscurity in the final decision on the Yap District Legislature. When the legislature tabled the municipal charter issue, it extended the life of the unchartered council for an indefinite period, but the leadership role of the council in Yapese affairs has been severely shaken. In contrast, the new district legislature has acquired even more prestige and power. In Yap, the number of legislators was reduced from twenty in the local congress to twelve in the new district-wide body, enhancing the prestige of a legislator. Even more important, however, the district legislature has continued the precedent of independent action established by the local legislature, and has expanded its sphere of power to include all of Yap District. Legislators trained by the Peace Corps lawyers have transmitted these skills to their new local and outer island peers.

Analysis

The American intervention and direction for change in the governmental structure of Yap employed three distinctive models. The naval government established a military regime, including a chain of command with elected chiefs supplying the connecting link between military government and the people. The civilian administration first introduced a model patterned on small-town government in the United States. In this model, all functions of government were handled by a magistrate and a council. The magistrate was judge, local executive, and head of the municipal council that passed ordinances. After a number of years, the Office of the High Commissioner, in response to demands from the U.S. Congress, embarked on a long-range program for political development centered around the "holy trichotomy" (Singleton, chap. 5, this volume) of executive, legislative and judicial branches of government. The model included a unicameral elected district legislature to balance the already existing executive and judicial branches of the administration and a municipality system based on a U.S. metropolitan model with separate executive and legislative branches.

It is rather obvious that the agents for development drew all of these models directly from their experience and ethos, with no reference whatever to the indigenous culture of Yap. Moreover, each model employed belonged to a distinctive level or group in American society and culture, and would not in any case be randomly substituted for each other in their original contexts. Further, the officials who defined these models and sought to implement them in Yap made no effort to investigate traditional Yapese government to find which model, if any, would be most applicable to Yap, or to compare what they knew of Yap with what they knew of the contexts from which the models were drawn. Finally, when the small-town model did prove adaptable and effective in Yap, the administration abandoned it for another that was more pleasing to the ideology of highly placed colonial officials.

The application of such diverse models for directed political change had the dysfunctional results that one might expect. The military model frustrated Yapese leaders because the chain of command was completely incompatible with accepted Yapese rules for mobilizing labor and support. The small-town model was no more successful until the district administrator allowed Yapese leaders to define their own functions and procedures for decision-making and mobilizing local support. Once the colonial and local officials reached a mutual understanding of the authority and power of the council, the model furnished a very effective governing organization. The trichotomy with its unicameral legislature and metropolitan-type government posed a serious threat to established leaders on Yap. Initially, they were able to absorb the threat by creating an inconvenient but subservient legislature. Later, however, when the legislators discovered their independent power, the legislature became the dominant governing body on Yap. The metropolitan-type municipal system has yet to be translated into an effective local government.

It seems evident, then, that the key variable for adaptability of any model for change is not its formal structure, although this is important, but rather the content of the organization and regime, or the rules and procedures for distribution of power. Those agents who concentrated primarily on revision of regime as opposed to revision of organization were most effective.

From the cases presented, it is evident that the goals motivating colonial agents to alter the organization and rules of Yapese government have varied considerably. Three particular types of goals stand out: functional, ideological, and problematical. Functional goals are simply the desires of officials to make the system work in a manner satisfying to the official and to the other participants. A functional administrative system is dependent upon mutual compromise between the colonial administrator and the administered. Because cooperation between participants is critical, the administrative plans and polities must be flexible and frequently adjusted until a degree of satisfaction is obtained that is acceptable to the participants. In the cases cited, the naval officers, district administrators, and Peace Corps lawyers emphasized functional objectives in their working with the Yapese.

Ideological goals are those designs that have no relationship to the concrete situations of the administered communities but are derived from the ethos of the officials who make major policy decisions and who frame the general course of administrative action in their territories. Because the foundations of such goals lie in the ethos of the colonizers, they are necessarily rigid in character and unresponsive to administrative experience. Although all officials have ideals toward which they strive in their administration, the critical variable is the degree to which their ideals govern their choices for action. From the cases observed, it appears that officials farthest removed from the situational demands of daily contact wth the indigenous peoples rely most heavily upon their ideals for establishing policy and making decisions. The Office of the High Commissioner, for example, is subject to minimal negative feedback and can therefore maintain a constant pressure through its intermediaries without experiencing the tension and stress incumbent upon the local administrator and the administered.

Problematical goals are those defined in specific situational contexts of temporary duration with particular reference to a problem to be resolved. The situational context includes both administrators and indigenous participants. The problem has a narrow focus with expectation of solution in a relatively short period of time. In the cases considered, problematical goals are most characteristic for the specialists, those outsiders brought in for short- or long-term consultation. The specialist endeavors to resolve difficulties created by the grand design, incorporating as much participation among the indigenous leadership as possible. His goals are limited primarily by the definition of the problem and not by his ideals or by a perception of how particular alternatives function over a long period of time.

The variation possible in types of goals sought by colonial agents is critical for an understanding of the models and strategies they employ in directing political change. Those sitting in the high commissioner's office, charged with the overall planning for the Trust Territory, formulated a grand design for development following a narrowly defined model derived from American democracy. The local-level administrators, in contrast, sought workable solutions that allowed effective administration and maintained cooperation and some good will with the indigenous people. These differences are directly related to the source of anxieties and concerns of the officials. Local officials are confronted by local people, whereas high-level officials must confront the powers of home.

In addition to the variation in goals and models employed by the agents of change, each official developed particular strategies in attempting to achieve the types of innovations desired. The strategies fall roughly into two categories that may be labeled *coercive* and *persuasive*. The former included edicts and threats of economic or political retaliation, whereas the latter emphasized education, discussion, participation, and example.

Perhaps the most important observation about strategy is that the type of strategy employed appears directly related to the kind of goals endorsed by the specific officials in question. Those seeking ideological goals attempt to enforce the formal structural changes they desire. In the Yap case, the Office of the High Commissioner, desiring a unicameral district legislature, sent down a ready-made charter, a professional trouble-shooter, and official directives to force the creation of such a legislature. In contrast, those with functional or problematical goals perceived the necessity for cooperation with Yapese people to achieve their objectives. They emphasized participant decision-making with guidance, consultation, and discussion.

The basis for such correlation between goals and strategies appears to be a variation of the *Gemeinschaft-Gesellschaft* dichotomy, and might be labeled the principle of bureaucratic distance. The greater the hierarchical and communicative distance between colonial officials and the colonized, the greater the commitment of these officials to ideological goals derived from their own ethos and the greater their dependence upon coercive strategies to obtain those goals. The converse would also appear to be true, namely, that the less the communicative distance, the more functional the goals, and the greater reliance officials place upon persuasion and participation as basic strategies to achieve change.

Although this principle may have general relevance to all types of bureaucracy, there are some critical differences between a colonial bureaucracy and others. One of the most important characteristics of a colonial bureaucracy is the contrast in ethos between officials and the people. In other types of bureaucracy, officials and the general populace for the most part share a common ethos. A second distinction of a colonial bureaucracy is the absence of accountability of the officials to the indigenous people. Athough high-level government officials in the United States are also committed to ideological goals and coercive strategies, they or their leaders are accountable to an electorate that may remove them from power. A colonized people lack the power to remove unresponsive leadership. This unresponsiveness is further reinforced when the high-level officials in a colonial bureaucracy are not free to direct themselves but must answer to a distant, and less knowledgeable, bureaucracy and constituency.

The responses of indigenous peoples to colonial policy must then be essentially protective in character. The strategies employed by the Yapese to counter those of the colonial officials were generally of the same kind. Coercion was met with counter coercion, demands countered with delays, ready-made solutions accepted but ignored. Likewise, persuasion was met with counter persuasion. When the administration extolled the merits of a legislature, the magistrates responded with a greater demonstration of their own ability to produce legislation.

With regard to goals, similar generalizations appear valid. Yapese were never impressed by new forms of government. From their own ethos, the land was chief. However, new rules for allocating power and mobilizing support were readily accepted after they were understood and tested. Further, when new leadership positions and organizational structures were demonstrated to confer greater power, prestige, and authority, they were quickly adopted and became a viable reward in the political contest. The forms from their ideological past were adjusted to a new content that allowed greater exercise of power.

Conclusions

In summary, we have observed wide variation in the goals, models, and strategies applied by numerous agents for political change in Yap. The most influential and "successful" agents were the Peace Corps lawyers and the district administrator of 1955-59, whose programs were addressed not to superficial forms but rather to explanation and exercising of new rules for organizing and allocating power. The least "successful" and most rigid were those agents who dictated policy from a distance.

It must be concluded that different agents within the same colonial system will frequently seek different goals and apply different models and strategies within the same long-range objectives for political change. The significance of the different inputs lies not in final forms, which may appear to vary only slightly, but rather in the processual movement toward those forms, and in the conceptualization of the colonized of the concomitant alterations in the rules. For example, the formation in Yap of municipalities and magistrates was a formal alteration in structure, but Yapese leaders saw no significant alteration in rules for behavior until the Distad had them define the relationship of elements within the form, and their respective responsibilities, and then exercise the new authority. In the same manner, the Peace Corps lawyers showed the legislators the content and scope of their power, drastically modifying their relationship to the council.

Finally, though the cumulative formal effect of directed change may appear the same, the actual interpretation and conceptualization of rules allocating power are subject to wide variation. The formal appearance of the Yap Islands Congress remained the same from 1959 at its inception until it was dissolved in 1968. However, Yapese understanding and behavior in the congress changed drastically during that period of time.

Two of the implications of these conclusions should be noted. First, in a multi-ethnic area like Micronesia a common "model" of district governments is a colonial myth. Even if they were structurally the same, and they are not, they would vary significantly at the conceptual and behavioral levels. Second, if models of government in colonial systems were less rigid, they would serve more effectively, because inherent conceptual differences could be made more explicit and adaptation more effective and satisfying for those undergoing change. On Yap, for example, chartering of the council in 1956 would have permitted both Yapese and American energies to focus on more effective government rather than on the sixteen additional years of flux and uncertainty that today is still unresolved.

1. The data for this chapter was collected as part of a larger research project conducted on Yap from October 1967 to August 1969. The research was supported by a fellowship (1 F1 MH-36, 672-01 CUAN) and a research grant (1 TO 1 MH-11213-01) from the National Institute of Mental Health, Public Health Service and a supplementary grant from the National Science Foundation.

2. In a personal communication, John Farrell, former Peace Corps lawyer on Yap, suggested that I have not given proper recognition to the influence of the Congress of Micronesia on the development of the Yap Islands Legislature. Senators Petrus Tun and Francis Nuun, among others, had been exposed to the workings of the congress for several years and recognized the value of a supporting staff and legislative counsel. Senator Tun was also vice-president of the legislature during this period. These men greatly implemented the creation of a full-time staff for the legislature, promoted the extensive employment of the Peace Corps lawyers on the staff, and furnished personal examples of how effective legislators work.

5

Education, Planning and Political Development in Micronesia

John Singleton

In this chapter, I use some personal experiences with formal schooling and educational planning in the U.S. Trust Territory of the Pacific Islands to assess the relevance of these processes to Micronesian political development.[1] In order to do this, it will be necessary to (1) specify the meaning that I attach to the concept of political development in the Micronesian context, (2) review the history of formal schooling on Truk as an example of Micronesian educational development in its political context, (3) suggest some goals for Micronesian schooling that might facilitate processes of political development, and (4) describe an exercise in stimulating broader participation in educational planning in Micronesia.

The problems with which this chapter deals come from the field of development education, where we are concerned with organized programs of teaching and learning, or schooling, in the context of planning for economic, social, or political change. While assuming the relevance of educational organizations and strategies to individual, community, national, and international development, we have sought to understand the effects of educational interventions in specific cross-cultural contexts (AERA 1968). The anthropologist, in this field of development education, is expected to assess education as a social institution and a social process—unlike our psychological colleagues in education, who look at education as a process of individual changes in behavior irrespective of context.

This chapter is, then, an anthropological perspective of educational data derived from professional experience as teacher, supervisor, and consultant, rather than from premeditated anthropological field research. From 1955 to 1959, I was an "educational specialist" on Truk working as a teacher, supervisor, print-shop director, and general handyman in the elementary and intermediate schools of the Truk district. It was a unique opportunity to know the school system at all levels before the influx of American educational administrators and Peace Corps volunteers. Only five Americans were then employed by the district's Education Department. As part of my professional assignment, I was responsible for developing a working command of the Trukese language. At the same time, my wife was a teacher in the Trust Territory–wide Pacific Islands Central School, then located in Truk and later to evolve into the first public senior high school in the Trust Territory.

In 1966-67, I was involved in the design and execution of a special project in educational planning for the Trust Territory carried out by the Stanford Research Institute. As the most comprehensive and extensively organized attempt to use outside consultants in devising plans for educational development, there were good opportunities to assess the evolution of Micronesian schools and educational policy. In political terms, it was an opportunity to promote new patterns of Micronesian participation in development planning. And, it was also an opportunity to infiltrate educational planning with some anthropological contacts and values.

Since then I have had one more opportunity to visit in Truk and Ponape, but I have not been able to keep up with the details of recent institutional developments. Over the years, in Japan, Hawaii, and Pittsburgh, I have been able to keep occasional contact with a few Micronesian friends—most of whom now wield considerable political or administrative power. Even my anthropological field research in Japan ten years ago was facilitated by contacts based on my previous association with the Trust Territory. Local Japanese who had lived on Truk during the Japanese mandate helped me to move into a rural community and introduced me to the network of repatriated Japanese soldiers and civilians from Micronesia. Thus, the ties with Micronesia have been reinforced over the years since I lived there.

Political Development in Micronesia

Before describing the relation of education to political development in Micronesia, it is necessary to specify the concepts of political development I shall use.

Political Development and Micronesia

Concepts of political development have changed over the years, especially as political scientists have attempted to objectify the meaning of this concept in a culture-free or value-free manner. At the height of the cold war with Russia, there was a strong tendency among American social scientists to equate political development with "democratization" of nation-states in which the definition of democracy had to be contrasted with communism or socialism. One example of this stance is the book by Staley (1961). In application, "political development" seemed to mean that the more the formal structures and symbols of national governmental systems corresponded to the U.S. pattern, the more developed they were considered. In Micronesia in the late 1950's, there was, in similar fashion, a strong push to establish formal systems of community and district government in which the seemingly holy trichotomy of administrative, legislative, and judicial functions would be formally separated and in which individual political roles would be sharply defined, or redefined, to include only one such function. Such symbolic role development for individuals and for political bodies was considered a most important task.

In one of the earlier "political education" programs, in fact, one of the first returning Trukese college students was put to work translating and then transmitting to village councils *Robert's Rules of Order*. The political chartering of municipalities in Truk District was made dependent on their willingness to establish local government based on the U.S. model and their ability in legislative councils to follow *Robert's Rules of Order*. There was an implicit assumption that local patterns of political decision-making were not relevant to the new purposes of community, district, and territory-wide political mobilization.

In one outstanding exception to this pattern, for a local community that was a political thorn in the flesh of the American district administration, the granting of a municipal charter was delayed, even though the local council had been systematically developed on the forms translated from an American civics textbook. Making use of the U.S. national governmental institutions as models, they even had a Department of State to issue visas for individuals from other communities who wanted to visit the reef islands under their control. Their early truculence with the administration seemed to be the major reason for withholding their charter. Thus, one would have to add willingness to accept the district administration's authority to acceptance of symbolic forms of U.S. local government as the requirements for political recognition.

The transmission of U.S. formal structures in rigid patterns to Micronesia was ironic in the lack of any recognition of alternative political structures existing in other nations and, in the Pacific, in the colonial extensions of France and England that did not pay equal homage to the U.S. forms. As Meller indicates in chapter 14, there have been more flexible approaches elsewhere in the Pacific. Equally ironic was the reaction of U.S. political scientist Robert Scalapino, who, in a 1960 radio news commentary about Micronesia, took the U.S. government to task for not adapting its Trust Territory administration to the expressed needs of Micronesians and then suggested critically that the development of the Marshall Islands Congress was "undemocratic" because it included representation based upon locally ascribed noble status together with popularly elected representatives. That the Marshall Islands Congress was one of the very few examples of successful accommodation to local interests and social structures in the Trust Territory political development program was unrecognized (Meller 1969: 132–41).

In the current consideration of concepts of political development, it is not surprising to find little consensus among social scientists about even the possibility of an objective value-free definition. Apter and Mushi (1970) suggest that there are currently three dimensions of a general theory of choice or development—normative, structural, and behavioral.

One definition, for instance, suggested that political development

> can be regarded as the acquisition by a political system of a consciously sought, and qualitatively new and enhanced, political capacity as manifested in the successful institutionalization of (1) new patterns of integration regulating and containing the tensions and conflicts produced by increased differentiation, and (2) new patterns of participation and resource distribution adequately responsive to the demands generated by the imperatives of equality. (Coleman 1965:15)

But there are inevitable value assumptions. As Goulet has noted,

> "Development" is above all a question of values. It involves human attitudes and preferences, self-defined goals, and criteria for determining what are tolerable costs to be borne in the course of change. . . . [The representative of a developed country] can never accurately observe underdevelopment in the detached mode of a spectator. Nor can he properly treat it as a mere problem: he himself is part of the problem. His society is responsible at least for the alteration in the other's aspirations—to achieve dignity and autonomous agency in its own development. . . . This means that researchers, no less than planners, must, *before taking action*, engage in critical dialogue with the interested populace itself, taking the limits posed by that populace as their own point of departure. (1971:205-27)

Under these considerations, I can only view political development as an increase in the opportunities for people to participate effectively in the political decisions that will affect their local, national, or international community. I do not assume a necessary political form within which this increase will take place, nor do I assume a correlation with increasing complexity or differentiation in formal political institutions. Successful adaptation in the furtherance of a society's political interests would, therefore, be counted as political development.

In the case of Micronesia, the definition of dimensions of political development can only be determined by Micronesians within those collectivities that are significant to them.

Gladwin's work as a consultant to Micronesians interested in the alternative political forms now open to them is an excellent example of an "educational" program to increase the options for political development. He tried to communicate the implications of an alternative political structure—one-party socialism on the Tanzanian model with independence from the United States (1971a, 1971b). In an article prepared for *Met Poraus*, the weekly mimeographed newspaper for the Truk District, he suggested the need for a broad educational-informational program to disseminate the implications he sees for Micronesian national political independence, especially in the light of Chinese, Cuban, and Tanzanian experiences with socialist-directed development. In that article, he said, with what I believe to be appropriate anthropological acumen,

> Americans often appear to believe that education is only what happens in school, and that political education is the same as propaganda, which they consider bad. Americans actually engage in a lot of propaganda themselves. For years they have been teaching Micronesians the virtues of the American form of government of free-enterprise capitalism, of the evils of communism and even socialism, but this they call education because they teach it in the schools they control. (1971a:2–3)

Another example of relevant political education is the work of Meller in helping to convey both the formal and informal patterns by which legislative systems operate to members of the Congress of Micronesia (Meller 1969).

Thus, even while concentrating upon the role of schooling in Micronesian political development, it is important to recognize that the formal curriculum of the schools is only one of many educational relations to political change. That part of the curriculum devoted explicitly to the transmission of political values and knowledge is only one dimension of such relationships between educational and political systems—one that, I am convinced, carries little weight. More deserving of consideration is the way in which the experiences of schooling have contributed to the skills necessary for effective political participation, the ways in which the system of schooling have had direct impact upon the political system, and the political effects of educational policy decisions.

I will discuss these aspects of education next in the context of that part of the Micronesian school system with which I have had most contact—the elementary and secondary schools of the Truk District.

Schooling on Truk

Formal schools on Truk are, of course, institutions imported from the Western world—first by American missionaries and later by Japanese and American government sponsorship. They bear little relation to indigenous forms of cultural transmission and have always been oriented to foreign languages and knowledge. They have been interface institutions between the external colonial authorities, whether government or missionary, and the Trukese community—with teachers acting as cultural brokers (Hunt and Hunt 1967). Though guided by policies based on assimilation of Trukese students to larger religious or political collectivities, for many Trukese, the schools have often been, in themselves, the limit of possible contact with the outside world.

The arrival of American Protestant missionaries on Truk under the sponsorship of the American Board Commission for Foreign Missions in 1884 marked the beginning of schooling in the Western tradition.

The Reverend R. W. Logan, describing his pleasure at the results of a missionary school examination held just two years after the beginning of mission work on Truk, wrote:

> Forty-eight scholars can read, and it was a joy to see the whole number stand up and read, each from his own copy of the Scriptures; many of them are getting beyond the stage of word-calling into that of intelligent reading. The school also did creditably in singing, writing, and the beginnings of arithmetic and geography. (Bliss 1906:60)

The Spanish and German administrations made no attempts to set up schools of their own, but allowed and encouraged the missionaries to keep on with their system. The Japanese, though allowing the missionaries to continue their schools, established a separate public school system.

The Japanese administration stressed Japanese-style public elementary schools for the native children that taught the Japanese language and the usual elementary skills. Japanese teachers taught the upper levels of the Trukese elementary schools, but Trukese teachers gave the beginners their first instruction in the Japanese language. Enough schools were set up to provide instruction for the major centers of the Trukese population, including the outer islands, but not all of the children on the smaller islands had an opportunity to attend. After four years of elementary education, selected pupils attended an advanced intermediate school for a couple of years of further education (Fischer 1961). The intermediate school was located on Truk Atoll and brought its students in from the islands of the Truk District. Further vocational education, particularly in carpentry and agriculture, was available to some of the intermediate school graduates in a vocational school for older students from all parts of the present Trust Territory. The vocational school was located in the Palau Islands about a thousand miles west of Truk.

The purpose of the Japanese educational system was to bring the Trukese people into the Japanese historical and cultural tradition, to make Truk a functioning part of the Japanese Empire. However, there was always a separate school system for the children of Japanese immigrants, and no Trukese student was ever sent out of the mandated islands to continue his formal education.

When the U.S. Navy administration for the Truk District arrived after the Japanese surrender, it began the program of American-sponsored education. The first step on the part of the navy was to establish a school for the teaching of English to promising young Trukese, most of whom had already gone through the Japanese schools. These young men and a few women were to be prepared as elementary teachers and for work in the civil administration of

Truk. After two or three years of such schooling, the graduates were to be sent to a teacher training school on Guam, or, in some cases, were to be put to work immediately as elementary teachers or administration workers.

With much U.S. Navy encouragement and assistance, villages provided buildings, and the navy sent out supplies and recruited teachers for elementary schools. As quickly as possible, a six-year, universal, coeducational, elementary school system was set up for the teaching of reading, writing, arithmetic, and the English language. Established by the navy, the schools were viewed by the Trukese community as a part of the "American" program, and they did not necessarily feel responsibility for the continued operation of the schools. The people were anxious, however, for their children to learn English, a skill that would help them to get a paying job with the American administration, and so they provided support for the schools when directed to do so by the American authorities. In a few years' time, schools had been established and teachers appointed for every village or island with enough children to justify a school. School buildings and teacher salaries in the 1950s came from local and district taxes rather than the administration's budget. Local magistrates were expected to ensure that teachers kept the schools open and were consulted about the assignment of particular teachers to their communities.

While close to 100 percent of elementary school children have been consistently enrolled in the village elementary schools, the experience of that schooling has changed in a number of ways. Local schoolhouses furnished and maintained by the community have been replaced in the last decade by modern concrete-block school buildings built and maintained by the administration—often with imported construction laborers from the Philippines. Native teachers have gradually acquired skills and knowledge to carry out more meaningful programs and have been furnished an increasing, though small, amount of educational materials and texts designed for Micronesian schools. Especially important has been the shift from nondescript teaching of English by non-English-speaking teachers using castoff Red Cross imported "Dick and Jane" readers to the introduction of modern linguistically oriented methods and materials for the teaching of English as a second language together with increasing exposure to competent speakers of English.

In the early 1960s, the first American elementary teachers were assigned to some elementary schools, and the larger schools have had continuous contact with such teachers since then—augmented in 1967 by Peace Corps volunteers. American teachers have found it difficult to work under Trukese principals, but they have been expected to do so over the years by Micronesian educational supervisors and administrators in many of the district education office positions. Since 1955, there has been a Trukese superintendent of schools, but a Trukese district education administrator, the top education job in the district, was appointed only four years ago to replace an American.

The schools have been put more firmly and completely under the control of the district education office, as Nagao and Nakayama have reported:

> In 1964 the Administration undertook total payment of teachers' salaries. Perhaps the most significant thing about this development was the Administration's acquisition of the right to hire, place, and transfer teachers without prior consultation with the communities in which schools were located. . . . The practice of seeking the consent of community leaders before specific individuals were assigned to their schools was ended. (1969:5)

In addition, a program of elementary school consolidation has further removed the elementary schools from identification with their local communities. The introduction of significant numbers of American teachers has also signaled a change in the external orientation of the schools.

The central district boarding school—established by the navy administration to train the first teachers and administration officials—has survived many functional changes. Quickly turned into a three-year intermediate school for selected Trukese elementary school graduates after the first classes of teachers and clerks had been graduated, it has always had a double vocational purpose. It has prepared a few Trukese students for further education, and it has had a local vocational orientation with some kinds of skills in agriculture, carpentry, boatbuilding, and construction being included in the curriculum.

Early in the 1950s, the Pacific Islands Central School (PICS) was established on Truk as a central public secondary school for students from the whole Trust Territory. PICS was the successor of the Pacific Islands Teacher Training School (PITTS) originally established on Guam and moved to Truk in 1948. Recognizing that PITTS had become in fact, if not in name, the source of public general secondary education, the name was changed about 1954 from PITTS to PICS, and the official rationale for the school caught up with its function. It was, at that time, providing two years of post-intermediate education and the staff soon moved to implement a three-year program that would more readily be acknowledged as college-preparatory for those graduates chosen to continue their formal education overseas. Moved to new quarters on Ponape in 1960, PICS was the only Trust Territory high school until 1962 when district intermediate schools were upgraded to high schools and elementary schools were given increased responsibility for eight years of schooling.

By then, the facilities of the intermediate school and PICS on Truk were combined to make the Truk High School. Originally staffed by American and Micronesian teachers together, the central district school has continued to be a culturally mixed institution with inevitable tendencies toward an academic orientation. It has never been able to accommodate more than a small fraction of the elementary school graduates in the district.

In 1967, the local demand for expanded secondary education opportunity led to the establishment of "post-elementary" schools on several of the outlying islands. Established cooperatively by administration, Peace Corps, and local officials for secondary education of a locally relevant vocational nature, these schools have had a somewhat tenuous existence, but probably they receive more direct support than other public schools from the local communities they serve—if only by default because the administration had no budget or fancy buildings for them. The first such school, which I visited shortly after it opened in 1967, was staffed by Peace Corps volunteers and local vocational specialists in a Trukese thatch building erected by the local people without benefit of imported materials.

Higher educational opportunity has always been open to a few Trukese outside of the district, usually sponsored by government scholarships with some funds coming from locally administered tax revenues. The earliest and best higher education received by Trukese was in the medical field. Medical practitioners trained in intensive programs on Guam and Fiji were already carrying the major responsibility for modern medical services in the early 1950s. My first child, in fact, was delivered by such a doctor in 1956 on Truk.

The first Trukese to study outside of Truk in nonmedical fields returned to teaching jobs at the intermediate school in 1955. But the first Trukese college graduate did not come back until 1967. The University of Guam, the University of Hawaii, and, for a few students, the University of the Philippines have been the major centers of outside higher education.

Other training programs for a variety of vocational fields have been developed in the Trust Territory from time to time in fields such as nursing, radio operation, auto mechanics, and weather station operations. Further vocational educational training outside of regular college degree programs has also been offered since 1961 at the East-West Center of the University of Hawaii.

The present political leaders of the Trust Territory who do not derive their positions from age or chiefly status first met as students at the old Pacific Islands Central School, but the second generation of Micronesian political elites are apparently meeting each other in Guam and Hawaii.

Micronesian Schools and Political Development

In order to assess the political implications of this schooling on Truk, I will turn to outlines by anthropologist Margaret Mead and political scientist James Coleman. Mead (1946) has suggested that curricular concerns for those skills that would facilitate world mobility are most appropriate to Pacific island territories. Coleman (1956), on the other hand, has suggested that the political development functions of schooling include political socialization, integration, and recruitment. These formulations help to put the curriculum and the social structure of the school into the perspective of political development.

Mead's concern for the people of developing areas in the Pacific was that they acquire those skills and understanding that would enable them to interact effectively with the world outside of their communities so that they would have more control over the political and social decisions affecting them. She was not concerned about developing substitute mechanisms for cultural transmission in communities with well-integrated patterns already established for local cultural transmission and change. She was, however, concerned about how people in small, politically weak communities and territories would defend their real interests in their increasingly inevitable transactions with the rest of the world—with alien governments, colonial authorities, commercial entrepreneurs, and other representatives of outside interests.

Mead's outline of the skills and understanding that might be transmitted through schooling (1946:347) included:

1. the ability to speak, read, and write a world language that would provide a medium of communication with those who would come to the islands and would provide for islanders to move about freely in international affairs;
2. a grasp of the framework of Western and international economics, including the notions of contractual responsibility;
3. that cross-cultural sophistication which would enable an individual to deal with others holding different cultural codes and standards;
4. an ability to act within the framework of the scientific attitude and to understand its premises in political, economic, and technological contexts;
5. a concept of history that would make it possible to understand the relation of one's community to the time perspectives of other civilizations;
6. the ability to exist independently for varying periods of time away from one's immediate community and its cultural and psychological supports.

These educational goals provide a rationale for much of the conventional curricular purposes of Trukese schools, but there has been little systematic evaluation of educational achievement in such terms. Only in the case of English-language instruction has there been a functional drive for instruction and evaluation consistent with the goal of world mobility through the English language. More importantly, perhaps, there has been no teaching of alternative languages of international importance to Micronesians. Because of the strong economic ties with Japan, one might well suggest the necessity of developing a new generation of Japanese language–speakers to replace the adults over forty who were schooled under the Japanese and who now carry the burden of communication with Japanese in Japanese.

I would add to Mead's list the need for systematic attention to vernacular Trukese literacy so that the schools may more efficiently teach the skills of reading and writing separately from the processes associated with mastering communication in a foreign language. Given the need to transmit a variety of functional skills for world mobility—or political development, in our current terminology—there is no excuse for making English the language of all instruction in elementary education. To do so is to imply that foreign-language skill is the only necessary skill in achieving the potential for world mobility. It also conveys an undeserved disparagement of the vernacular languages.

Unfortunately, educational achievement in Micronesian schools has been most often evaluated by achievement tests developed and standardized for American children in U.S. schools. Even when teachers administering the tests have insisted that they were only accumulating comparative data for assessing individual achievement, there has been an inevitable and invidious comparison with the performance of American children on the same tests. There has been little understanding by either Micronesian parents or American teachers of the double standard in this comparison where one group of children is tested in their vernacular language on subject matter associated with their long-established patterns of schooling and another is tested in a foreign language on subject matter from a foreign area—to which their only exposure has often been through the medium of a second language.

I am here suggesting what has not yet been done: that Mead's list of skills be used for developing a new kind of educational evaluation in Truk based on goals that would more closely approximate the functional requirements of Micronesian political development.

In somewhat larger perspective, it is necessary to look at the ways in which the educational system interacts with the political system. Coleman's suggestion that political socialization, integration, and recruitment are three basic processes of political development relevant to education provides an appropriate framework for this analysis (1965:17–18).

Political socialization is seen as the process by which individuals acquire understandings about, and attitudes toward, the political system and toward their role within it (Coleman 1965:10). In the context of Trukese schooling, the school is most relevant to the newly introduced systems of municipal, district, territorial, and international government. Indeed, the symbolism of the United Nations has received much emphasis in the schools—the most exciting event of the school year was often the United Nations Day interschool athletic competitions. Meller has observed in historical context that the "schools played an important role in conditioning Micronesians for accepting and participating in assemblies with law-making power" (1969:46). But the schools, like the political education program for transmitting *Robert's Rules of Order* described earlier, have more often transmitted the symbols than the content of political institutions. I do not believe that they have developed the basis for the necessary adaptation of indigenous patterns to the highly differentiated and complex institutions within which the Micronesians are now expected to make sophisticated political decisions about their future. The current crop of Micronesian political leaders probably learned most of the formal patterns of legislative political strategy from astute observation of American local politics while they were college students in Guam, Hawaii, and on the U.S. mainland. Their political goals and strategies are, of course, a function of their Micronesian community experience.

The primary role of Trukese schools in political socialization would seem to be transmission of the skills listed by Mead for world mobility and communication. Standards of evaluation based on U.S. models have probably subverted their potential for achieving Mead's goals in the past.

Political integration refers to the development of an integrated political process in which the gap between governing elites and the masses is diminished (vertical integration) and in which previously separate political communities are amalgamated into a larger political collectivity (horizontal integration) (Coleman 1965:30). As Ivan Illich has pointed out so forcefully for Latin America, the extension of schooling can be a mechanism for maintaining rather than diminishing the elite-mass gap (1968). Likewise, the placement of schools and the processes by which they identify and organize students may strengthen, rather than weaken, local parochialism.

In Truk, the central district boarding high school provides the first major setting for many students to meet individuals from across the district. The association of these students promotes a horizontal integration in the Truk District while promoting a mass-elite gap by the privileges it bestows on those few students it is able to admit. Before 1962, the Pacific Islands Central School served a similar important function of horizontal integration for Micronesia while promoting an ever more pervasive elite-mass separation for the Trust Territory as a whole. In the last decade, the district high schools have furnished district-level secondary education, eliminating the territory-wide secondary school. In place of the Pacific Islands Central School, the University of Hawaii is now the major point of elite horizontal integration for the Trust Territory, with the University of Guam serving as a second-level, less prestigeful meeting point for other students. Neither Hawaii nor Guam has effectively replaced the former Pacific Islands Central School as an intensive institution for the development of Micronesian political unity, for within each institution, Micronesian students are a minority group more or less integrated with the total student bodies for most of their activities there. The presence of a separate dormitory for Trust Territory students in Guam probably provides closer contacts for students there. In Hawaii, the Micronesian Club has been the central focus for Micronesian student interaction.

There is also a potential curricular input to political integration of the Trust Territory when, and if, the schools systematically convey some sense of the multicultural political unit that is Micronesia. The ability to deal with, and identify with, Micronesia, the Pacific, and other regions of the world might well be enhanced within the schools.

Political recruitment is a function of social stratification (Coleman 1965:25), and it is obvious that school systems are important in selecting those who will be upwardly mobile in contemporary societies. The limited access to secondary and higher education—the experience of which is especially associated with political leadership in the new political organs of the Trust Territory, as discussed in several other chapters in this volume—indicates the importance of this function of the schools. Although elementary education is universal in Truk, academic success is the key to admission to the higher levels of education. Academic success in high school, often measured by individual scores on U.S. achievement tests, is the key to scholarships for university study in Guam and Hawaii. Before the development of the Congress of Micronesia, the graduates of higher education were almost exclusively absorbed into the higher-level positions of the Trust Territory administration. With the forced option between administrative and legislative positions after the founding of the Congress, many of the new elite—those who have moved up via higher education—have chosen to identify themselves with the Congress and have resigned from their administrative positions. Few of the educationally selected elite have gone to work for commercial enterprises, though this is now changing.

The schools have, therefore, served as a channel for recruitment and identification of new political leaders. No longer, however, is high school graduation sufficient for entry to elite status jobs. The first generation of Trukese elite jobholders is still young and not yet ready to retire. Employment opportunities have by no means kept up with the increasing supply of educationally certified aspirants for elite employment.

Nevertheless, the political functions of schooling have developed in an unplanned and erratic way based upon such educational policy decisions as the elimination of a territory-wide secondary school and the assumption by the administration of responsibility, for elementary schoolteachers' salaries.

Closer attention to the social processes and functions of the school system in ways such as Mead and Coleman have suggested would help to more constructively direct educational policy decisions in Micronesia.

In order to further pursue the political development potential in Micronesian education, new patterns of educational leadership and planning are required. One attempt to develop new forms of educational planning for the Trust Territory was undertaken several years ago.

Micronesian Educational Planning

The political dimensions of contemporary exercises in development planning are not usually considered in relation to political development. They are, however, potentially important political processes, and this is nowhere more evident than in the Trust Territory. Planning for economic development, health, education, and several other areas has been emphasized since 1966 by a series of special planning projects during which outside consultant groups have worked with the administration, and occasionally, with the Micronesians, themselves, to recommend long-range plans for action.[2]

Of particular relevance to political development has been (1) the extent to which the planning process has encouraged and enhanced the ability of Micronesian communities to define and promote their own developmental goals and (2) the way in which recommendations have begun to define the options that will be open to Micronesian individuals and communities in the future. More specifically, the extent to which alternative political futures have been implicitly assumed or explicitly enumerated will help to determine the future options of a Micronesian community or polity.

During 1966 and 1967, the Trust Territory administration initiated a brief, but intensive, program for long-range educational planning in Micronesia. The decision to initiate such a project was based upon many considerations, not the least of which was the availability of funds for educational planning from the U.S. Office of Education outside of the regular Trust Territory budget.[3] The Stanford

Research Institute (SRI) was asked to develop a proposal for initiating a master plan for education and training in Micronesia. Its proposal was accepted and made the basis of a contract that provided for an SRI consultant team to spend four months in the Trust Territory.

Two major purposes were associated with the project. The first was to initiate a series of interviews and conferences in each district culminating in two territory-wide conferences on Saipan, during which Micronesian communities and leaders would be brought into a multilevel goal-setting process for educational development. The second was to conduct a manpower study for the Trust Territory delineating both future social demand for education (on the basis of demographic data) and manpower needs (on the basis of economic and social development projections). The first function was primarily that of community organizing, in which it was assumed with Goodenough (1963:58) that "what a community *needs* for its development is not so much a matter of fact as a matter to be negotiated." The second function required technical expertise in the collection and analysis of manpower data.

The final report of the SRI team was dated December 1967 (Platt and Sorenson). It summarized the planning process, provided the required data, and made a series of formal recommendations. As is often the case, the printed report was perceived by most observers as the major product produced by the planning activities. On this basis, the SRI project could hardly be justified. As a Trukese magistrate, critical of the large expenditure on the SRI project, said during 1967 graduation exercises at the Truk High School, "We know what our educational problems are—give us the money and let us get on with the job."[4]

What, then, were the important political development functions of this project that might have justified the seemingly irrational expenditures on it?

First, and most important, the project was a necessary political and administrative antidote for the Nathan Report on Economic Development Planning issued early in 1967 (Nathan 1967). Nathan Associates had implicitly assumed physical resource development to be the prime goal of U.S. policy in the administration of the islands. Their plan, for example, called for developing a disciplined and productive labor force that could be concentrated in accessible urban centers and used in a profitable manner by both traditional and modern industries, including the exploitation of resources for tourism. Reminiscent of the development of Hawaii, Fiji, and the mainland United States, it was proposed, in all seriousness, that laborers be imported from countries like the Philippines where people were accustomed to the "real" value of their labor and would not demand the "unrealistic" wages currently paid to Micronesians by the island government bureaucracy and would be willing to put forth intensive efforts in their labor.

The SRI Report, on the other hand, proposed the alternative goal of human resource development as the measure of development planning (Pearse and Bezanson 1970). The development of physical resources was seen as justifiable only in terms of the increased abilities acquired by Micronesians to contribute to, and share in, the profits of such development. The importation of foreign laborers made no sense when there were unemployed Micronesians, and the importation of foreign-organized businesses to provide opportunities for the exploitation of cheap Micronesian labor were equally reprehensible in this view. In addition, the SRI report deliberately included consideration of the political alternative that the Trust Territory might opt for some form of independence rather than continuing status as a U.S. territory. The Nathan Report had called for closer integration with the U.S. economy, ignoring the possibility of political alternatives that would substantially change the political relationship of the Trust Territory to the United States.[5]

A second result of the educational planning project was the creation of a manpower planning board inside the administration to oversee and implement the strategic goal of human resource development in all developmental activities of the administration. The particular purpose of this board was to provide authority over Trust Territory dealings with outside agencies and employers—to make sure that requirements for Micronesian participation and training in all projects were actually carried out.

Third, an informal pattern was established for territory-wide consultation with Micronesians on development policy determination. Without a new formal organization, there may be some question about the long-range influence of this project. It was, at least, a demonstration that such consultation could be effected in a manner not previously initiated by the administration. It was, seemingly, not in conflict with the Congress of Micronesia, for many congressmen participated in the consultations, and the congress, itself, commended the final report in a formal resolution. One had the feeling at the time that the congressmen appreciated a process of consultation and negotiation that did not rely exclusively upon them when they were very much concerned with the large range of issues demanding the congress's attention.

Fourth, the plan did provide a technical basis for administrative and legislative policy decisions in education, as well as a justification for continued allocation of finances in the Trust Territory budgeting system.

In larger political and development perspective, the SRI project was only justifiable to the extent that it contributed to a self-generating process of educational planning and concern.[6] It was, of course, neither a necessary nor sufficient impetus for the generation of such a process; rather, it was one attempt to move in this direction with the aid of outside consultants not committed to current administrative patterns.

Conclusions

This paper has suggested that education, schools, and educational planning have a direct relevance for Micronesian political development over and above that which is taught explicitly to Micronesian children in a formal social studies curriculum. The extent to which Micronesians are able to acquire the skills for world mobility—the skills that lead to effective political participation in regional and international affairs—and the extent to which schools and their affiliated administrative systems deal with political socialization, integration, and recruitment will determine the effectiveness of formal education as an instrument of political development. Undoubtedly more affected by, than affecting, their political context, the schools are, nevertheless, engaged in a social transaction with their society and the various political systems that exist within it or act upon it.

Conventional, by U.S. standards, evaluation and administration of the schools has been a hindrance to the development of more sophisticated political awareness in Micronesian education. The SRI educational planning project was, in some part, an attempt to make more explicit and effective the relationship between schools, educational administration, and the Micronesian society. It was, obviously, of only minor historical importance in the evolution of Micronesian education. It has been treated here, however, as an example of a kind of educational intervention different from the usual missionary-like efforts to extend schooling for the sake of schooling.

This chapter has, then, suggested some of the dimensions by which we might evaluate the contributions and relations of education to the political development of Micronesia. The evaluation is by no means complete; rather, there are a number of relevant researchable questions that have been posed.

1. To what extent have the skills associated with world mobility been transferred to Micronesian students by the schools?
2. In what specific ways have the functions of political socialization, integration, and recruitment been served or subverted by the schools?
3. Has the process of educational planning initiated in 1967 had any effect on increasing Micronesian participation in the setting of development objectives and plans?

In many ways, Micronesians have become a minority ethnic group in the U.S. political system. Unlike the Hawaiians, Indians, Blacks, Chicanos, and others who have been permanently incorporated into American society, Micronesians are faced with a symbolic and, perhaps, real option about their future political status. It is necessary that the school's role be considered as choices are made and that Micronesians become aware of the experience of other incorporated minorities in the American system. They already have much in common. One recent graduate of the current system of Micronesian schooling put the issue very directly:

> As it is now, the educational system in Micronesia is designed to make Americans out of the Micronesians. This Americanization of Micronesia is done in the name of modernization. Micronesians unknowingly are being robbed of their value systems which are replaced by the white man's value systems. (Uludong 1969:3)

1. Parts of this chapter were originally presented under the title "Cross-Cultural Strains in Development Education: An Analysis of American-Sponsored Schooling on Truk" at the Interdisciplinary Conference on Processes of Change in Contemporary Asian Societies at the Center for Asian Studies, University of Illinois, Urbana-Champaign, 5–7 November 1970. Helpful comments have been received from Daniel Hughes, A. Richard King, Thomas Gladwin, David Ramarui, and John Fischer.

2. There have also been, of course, plans developed within the U.S. government for military and political purposes that have been kept secret. The Solomon Report commissioned by the Kennedy administration is one example.

3. As Meller mentions in this volume, the Hawaii congressional delegation

had begun to add the Trust Territory to a variety of appropriations bills for regular U.S. government programs. This had the effect of making funds available for special projects outside the Territory's regular budget.

4. Even though I later learned that a Peace Corps volunteer had written the magistrate's speech, he had a point. It was, however, embarrassing because I, a member of the SRI team, was the commencement speaker—a last-minute replacement for the irreplaceable Dwight Heine, who had been caught by a quarantine in the Marshalls.

5. Neither of the reports pursued the specific possibility of significant political replationships with Japan being redeveloped through the natural economic ties that might again be mutually profitable.

6. I have not personally been able to observe the longer-term results.

6

Obstacles to the Integration of the District Legislature into Ponapean Society

Daniel T. Hughes

On Ponape, as in the rest of Micronesia, the most significant political change in the past twenty-five years has been the introduction to some extent on all levels of government of democratic institutions and procedures modeled largely on the political system of the United States. This is not to say that traditional Ponapean society was completely "undemocratic." If we acknowledge the most essential characteristic of a democracy as a relatively high degree of control exercised by people over their leaders, then we must conclude that there were definitely democratic elements in the traditional Ponapean society. Ponapean chiefs rarely made unilateral decisions on important issues in their chiefdoms. They sounded out public opinion by consulting their subordinates, who in turn were in constant contact with the ordinary people. Moreover, important titles were distributed among various clans and sub-clans, and this practice dispersed authority throughout the society. Granted then the presence of democratic elements in traditional Ponapean society, still the democratic system introduced by the Americans was a totally different one basically in imitation of their own political system. The introduction of this new political system has deeply affected Ponapean society.

Previous foreign administrations also effected political change on Ponape (Hughes 1970:41–45). But the American administration, for better or for worse, has altered the traditional system far more profoundly than any previous administration. It has introduced elections widely, established elected and appointed Micronesian officials on all levels of government, and has insisted on the division of legislative, executive, and judicial powers among distinct branches of government on all levels. Such innovations have significantly altered the traditional social and political systems on Ponape and in the rest of Micronesia.

In recent years, political change in many societies has increasingly involved the introduction of new political systems. Because the viability of a new political system depends in large measure upon the successful integration of new leadership roles into a society, the interest of social scientists has turned to factors aiding and inhibiting such successful integration.

In 1966, I conducted a research project on the Island of Ponape studying the integration into Ponapean society of the four elected leadership roles of magistrate, councilman, district legislator, and territorial congressman. In previous reports, I have focused on the roles of magistrate (1969b), councilman (1969a), and territorial congressman (1972). This chapter focuses on the role of district legislator. In it, we shall: (1) trace briefly the setting and historical background of the role of district legislator; (2) see how this role functions in Ponapean society by examining the role elements of recruitment, activities, and position in the political system; and (3) discuss some reasons that this role is less accepted and less integrated into Ponapean society than the other three elected leadership roles. The reader is asked to bear in mind that this chapter describes and analyzes the situation in Ponape at the time of my study in 1966.

Setting and Background

Ponape, a rich, mountainous island in the Eastern Carolines, has a population of about 13,000. Here the traditional political system still functions quite vigorously and is centered in five chiefdoms or autonomous states. A primary ruler called the *nahnmwareki* 'paramount chief' and his principal adviser called the *nahniken* 'minister' govern each chiefdom. Below both of these rulers in each chiefdom there is a line of titleholders, with the first twelve men in both lines constituting a privileged noble class. People with lower kingdom titles or with no kingdom titles are commoners. The five kingdoms are divided into geographical areas known as *kousapw* 'sections' each of which is governed by a *kaun en kousapw* 'section chief.' The paramount chief and the minister must appoint the section chief, and they often designate the head of the leading lineage of the section for this position.

Under the American administration, Ponape is divided into six municipalities, five of which are coextensive with the five traditional chiefdoms. The sixth was established in 1965 when the town of Kolonia, which has always been the base for foreign administrations, separated from the chiefdom and municipality of Net. Each of the six municipalities has an elected magistrate as its chief executive and an elected council as its legislative body. A councilman typically represents an area coextensive with several traditional sections of the chiefdom. On a higher level, the elected district legislature has legislative authority over the entire Ponape District, which includes the islands of Ponape and six others. The highest executive official at this level is the district administrator, who is appointed by the high commissioner. The high commissioner, designated by the president of the United States and responsible directly to the secretary of the interior, is the ranking executive official in the Trust Territory. The legislative counterpart to this office is the Micronesian Congress, with members elected from all six districts of the Trust Territory.

The traditional Ponapean political system extends only to the municipal or chiefdom level. On this level, the magistrate parallels the traditional 'paramount chief,' and the councilman parallels the 'section chief.' Though the present chapter focuses on the position of district legislator, this position should be viewed in the context of the whole system of which it is a part.

Before discussing the district legislator role, it may be useful to review the historical background of this legislative body. Here "congress" refers to legislative bodies on a district-wide basis: beginning with the Palau Congress in 1947, all six Trust Territory districts established such district-wide "congresses" (Meller 1969: 59). However, in 1965, a territorial congress, the Congress of Micronesia, was formed, and the district "congresses" became known as "legislatures." If this switch in terminology confuses the reader, he might take some comfort from knowing that it also confuses the Ponapeans.

Ponape took its first step toward setting up a congress with a referendum in 1949 to determine whether the congress should be district-wide or limited to Ponape Island itself. The referendum favored a district-wide congress, and the following year a charter was submitted to the high commissioner for a Congress of Ponape District. The high commissioner rejected this charter because he felt that differences of language and difficulties of travel in the area made a district-wide congress impractical at that time (Richard 1957 III:400). In 1952, the high commissioner approved a charter establishing the Ponape Island Congress, which was limited to Ponape Island.

The Ponape Island Congress (1952-58) consisted of two houses, the Nobles' House and the People's House. The Nobles' House was composed of five nobles from each of the five municipalities of Ponape Island. The first two titleholders in both noble lines from each municipality automatically took seats in the Nobles' House. The 'paramount chief' and the 'minister' of each municipality jointly appointed one other high-ranking titleholder outside of either noble line.

All representatives to the People's House were elected. Each municipality had one representative in the People's House for every 300 residents. Those nobles automatically seated in the Nobles' House were excluded from the People's House, but other nobles were eligible for election to the lower house. Both houses had the right to seat delegates from the outer islands on a nonvoting basis.

The early domination of the Nobles' House over the People's House can be seen in the record of the 1952 session of the legislature. In that session, twelve resolutions sponsored by the Nobles' House were approved, and only three sponsored by the People's House were approved. As time went on, the business of the congress became more complex, and many of the Ponapean chiefs ceased taking part in the sessions. Many were handicapped by not knowing English fluently and by a lack of formal education in dealing with legislative affairs. They were also unaccustomed to stating a position positively and having the position challenged or opposed. In the 1956 session, only three 'paramount chiefs' and one 'minister' attended the meetings. At this session, the congress approved four out of six resolutions proposed by the People's House and only one out of three proposed by the Nobles' House. By and large, the Ponapean chiefs were withdrawing from this institution and relinquishing it to the younger, more educated Ponapeans (Meller 1969:125–26).

In 1958, a new charter was approved, and the Ponape *Island Congress* became the Ponape *District Congress*, a single legislative body with elected representatives from all the islands of Ponape District. The charter for the Ponape District Congress (1958) provided for the election of representatives from all the municipalities of the district, with no nobles automatically included in the congress. In 1963, the Ponape District Congress revised its charter and established the Ponape *District Legislature*—really a continuation of the Ponape District Congress (1958–63). At that time, all district "congresses" became "legislatures" to prevent name conflict with the "Congress of Micronesia."

Recruitment

The Ponape District comprises twelve municipalities. Six are on Ponape itself, and six are outer islands. The people of these municipalities elect twenty-four legislators for four-year terms, with the number of legislators from each municipality proportionate to its population.

At the time of the study, the legislature was a relatively young group with three members in their twenties, fourteen in their thirties, and seven in their forties. Only three were nobles, and one was a section chief; but we must remember that nine legislators represented municipalities outside Ponape Island and thus could not possibly be nobles or section chiefs of Ponape. Three legislators were also municipal councilmen, and two were members of the Congress of Micronesia. The occupations of the legislators were somewhat varied, with teaching predominating. Eight were teachers, four were medical personnel, four were in other positions with the American administration, and three were with cooperative companies. Two legislators were Protestant ministers, one owned and managed a bar, one was a farmer, and one had no occupation.

Ten legislators had gone to high school, two to medical school in Fiji, and seven to college (this included two with only one summer at the University of Guam). The district legislators had traveled far more than their counterparts in the municipal councils. Twenty-two had gone to other districts of the Trust Territory, sixteen to Guam, ten to Hawaii, three to the mainland of the United States, three to the Philippines, three to Fiji, and two to Japan.

Two legislators who spoke excellent English were asked to rate all the legislators on their English-speaking ability. One rated seventeen and the other rated nineteen as "good" or "very good." Since they did not know all the chief magistrates or councilmen, they were not asked to rate the English-speaking ability of these leaders.

However, from my own observation it was evident that very few of them except those in Kolonia spoke English well.

An extensive pilot study revealed that some Ponapeans considered formal education, travel, and English-speaking ability as forms of exposure to Western ways and helpful qualities for the occupants of elected positions. These qualities are in clear contrast to the main qualifications for traditional leadership positions—noble rank and age. Therefore, an attempt was made in this study to focus on education, travel experience, and English-speaking ability as well as on traditional rank and age to determine if these qualities do in fact vary in the occupants of the four elected leadership positions under study and to analyze the meaning of such variation that was found to exist.

In comparing the personal backgrounds of the legislators with those of the magistrates and the councilmen, it was found that the legislators were a much more Americanized or Westernized group than the magistrates or the councilmen. A lower percentage of legislators than magistrates belonged to the nobility. On the other hand, the legislators were a much younger group than either the magistrates or the councilmen, with more formal education, greater travel experience, and much greater English-speaking ability. Applying the same criteria, we found the territorial congressmen from Ponape District to be even more Westernized than the district legislators. The Ponapeans were clearly applying traditional norms of leadership more strongly in the election of local leaders and applying the Western norms more strongly in the election of higher-level leaders. The reason for this difference is that the magistrates and councilmen enact their roles almost completely within their own municipalities, immersed in the traditional social system. The legislators and the congressmen, however, enact their roles away from their municipalities and outside of the traditional Ponapean social system.

Activities

Campaigning for election is not yet an acceptable practice for legislature candidates. Only one legislator had personally conducted any sort of campaign before the previous election. He had "talked to friends about the election, and had sent out notes to be posted in various spots." However, he found that campaigning was "new to the people and many of them laughed." Another legislator had had a friend go around to kava-drinking gatherings to speak in his favor before the election. None of the others had campaigned in any way. Some said that campaigning would "embarrass them" because it was "against custom." As noted above, because the role of Micronesian congressman is enacted mostly away from Ponape and therefore outside of the traditional Ponapean social system, Ponapeans have accepted more nontraditional behavior with this role than with the legislator. Consequently, it is considered proper for a congressional candidate to campaign for office provided he does so "modestly" and avoids boasting (Hughes 1972).

Most legislators from Ponape Island, even those representing the municipalities outside Kolonia, lived and worked in Kolonia and had little time for contact with their constituents. It is not surprising, therefore, that of a random sample of 300 adult Ponapeans, 24 percent had heard their legislator speak at some public gathering, but only 6 percent had personally seen their legislator about any problem in the preceding year. The municipality of Uh was unusual in this regard. Many people from Uh had either seen their legislators personally or heard them speak at public meetings several times in the previous year. Uh is the smallest and most accessible municipality outside of Kolonia, and both legislators from Uh lived and worked in the municipality. Therefore, they had more opportunity to communicate with their constituents than their fellow legislators living in Kolonia. Although few other legislators had this much direct contact with their constituents, some did report to their municipal councils before and after legislature sessions and thereby kept up an indirect contact with the people.

In 1966, the legislature began to tape parts of its meetings and then broadcast the tapes from the radio station in Kolonia every evening that it was in session. Since many farmsteads throughout the island had transistor radios, this move enabled them to communicate directly with a large portion of the population. Seventy-six percent of the random sample had heard the previous legislature session on the radio at least once. Most of the people liked these broadcasts and hoped they would be continued, but some found it difficult to understand what was being discussed and voted on. One difficulty with the tapes was that they were mainly excerpts from the meetings with little or no commentary. In any case, the broadcasts did stimulate interest in the legislature meetings. On the few occasions when I was visiting a Ponapean home and the tape from a legislature meeting was played on the radio, the volume was turned up and everyone listened.

The district legislature held two sessions a year, but the exact time of these sessions depended in part on the availability of ship transportation for representatives from the other islands. There was no official legislature building, so the sessions were held in various buildings in Kolonia. They generally lasted about two weeks. I attended the April-May 1966 session, which was conducted in a large classroom of a new (though not yet completed) building at the district high school in Kolonia.

In their general meetings, the legislators sat at tables joined together in the form of a hollow rectangle. The Speaker and the secretary sat at one end of the rectangle, and other legislators around the other three sides. Two advisers or representatives from the district administration office (both Ponapeans) were usually present but seated somewhere along one of the sides a few feet away from the legislators. Often, five to twenty high-school students stood around the sides watching the meetings.

The sessions were conducted mostly in Ponapean; but this was not as simple as it might appear. There are three levels of the Ponapean language: (1) the common language, (2) the polite language, and (3) the royal language (Garvin and Riesenberg 1952:205–6). These three levels vary in complexity and are used in different social situations. Of the six non-Ponapean islands in Ponape District, only Pingelap, Mokil, and Ngatik have languages that are dialects of Ponapean. The languages of Kusaie, Kapingamarangi, and Nukuoro are mutually unintelligible to the language of Ponape. However, the representatives from these islands speak and understand Ponapean as a second language. This means that most have a good knowledge of the common language, a fair knowledge of the polite language, and no knowledge of the royal language. In fact, many Ponapean representatives do not know the royal language well. In the days of the Ponape Island Congress, the royal language proved a real difficulty in communication when the Nobles' House and the Peoples' House met in joint session.

One rule of the legislature states that the meetings are to be conducted in Ponapean, but any member lacking fluency in Ponapean may use English or any language of the other islands. All the legislators interpret this rule to mean that the royal language is not to be used. At the session I attended, the legislators used a combination of the common and polite languages, depending on their own fluency with the polite forms. All the legislators resorted to English for technical expressions such as "quorum," "resolution," and "committee," and once in a while a representative would break into English for a sentence or more in the middle of a discussion in Ponapean. Usually, if the English continued for more than a few sentences, a translation was provided. All rules, resolutions, and laws of the legislature were to be provided in English and Ponapean. In the beginning of the session, one of the representatives complained that some rules had been distributed only in English, and the following day a Ponapean rendition was provided.

During the legislature meetings, the traditional forms of deference were much less in evidence than in the municipal council meetings I had attended (Hughes 1969a:43). The traditional gesture of stooping down in passing a person (even in passing one of the three legislators who are nobles) was much less frequent and less pronounced here than in the council meetings. Very often, a clerk or a legislator distributed papers without crossing his right hand over his left wrist (another traditional gesture of respect).

The Speaker of the legislature was Bethwel Henry, a young man from Mokil Island. Almost all his peers considered Bethwel the most effective member of the legislature. They said that he was efficient in conducting the meetings because of his training at the University of Hawaii, his long experience in the legislature, and his diligent work. Many described him as "kind" and "humble," and some said that he "respects people," "never gets angry," and "likes to help the other legislators."

During the two weeks that I observed the meetings, the Speaker was consistently courteous and respectful to all the representatives, legislature clerks, and administration officials who appeared before the legislature. It was not surprising to find these "idealized" Ponapean virtues in the Speaker, but that they were present so consistently and to such a degree was definitely impressive. The administrative ability, which was coupled with these "idealized" virtues, was equally impressive. When only a few days of the session remained—after a slow, easy-going pace in the first week and a half or so—the remaining bills were assigned to committees, committees were called to task for their reports, and measures were voted on with a definite speed and efficiency. It was easy to understand why the legislators rated Bethwel so highly.

The acknowledged leader of the Ponape District Legislature was only thirty-two years old at the time of this study. He was born and reared on the island of Mokil and thus was not a native-born Ponapean. He attended four years of college at the University of Hawaii and had traveled to Guam, Hawaii, and the mainland of the United States. He had been a member of the Congress of Micronesia since it began in 1965. Presently, he is Speaker of the House of Representatives in the Congress and is also a teacher in the district high school of Kolonia.

After a few general meetings, the Speaker appointed all the legislators to serve on one of the four standing committees: (1) political, (2) social, (3) economic, and (4) appropriations. He also assigned proposed bills and resolutions to the committees for their consideration and recommendation. From then on, the session alternated between general meetings and committee meetings. The acting district administrator, an American named Manuel Sproat, gave a report in English (with a Ponapean translation) at a general meeting. Other administration officials gave reports to individual committees, often with many noncommittee members attending. The Ponapean officials in the administration generally spoke in Ponapean, and the American officials in the administration generally spoke in English. For two of these English reports, no translation was provided; and none of the legislators complained, although some of them could not understand the questions and responses following the reports.

Although the representatives were all generally most polite and deferential to each other, the exchanges could become quite heated; and invariably, in the middle of any heated discussions was Heinrich Iriarte, one of the legislators from Net. Heinrich is the brother of the paramount chief of the Net chiefdom and holds the fifth title in his line of royalty. At the time of this study, he was forty-seven years old, and his experience in the legislative bodies of Ponape Island and Ponape District was unsurpassed by any other representative. He had been a member of the Nobles' House in the Ponape Island Congress and had been an elected representative from Net since the beginning of the Ponape District Congress in 1958. During the legislature meetings in 1966, it was obvious that he enjoyed a special position of respect with his fellow representatives. Heinrich was clearly a forceful and dynamic person, and the respect of the other representatives seemed to be based far more on his experience and ability than on his status as a noble.

Bethwel Henry and Heinrich Iriarte were the legislators most frequently named as the ones doing the best job. Like the legislators themselves, many people admired Bethwel for his competence and his gentleness in conducting the meetings. One man, who had heard all the tapes from the past session on the radio, felt that Bethwel was doing the best job. "He can correct the other Legislators," the man observed, "but he still loves them. And he obviously loves the people." Many people felt that Heinrich Iriarte was the best legislator because he was the most "fearless." Others said that Heinrich was "interested in helping the whole district" and "understands the customs of both the Americans and the Ponapeans and wants both to succeed."

During the legislature session, almost all the legislators wore white, short-sleeved shirts, dark trousers, and shoes or zories (Japanese rubber sandals). In this dress, they were easily distinguishable from most of the people in Kolonia. The most elaborate machinery at the legislature meetings was the recording equipment placed in the middle of the rectangular formation of tables. Microphones rested on the tables in front of the representatives, and a technician turned the recording on and off at signals from the Speaker.

Aside from the recording equipment, the facilities for the meetings were totally inadequate. The lighting was insufficient for evening sessions; the mimeograph machine was not always working; and there was simply not enough room (or rooms) for all the necessary activities. At one point, three committees were meeting in one room. Added to the noise of the three simultaneous meetings were a clerk's typing in the same room and workmen's hammering in the next room. I was sitting only a few feet from one group of committee members and could hear almost nothing they were saying. Admittedly, conditions were usually not that bad; however, even at their best the surroundings were hardly conducive to a serious legislative session.

In the course of this session, the legislature passed twenty-eight bills and nine resolutions. One bill established a district economic loan fund, and others provided aid to municipal administrations, scholarships for study outside the Trust Territory, and a family allowance for Ponapean students already attending schools outside the Territory. Still other bills amended the district liquor law and tax laws. Some of the resolutions passed requested that: (1) the Peace Corps enter the Trust Territory, (2) a graduate nurse be assigned to each dispensary in the district, (3) a medical officer be on duty at all times in the Kolonia hospital, and (4) a commendation be given to Father Hugh Costigan, a Catholic missionary, for his services to the district by his work with the Madolenihmw Housing Cooperative.

Position in Political System

A survey of 300 randomly selected adult Ponapeans revealed the attitude of the Ponapeans toward the district legislator and the other leadership positions under study. The categories included in the survey questions and recorded in the following tables are the categories that appeared repeatedly, both in formal and informal interviews, during an intensive pilot study. Some of these categories are vague and some are overlapping, but they are the categories in which Ponapeans discuss the leadership roles in their society.[1]

Table 1 shows that the quality most highly valued in a legislator as well as in the other elected leadership roles is "love of people." Actually, this is the most highly valued quality in all leadership roles on Ponape, whether traditional or elected. This love should be manifested in such external characteristics as kindness, gentleness, and approachability, but it also includes a determination to work for the good of the people. However, the people rate the traditional quality of "love of people" as less important for the higher-level officials, the legislator and the congressman, than for the lower-level officials, the magistrate and the councilman. Because the legislator and congressman are in less direct and frequent contact with them, the people place greater stress on impersonal qualities like "capability in legislation" and "education" in these officials.

TABLE 1

Qualities Most Highly Valued in Elected Leaders

	Magistrate	Councilman	Legislator	Congressman
Love of people	65%	65%	58%	56%
Capability in administration/legislation	44	53	52	51
Ability to foster cooperation	38	40	31	29
Education	34	24	39	44
Intelligence	20	19	20	20

The same questionnaire used in the survey of the general population was also given to political leaders on various levels of the traditional and the elected systems. In their responses, the twenty-four legislators chose "capability in legislation" and "ability to foster cooperation" as the two most important qualities for a legislator. "Love of people," "intelligence," and "education" were all tied for third place. Because they are directly engaged in the legislature session, they tend to stress a legislator's professional competence. They rate "ability to foster cooperation" very highly, because this quality is necessary to keep the sessions running smoothly.

Tables 2 and 3 show that the Ponapeans consider "representing the people at meetings," "making laws," and "reporting to the people" as the most important tasks of a legislator. They also express a strong desire for the legislators to "reduce taxes" and "repair the roads." As with the other elected leaders, the basic assumption concerning the legislator is that he is elected to represent the interests of his constituents and is responsible directly to them. The Ponapeans are quite strong in their praise of those legislators who regularly report to them what happens at the legislature meetings. They are equally strong in their criticism of those who do not.

TABLE 2

MOST IMPORTANT DUTIES OF LEGISLATOR

Duty	Percentage
Represent people at meetings	49
Make laws	30
Assist district administrator	15
Represent government to people	4

TABLE 3

WAYS LEGISLATOR CAN BEST HELP PEOPLE

Activity	Percentage
Represent people at meetings	71
Report to people	53
Reduce taxes	38
Repair roads	34
Preserve traditions	4

Neither the general population nor the legislators themselves gave much stress to the task of "assisting the District Administrator" in governing the district. However, the legislators do see their relationship to the district administrator as being very important. The legislators and the district administrator are the two counterparts of the district level of government. The district administrator is head of the executive branch of the district government, paralleling the chief magistrate on the municipal level and the high commissioner on the territorial level. He must approve or veto all bills passed by the legislature. According to the 1958 Legislature Charter, the district administrator would forward any bill he approved to the high commissioner. If the high commissioner also approved, the bill became law. In 1966, the high commissioner granted the district administrators authority to approve some bills as laws without sending them on for higher approval.

Both in interviews and in informal conversations, the legislators expressed great admiration and respect for the district administrator, Robert Halvorsen. The Ponapean personnel of the district administration expressed the same feelings toward the district administrator. Many ordinary Ponapeans all around the island praised Halvorsen as one of the few American officials who understood them. Halvorsen was very different from most American officials in Micronesia. He could understand both written and spoken Ponapean (I am not certain of how well he could speak the language) and had an impressive knowledge of Ponapean traditions and customs.

The last item in table 3, "preserving traditions," came up repeatedly in the pilot study. But the survey responses indicate that this is considered the responsibility of the traditional leaders and not of the elected leaders. It is also clear from the survey that the people are more concerned with "joining the traditional and modern systems" than with "preserving traditions."

The responses of the legislators corresponded very strongly with those of the general population shown in table 2, but they differed noticeably from the responses of the general population shown in table 3. The general population put much greater stress than the legislators on "reducing taxes" and on "repairing roads."

The survey indicated that the Ponapean legislators enjoyed wide support and respect among their constituencies. Eighty-five percent of the sample rated the position of legislator as "important" or "very important," and 68 percent rated the legislators from their own municipality as "diligent" or "very diligent" in performing their jobs. However, the validity of this part of the survey was rendered suspect by comments of many respondents showing that they still confused the Ponapean District Legislature with the Micronesian Congress. This confusion is not surprising; as was noted earlier, the District Legislature had been known for so many years as the District Congress. The above figures were also rendered suspect by the fact that, in the same survey, although 94 percent of the respondents named their chief magistrate correctly and 60 percent named their congressman correctly, only 44 percent could name even one of their legislators correctly.

Both in formal interviews and in informal conversations, many Ponapeans expressed hostile and negative feelings toward the district legislature. This reaction was in sharp contrast to their reaction toward other elected leadership roles. Their esteem of the Micronesian Congress was extremely high. In ten months on Ponape, I almost never heard a Ponapean speak the slightest bit unfavorably about the Micronesian Congress as a body or its members as individuals. Criticism of a councilman or a chief magistrate was not at all uncommon, but such criticism was invariably leveled at the individual holding the office and not against the office as such. Criticism of the district legislature was quite different in that it was much more frequent and severe, and it was often leveled at the legislature as a whole. Some people discussed other elected roles quite readily, but simply refused to talk about the legislators, saying bitterly: "They meet in Kolonia, but they never come and tell us what happens."

To understand the hostility of many Ponapeans to the district legislature, we must go back to the founding of that body (as the Ponape Island Congress). Fischer reports that from the very beginning the people misunderstood the function of the Ponape Island Congress (1957:184). The administration intended the Congress to serve as an advisory group to the district administrator concerning any laws he might enact for the district (Meller 1969:94). The Ponapeans could not understand why so much fuss had been made and elections held merely to set up an advisory group, and they concluded that the congress was a new executive level being added to the administration. Their conclusion was strengthened when some congressmen took over such duties as seeing that their constituents did their share of road building and repair and made reports to the district administrator about such matters. It was further strengthened by the fact that originally the congress was not granted any legislative power whatever, and most of its recommendations had to wait for months to be cleared by the high commissioner.

At present, a great source of friction between the legislators and their constituents is the failure of many legislators to communicate sufficiently with their constituents. Ponapeans consider communications with them to be one of the most important obligations of their elected officials (Hughes 1969b:283–84; 1969a:36), and many accuse their legislators of failing in this obligation. Unlike the municipal councilmen, who generally live in the area they represent, most legislators live and work in Kolonia. Because they are employed full time in other occupations, they have little time for contact with their constituents.

The territorial congressmen enjoyed wide popularity despite the fact that they too lived and worked in Kolonia and had relatively little time for direct contact with their constituencies. People have been favorably disposed toward the Micronesian Congress by intensive publicity from the administration concerning the importance of this body. Because they realize that he deals with the upper levels of the American administration and enacts his role largely outside of Ponape District, the people are generally satisfied to have the congressman communicate with them by radio broadcasts. They were very favorably impressed in June 1966 when groups of congressmen visited each municipality on the island to report directly to their constituencies and to solicit suggestions for legislation at the forthcoming session of the Congress of Micronesia.

Another reason for the negative and hostile feelings of many Ponapeans toward the legislature is the poor image projected by that body. No doubt this poor image first took shape in the early 1950s when the function of the legislature (then the Island Congress) was so unclear. Unfortunately, this poor image has been perpetuated. The continued failure on the part of the American administration to take the district legislature seriously is abundantly clear to the Ponapeans, who are fully aware of the humiliating conditions in which their legislature is forced to hold its sessions. Finally, in an indirect way the establishment of the Congress of Micronesia may also have downgraded the image of the legislature. Since 1964, the Ponapeans have been bombarded with publicity—especially on the radio—about the Congress of Micronesia and the importance of this territorial legislative body. This publicity has tended to minimize the role of the district legislature. Moreover, the official relationship between the Micronesian Congress and the Ponapean District Legislature has yet to be worked out in more detail (Meller 1969:118), and has certainly not yet been explained clearly to the people.

Conclusion

It is not my intention to disparage the membership of the Ponapean District Legislature. In the two weeks I spent attending the legislature session in 1966, I was deeply impressed by the obvious competence of many of its members. Bethwel Henry and Heinrich Iriarte were perhaps the two most outstanding members, but many others could be accurately described as competent and concerned legislators. Nor do I intend to imply that the majority of Ponapeans are unfavorably disposed toward the legislators; this is not true. But it is true that, during the course of this study, a far greater number of Ponapeans expressed negative and hostile feelings toward the legislators, both as individuals and as a group, than toward the chief magistrates, councilmen, or congressmen. Such expressions of hostile and negative feelings indicate that the role of district legislator is not as well accepted and integrated into Ponapean society as the other elected leadership roles. In this report, I have merely tried to analyze some factors that explain these negative and hostile reactions.

The main reason for the negative feelings on the part of some Ponapeans toward the district legislators are: (1) the unclear and uncertain definition of the nature and purpose of the district legislature when it was first established (as the Ponape Island Congress); (2) the lack of sufficient contact of many legislators with their constituents; and (3) the poor image the legislature continues to project. Generalizing from the case of the Ponapean legislators, I would suggest that three factors that play an important part in the acceptance of any new leadership role are: (1) a clear explanation of the nature and importance of the role; (2) sufficient contact between the new leaders and their followers; and (3) the projection of an image of importance and power.

1. In the questions corresponding to tables 1 and 3, the respondents were asked to select two items. In the questions corresponding to table 2, they were asked to select one item.

PART TWO

Perspectives of Traditional Societies

7

Introduction to Part Two

A traditional society is one in which the primary meanings, modes, and motivations are defined in an authoritative past. Members of such societies conceive the past as the source of truth and of rules and examples for right conduct. The ancestors are frequently the guardians of these precepts and lend to the past its aura of sacredness and its power to impose sanctions on those who deviate from the right path.

Micronesian societies are traditional in perspective. Their primary organizations are unilineal kinship groups that trace descent from common ancestors. Authority in these societies is most often assigned to the founding clans or lineages of the community that enjoy superior rank and provide the organization through which the community functions. The elders of these kin groups supply the leadership for the community. Regime, or rules for making decisions and distributing power, is defined in tradition, and includes codes of strict respect, public humility and restraint, and a consensus model for decision-making.

In chapter 8, Nason suggests three areas in which one might examine the political perspectives of local Micronesian communities: "political space," "political integration," and "political responsiveness." The primary spatial orientation of Micronesian groups is local. The kin groups of lineage and clan are the basic social unit, and the villages or local sections of dispersed communities are the basic geographical units supplying the primary arena for social and political interaction. Both in high islands and atolls, the villages or sections affiliate with other adjacent localities and often unite for the common good under a common leader for production, protection, and ritual observances. Beyond these local affiliations, most communities ally themselves with geographically more distant entities, creating regional political networks utilized for purposes of war, disaster relief, and trade. The regional networks generally define the outer limits of the politically significant space of any Micronesian community.

Political integration of Micronesian communities is principally internal in perspective. The most important concerns are parochial, and unless situations dictate otherwise, political activity is confined to village or to local island affairs. The authority and responsibility incumbent upon both leaders and people issue from the traditions of their ancestors. These prerogatives and duties command the courtesy and deference reserved for those things deemed sacred, and require behavior, particularly of leaders, that demonstrates such respect. Deviation from these principles provides cause for conflict and public or supernatural sanction against the offender. Wider affiliations, however, entail only sporadic obligations, based primarily on mutual good will and anticipation of future returns in the form of economic aid or military alliance. Such bonds are maintained by occasional contact for trade or social purposes, and by rendering assistance when the ally is in need. The ties are purely political and economic and may be ignored if local interests dictate otherwise.

The assignment of leadership to royal clans and lineages creates a dynastic image of Micronesian polity. The nature of political responsiveness within this polity, however, denies the possibility of a royal hierarchy with unrestrained power. Selection of leaders is rarely so rigidly defined that competition and conflict are excluded. In fact, a number of cases in the following chapters show the opposite is true. Heirs apparent face intense competition for the throne and in past history often lost. Such rivalry forces leaders to win the support of the people and to maintain this support through continual attention to their needs and wishes. Although Micronesian leaders receive great deference and respect, they are not able to remain aloof from the will of their constituents. They rarely make any decision without first discussing the issues in a council of chiefs and elders and obtaining a consensus. Leaders usually maintain face-to-face contact with their people.

Goals of Traditional Societies

When a colonial power envelops traditional societies with vast military and economic power, its administration induces changes to draw these small social systems into their network of dependency relationships. The ultimate goal of the colonial government is to serve its own ends, whether economic or political, and the traditional societies are manipulated to further these ends. A traditional society is then faced with a struggle for survival. Because of its limited power, it cannot resist by force and is dependent upon wit and flexibility to assure its continued identity. In each case considered in this volume, the traditional leaders fought hardest to retain or to regain control over policy formation and the distribution of power in their traditional spheres of influence. This goal stands above all others in importance. Although it is certainly motivated by personal desires to retain power and influence, it is rooted much deeper in the system of beliefs that defines their right to power and their responsibility to serve the interests of their people. Without such commitment to their own political ethos, they would quickly succumb to the pressures of the colonial government. Instead, these beliefs supply the resilience to survive and the currents that ultimately erupt for independence.

Survival, however, is very much a matter of wit; and most traditional leaders are quite willing and eager to tap the new sources of wealth, power, and prestige. The requirements for successful manipulation of new sources of power are accommodation and absorption. In cases presented in chapter 8, the traditional chiefs purposefully conceded to colonial demands they considered advantageous and managed to absorb or ignore demands to their disadvantage. Throughout their history of subservience, they never appear to relinquish command of their own interests. The Ponape case presented in chapters 10 and 11 illustrates similar effort to retain control and tap new sources of power. In this case, the paramount chiefs used traditional obligations incurred with the bestowing of titles to draw new economic and political leaders into their sphere of obligation. The chiefs then distributed the economic gain acquired to broaden their base of support. This action reflects the ultimate objective of traditional leadership: to enjoy the approval, respect, and support of the people.

Adjustment and Adaptation

In the following chapters, the authors have examined the responses of traditional societies and leaders to changes introduced by German, Japanese, and American governments in Micronesia. From these cases, generalizations may be drawn about Micronesian responses to new forms for the organization of political process, new rules or regime, and new leaders and methods for selecting them.

Changes in the organizational structure of Micronesian societies followed two different approaches. In the first, the policies of German, Japanese, and American military governments decreed a new mediating status at the top of Micronesian political systems, but no structural change below. Frequently, the individual appointed to this position was a paramount chief; but if not, he did not interfere with the jurisdiction of that chief. The example from Ponape in chapter 10 suggests that the paramount chief actually rose in the esteem of the people when he ceased to function as an official for the Japanese and became more of a spokesman for the people. The new leadership position also appears to have created few problems. In most cases, the position was accepted, redefined to fit into the traditional framework, and things continued as usual. For example, the position of magistrate, introduced on Etal in the Mortlocks, was defined as messenger, and the paramount chief and lineage chiefs continued to make the decisions. Micronesians capitalized on administrative ignorance of their languages and conducted affairs as much as possible in their own way.

The American government introduced the most far-reaching organizational changes with completely new forms of local and district government. Micronesian responses to such drastic innovation varied widely. The case presented earlier of the Yap Council illustrates how even a new form of government may be filled with traditional content and adapted to create a very effective organization. The case from Etal, described in chapter 8, is remarkably different. There the traditional organization decided to adopt a new system and established an elected municipal council to serve as a check on the power of the magistrate. Membership on the council included mostly younger, educated men thought to be knowledgeable in dealing with the alien administration. The cases described from Palau, Ponape, and the Marshalls show less successful patterns of adaptation. The situation of Arno atoll, described in chapter 9, suggests a complete breakdown in the political process.

Change in the organizational structure itself does not then appear as a critical variable in explaining Micronesian adaptation. The government introduced similar structures across Micronesia, which stimulated widely varying responses. Perhaps more basic than changes in organization are changes in regime.

Regime lies at the very core of political process. Changes in regime may completely reshape the alignment of power, whereas continuity in regime may withstand any number of organizational alterations without significant change in power. Two cases are especially pertinent. In chapter 4, Lingenfelter describes the Yap Islands Legislature as an inept organization, dependent upon the Yap Council for guidance until Peace Corps lawyers instructed them in the procedures for utilizing their power. Within a very short time, legislators manipulating these new rules assumed the central role for making policy on Yap. In chapter 8, Nason presents a case in contrast. On Etal, the people established a new organization with an accompanying set of new leaders, but retained the same set of responsibilities, obligations, and procedures for reaching decisions. The relationship of new leaders to the people was defined essentially in the same way, and Nason concludes that in goals and methods of reaching goals the regime on Etal has changed little, if at all.

Changes in regime can have drastic effects on traditional systems. The traditional leaders of Yap have yet to recover from their very abrupt loss of power, but the new legislature has moved rapidly into the vacuum. The case Rynkiewich narrates for Arno portends more disastrous results. After the government courts intervened to resolve conflicts of succession to paramount chief, the society suffered a complete loss of leadership and rule. The court intervention superseded accepted procedures for resolving such conflict, and consigned such issues to the court. The court's decisions obviated the need for supportive ties between chief and commoner that were mandatory for succession to title in the past. The consequences of this change are political vacuum. Neither traditional chiefs nor the American-introduced council are able to lead the people of Arno.

The implications for change in regime extend one step further to the recruitment and legitimacy of the political elite. When traditional methods for recruitment are ignored or revised according to new rules and procedures, the new elite may fail to obtain legitimacy in the eyes of the community. The consequences of this failure are the refusal of the people to support the leader, insecurity and ineffectual leadership from the elite, and a general breakdown in the political process. The American administration intervened in the question of succession on Arno (chapter 9), and the solution proved more painful than the problem. The winner was unable to mobilize support from his constituents, and his community lapsed into a directionless political vacuum.

In marked contrast, the criteria for recruiting leaders on Etal were changed drastically, but by the people themselves. Working through the traditional regime, public discussions and consensus, the Etalese decided that their leaders should be younger, educated men, experienced in the ways of the alien administration. They were to be elected, form a council of six, and exercise the authority once held by the chiefs. They were given complete control over island affairs, and led the people. First and foremost, they were legitimate, selected according to procedures approved by the people. They enjoyed the complete support of the people, and they were responsible and responsive in the same manner as the old traditional chiefs.

Successful adaptation to change for traditional societies may be defined, then, as retention of control over regime. Changes in organization and in officials may be assimilated with relative ease if regime remains constant. Changes in regime, however, destroy the canons of legitimacy and undermine the mechanisms of support essential to a dynamic political system.

8

Political Change: An Outer Island Perspective

James D. Nason

Awareness of the fundamental importance of political development in the United States Trust Territory of the Pacific Islands has been expressed in numerous governmental planning surveys, reports, and development programs carried out during the past two decades.[1] We find considerations of future self-government in studies of territorial economics (e.g., Hall and Pelzer 1946:108–10, Nathan et al. 1966:Parts I and III), in physical planning programs for district centers (e.g., HAE 1967), and in planning reports for education and future manpower requirements (e.g., Platt and Sorensen 1967). In virtually all of these, as well as in countless other discussions of the Territory's future, predominant focus is directed toward that limited number of island clusters or individual islands that constitute the present district centers. The converse of this, of course, is that the comparative multitude of so-called outer islands have commonly received little substantive attention or notice. When the outer island situation has been considered, it has usually been within the framework that these islands present special and difficult problems that are not clearly or immediately amenable to administrative solution. This, in turn, has led to two distinctive orientations toward these islands: (1) because measures to ameliorate or obliterate these difficulties are not imminently foreseeable, the concentration of developmental effort will be directed toward the district centers; or, (2) the only effective manner in which to deal with the outer island populations is to encourage and promote their removal to district centers, thus negating the essence of the problem.

It is not surprising that these outer island communities have been of but modest import in deliberations on general territorial development, or that they have assumed a secondary importance in discussions of political change. Taken as a group, the outer island category consists almost entirely of coral islands that are characteristically small in land area, population size, and relative economic importance. They are indeed the hinterlands of Micronesia when compared with the larger and more populous islands that are the district centers. Although this hinterland status is a reflection of their absolute geographical separation from these centers, it is reinforced by the continuing isolation that results from minimal lines of communications between islands. As the hinterland, the outer islands are removed from nexus points of political power and decision-making as well as from important mercantile endeavors with which the district centers are now virtually synonymous. From almost any regional viewpoint, outer islands are now and have been for some time of relatively little importance in the territorial scheme of politics and economics.

The predominant administrative concern with the territorial or national view has obvious merit. To take a more limited perspective would lead to decisions and plans for further development lacking coherence and thus of questionable validity. It is also clear that the district centers, the urban areas of the Territory, are the most apparently significant units for national analysis and comparison because they do in fact represent the political and economic nuclei of the area. But this does not lead us inexorably to the equation of district centers with territory or nation. As Mason has recently pointed out, the "urban" and "semi-urbanized" islands account for only some 57 percent of the territory's total population; the remaining 43 percent are residents of the "traditional rural" outer islands. (1971:20).

If we exclude the outer islands from our perspective, we accordingly limit ourselves to dealing with only half of the people directly concerned with, and affected by, regional development. Such a limitation is perhaps unwarranted on grounds of population alone, although it could be argued that the district centers will be the sole determinants of territorial change. This chapter will suggest, however, that any exclusion of outer islands is an untenable position in discussions of future political development. Three reasons for this position are proposed: (1) the outer island "problem" as administratively seen will continue to exist regardless of what future developments take place in the district centers (assuming that population removal will not become a more attractive solution than it is at present); (2) the nature of outer island political organization is distinctive in a way that tends to disassociate outer islands from district centers; and (3) this disjunction will limit or even preclude outer island concern with, or participation in, district and territory affairs. Thus, though any future administration will continue to grapple with the perplexing difficulties engendered by the existence of this rural population, it will find its task complicated by an outer island political perspective that is inimical to understanding or interest in the workings and problems of the regional political organization. This will constitute a situation in which political change amenable to both urban and rural communities will be difficult to achieve, with corresponding effects at the territorial or national level.

To illustrate this minority perspective on political development, this chapter will examine one of the outer islands of the territory. This atoll, the island of Etal in the Mortlock group of Truk District, is only one of the many small outer islands that comprise the majority of landforms within this area. The essential physical characteristics of Etal Island suggest that it is representative of outer islands generally. It has a land area of only some seven-tenths of a square mile, a population of a little over three hundred, and a geographical position some one hundred and eighty miles from Truk, the nearest urban center. It has minimal contact with the district center and historically has been an isolated autonomous community with relatively few intensive outside contacts. One significant result of these influences is a present political system that corresponds to neither traditional nor contemporary guidelines. Instead, a series of adaptive responses have yielded a distinctive contemporary political scheme containing both traditional and nontraditional elements. A review of past colonial inputs at this local level will not only exemplify the ways in which this outer island community responds to external directives, but will also provide the background necessary for understanding those specific features of the present political organization important for future political development on the national scale. Throughout this review, the focus will be on three interrelated aspects of political organization considered from the perspective of the local community:

1. Political Integration—the degree to which the local community and its leadership comprehend, are willing to consider and/or participate in decision-making for issues or problems that transcend the island's own immediate boundary, i.e., the relative presence or absence of factors such as political allegiance to an external administration or political education in national affairs.

2. Political Space—the perceived geographical structuring and allocation of political responsibility and authority, i.e., the local community's view of its own political boundary or autonomy and the "density" of this boundary with regard to any other political unit of similar or greater size.

3. Political Responsiveness—the degree to which the local community perceives that its leadership, local or external, is not only accessible but also responsive to the problems and goals of the community.

Traditional Political Organization

Etal Island is a roughly triangular coral atoll of fifteen islets, only one of which has ever been inhabited. The smallest of the three atolls that comprise the Mortlock group, its area is sufficient to provide all plant foods required by the population. The inhabitants refer to themselves as *chon Etal* 'the people of Etal'. Their primary identification with the island is a strong and vitally important concept that is roughly analogous to our own notion of citizenship. This identification is founded in the ownership of land. It is unthinkable that someone born on Etal (or whose parents or other close kin are from Etal) would not have some direct land affiliation with the island. It is also inconceivable that an Etal islander, so defined, would disenfranchise himself by relinquishing these claims to land on the island. Besides providing the basis for a conceptual allegiance to the island, land rights also act as the major means for structuring social, economic, and political relations. This is achieved through the agency of clan organization. All islanders belong to one of eleven named matrilineal clans. All homestead land and most food lands are held in full title by these clans. Each clan is led by a chief who is the eldest male relation, either brother or son, of the oldest female clan member most closely associated with the line of the founding ancestress. This man has several well-defined duties and obligations to his fellow clansmen:

1. *Land.* He must hold meetings of senior men and women to discuss, and then must approve, continuations of usufruct land titles, or any transfer of clan land, whether by reassignment to a newcomer to the island or to balance land and membership needs.

2. *Work.* He must initiate and organize group fishing endeavors, the clearing of, or other necessary work on, land held by the clan, and the rebuilding or reconditioning of clan structures.

3. *Law.* He must approve any proposed marriage involving a member of the clan, insure that clan rights to property are maintained, see to it that restitution is made for injuries done a clansman or his property, and settle any dispute between a member of the clan and anyone else.

4. *Religion.* He must see to it that the proper first fruits are given to the appropriate island leaders at the correct times, that clan members are prepared for burial and mourned befittingly, and that clan members who are ill or in danger receive whatever assistance the clan spirits can provide.

5. *Trade.* He must organize clan contributions for the exchanges that mark the end of a mourning period, and approve either the acquisition or disposal of important properties, including land, items like canoes, and special knowledge.

6. *War.* He must see to it that the men of the clan are trained and prepared both spiritually and materially for either offensive or defensive combat with other islands.

In additon, any clan chief must try to live up to a set of ideal forms of behavior:

7. He must always seek or try to seek a decision by consensus after all adult men have expressed their own views, i.e., he must try to be the speaker for the clan.

8. He should not attempt to innovate new areas of decision-making to his role or new and different tasks and precepts for his fellow clansmen.

9. He should never set himself above others (i.e., be haughty or overbearing), but should always behave as a sibling of all other clansmen and as a fellow islander to all others. He should never show favoritism in allocations of clan land or services, or expect others to work for him.

10. He should always think of his people and the island first and foremost, exhorting them to cooperate with each other, not to

transgress any social or religious dictum, and always to demonstrate by good and proper public actions their clan solidarity as well as their pride in being from Etal. In this, he must set a good example.

These behavioral ideals are held to be proper for any adult male, but it is expected that those bearing uncommon social responsibilities are most obligated to live up to them. Clan chiefs, then, are viewed in two subtly different ways by their clan constituents. On the one hand, they are expected to live up to the clan's cooperative and egalitarian ethics. On the other hand, because they represent the clan to all other groups and bear the ultimate responsibility for proper continuation of the clan and its affairs, they should behave more properly and circumspectly than others.

It might be thought that this combination of a kinship-based egalitarian ethic with an ascriptively delegated role of no little responsibility would result in a torpid leadership position with little or no independence of action, subject to the shifting demands and attitudes of the constituency. This is prevented by the commonly held expectations of behavior due to a clan chief by his clansmen, as well as by some inherent aspects of this ascriptive role. No clan chief, for instance, can ever be deposed. If one should be lost at sea, no replacement can be made until a spirit medium certifies his death. If "lost" through senility or even exile, he remains as the only one who can be called the chief, although the next in line will actually perform his duties. The uncommon nature of the clan chief's position is also reinforced by respectful behavior clansmen are obligated to show his office. One should speak respectfully when addressing the chief and pay attention to, if not always obey, his wishes. One should give a token amount of the first of each new plant food to him and the largest or best fish when they are taken. The intention of these guidelines is to show respect not so much for the man as an individual but for the living clan through its representative. First fruits are presented not because the clan chief has allocation rights to land but to publicly signify proper behavior as one who is mindful of obligations to the clan for birth-to-death sustenance. Failure to observe the proprieties of respect would certainly merit the condemnation of the island community. It would also, more directly, lead to an angry reprisal by clan spirits against some clan member.

Two clan chiefs find themselves with authority and responsibility extending beyond clan lines because all clans are ranked according to the sequence of their occupation of the island. Thus, the first- and second-ranked clans are those whose female and male partners, respectively, made the first landfall on the island and in so doing claimed it. The clan of this first female settler gained full title to all of the island, her spouse's clan receiving half of the land as a gift. All succeeding clans were then given land as gifts from one of these original two clans and were ranked according to the order of their appearance. This ranking system provided the island with the foundation for its overall political organization.

To a casual observer, the residential area on the island would appear to be one continuous village settlement, but it is actually two distinct and separate villages: "south" village at the southwestern end and "north" village at the northeastern end. These two villages represent a complete division of the entire atoll into two political districts. These island districts are the result of that original division of the atoll by the first- and second-ranked clans. It will be remembered that the head of each clan is called the chief of the clan. The chiefs of these two top-ranked clans, however, also bear special titles that are held by their clans in recognition of this district division. The chief of the second-ranked clan is called the *marenu* to signify his responsibility and authority over all of the lands and inhabitants of the "north" district. The chief of the first-ranked clan is called the *makal*, a title that indicates his authority over the lands and inhabitants of the "south" district. In addition, as the representative of the original full titleholder to all of the island, the *makal* acts as the paramount chief of the entire island.

These two men not only carry out the duties appropriate to a clan chief but also perform district-oriented tasks. These include the arbitration of disputes within the district, planning and implementation of certain labor activities within the district, and food organization for district or island feasts. In other words, their duties and obligations are primarily district-level extensions of what is expected of a clan chief.

The paramount chief of the island has a further extension of authority. He holds the final veto or approval power over all island matters that pertain to food, including the right to taboo any island food resources for any period of time. His position is the most respected on the island and encompasses the right and the obligation to settle any dispute that cannot be otherwise resolved, to approve any marriage, and, most particularly, to direct the external relationships of the island in warfare, diplomacy, and trade. His position as the island's representative to the world is symbolically validated by the requirement that he, before all others, receive first fruit presentations from all of the people. Whereas failure to give such a presentation to one's clan chief would result in illness or disaster for a clan member, a similar lapse in the case of the paramount chief would bring misfortune to the whole community.

Both of these men, the "north" district chief and the paramount chief, are not only obligated to maintain internal island harmony and well-being but also should ensure the proper maintenance of custom and tradition by exercising their roles as the individuals most responsible for island welfare. They are, in fact, the only individuals who can do so. This aspect of their leadership places them in the position of being the living symbols of the island's autonomy and prosperity. They are the nexus points between the supernatural and natural world. Any lapse in respectful behavior toward them is not only an affront to another islander, which is contemptible, but an offense against a position backed by ancestral spirit regard and thus contumacious to these members of the supernatural world. It is this belief that underlies the adjudicative authority of these men as island district chiefs and the external political authority of the paramount chief.

The ability of these leaders does not, however, rest solely on their relationships with the supernatural world. Both men are fully expected to be capable of deciding land conflicts, for instance, through their knowledge of individual genealogies and legendry as well as historical precedents. Similarly, both men are shown the respect due any clan chief as well as some special prerogatives that surround their foremost rank in island society. These are deferences that are due their positions. As individuals they are not supplied with food or shown special favor when labor is required. Knowledge of esoteric lore or genealogical information is also not restricted to them; it is simply more incumbent upon them to know such things.

In summary, it is clear that the differential control of land rights by ranked clan units provides the island with its structure of political authority and responsibility, in increasing degrees of significance from the clan homestead to island district to the ultimate most significant territorial and political boundary of the island as a whole. Although any one individual's day-do-day concern is undoubtedly directed toward homestead or clan, one's primary allegiance is always to the island, to Etal, which is perceived as an autonomous political unit that makes war and settles issues with other islands.

Those external obligations it has as an island are not extensive and are based on considerations of alliance, mutual regard, and good will. Etal's closest ties are to Namoluk Island, thirty miles to the north. This island is considered to be the "child" of the "parent" Etal on the basis of people from Etal, at their paramount chief's request, having resettled Namoluk following a legendary disaster to that island. Because of this tie of kinship, the two islands are expected to aid one another in times of war or disaster, exchanging not only people but food, services, and other goods. At the next most inclusive geographical level, Etal is a member of one of two loosely organized alliances for warfare in the area south of Truk. Etal is not absolutely obligated as a member of this alliance, but it should, if able, render assistance to its three allies against their four common enemies. This division of the Mortlock area into two military alliances does not, however, affect the rights and obligations of any of these islands to expect or actually receive assistance from any other island, even in time of war, in the event of a devastating natural disaster, such as a typhoon. Relief assistance to any island community is not obligatory but considered to be a reasonable and appropriate action taken by paramount chiefs for their islands.

Beyond the Mortlock Islands, Etal has virtually no ties that entail political considerations or concern. The area of political space that is most tightly bounded and rigidly maintained is the island itself. The events that trigger a more inclusive degree of political integration are sporadic and can lead only to a theoretically nonobligatory stance. The island's leadership, in these situations, is fully cognizant of what effects to the island may or will result as a consequence of actions they take. The essence of these problems, locally occurring war and disaster, are comprehended not so much on the basis of island politics per se as on the basis of interisland kinship and mutual regard. The only leadership, in fact, that is anticipated in most instances to be most responsive and responsible to the island's needs and problems is its own. This expectation is virtually assured by the prevalent ideological constructs that surround leadership positions and the relations that characterize both leaders and led.

Initial Foreign Contacts

The period of Western discovery and first island contacts in Micronesia from 1521 to 1850 resulted in no known changes of significance on Etal. The first foreigner to have any sustained contact in the Mortlock area was apparently an Australian trader named John Westwood, who established residence on Lukunor in the late 1870s (Westwood 1905). However, it was not until after the arrival of American Protestant missionaries during this same period that we are certain of events on Etal. They established principal stations at Ponape, Kusaie, and Ebon in the 1850s, and native missionaries were trained and sent forth into neighboring islands. In 1872, three trained Ponapean couples came to Ta and Satawan to begin work in the Mortlock Islands, with the first church established on Etal in 1875 (Strong 1910:244; *MH* 1876:158–214). The first permanent minister arrived in 1877 through the actions of the paramount chief (*MH* 1877:118). By 1879, there were 86 church members, and the paramount chief's son had been to Ponape to visit the mission station, where he acquired Western clothes (*MH* 1879:219). The Mortlock Islands had, up to this time, been important to the missionary effort. By 1880, however, Truk became the focal point. At the turn of the century, the genuineness of the Mortlock conversions was in question, and the final conclusion reached by a missionary and by a German trader was that the people were indeed very slow to give up their customary behavior:

> . . . The good influences seem to have so little power and the powers of evil are so strong . . . ; the love for the old ways and the inclination to gratify the appetites and passions; the evil influences of traders and ships. . . . What folly to expect that these races can take on pure morals and Christian civilization in a few years! (Bliss 1906:56)

> . . . Until this very day the Mortlock Islanders have succeeded in maintaining their own peculiar customs and mores. . . . Neither missionary activity nor ship-carried civilization have changed their concepts and their mode of living. (Kubary 1880:226-27)

The First Colonial Administrations

Traders and missionaries continued to be the only effective external agencies operating in the Mortlock area throughout the period of Spanish administration in Micronesia. Actual contacts with a foreign government did not begin until the Germans instituted administrative control in the Carolines in 1899. During the fifteen-year period that followed, there was a steady decline in, and then a cessation of, missionary contacts in the Mortlocks. This was accompanied, in 1904, by a nativistic movement in the Truk and Mortlock Islands, apparently spurred by a rumor that the German government was opposed to the missionaries and wanted the people to return to traditional practices (*MH* 1904:251). In fact, the German governor interpreted this revival as a sign of defiance and had the most influential "offenders" arrested and imprisoned in Truk (Tolerton and Rauch n.d.:182-83). This did involve Etal, for there is an account that the chief of Etal expressed his sorrow to the missionaries for his conduct and promised that he would reform the following year (meaning 1908) (*MH* 1908:66).

The aims of the German administration in Micronesia were succinctly stated by H. Schnee in 1920:

> The most important problem of administration in these colonies is the exploitation of land, for most of it is still virgin soil. To accomplish this the most essential requirements are the subjugation of the natives, inclusion of them in our adminstrative system, extermination of disease, creation of financial resources, increase of schools, and spread of the German language. (1:352)

Not until the Truk Islands had been disarmed in 1904 did the Germans proceed to introduce changes in the outer islands. Their first interdiction into the Mortlock Islands resulted in the cessation of warfare and in the institution of "flag" chiefs to act as the governmental intermediaries between the administration and the local community. These flag chiefs were expected to convey the orders of the government to the people, enforce the various laws the administration promulgated, and fulfill the functions of peacekeepers, judges, and magistrates (Tolerton and Rauch n.d.:46–50). They were, in fact, crucial to the regular maintenance of any semblance of German rule, for the nearest administrative headquarters was on Ponape, the total number of resident Germans less than 200, and extremely limited communications possible (Yanaihara 1939: 26).

Appointment of the flag chief on Etal, however, had little effect on the island's political organization. When the Germans arrived, they asked for the chief of the island, as they wished to make him their chief. They were directed to the "north" district chief, not the paramount chief. Apparently, this was because he regularly and properly acted on many occasions as the "speaker" or "messenger" of the paramount chief. On Etal, the government ordered this man to oversee the construction of a stone jailhouse and lagoon shore privies as well as the clearing of bushlands for increased planting of coconut trees. All of these tasks were performed in the absence of the Germans, but not until the paramount chief, in a meeting with island clan chiefs and adult men, had discussed the matter, approved, scheduled, and then assigned the work. When the first flag chief died, he was replaced by a man in the paramount chief's lineage, chosen because of his knowledge of English and German. As before, decisions on matters introduced by the administration continued to be settled through meetings of island clan chiefs.

Some introduced measures were never carried out on Etal, but only on the larger islands under German control. For example, none of the following were ever effected on Etal: (1) the relegation of shorelands to a status for private purchase; (2) changes in the inheritance system; (3) regularized payment of taxes or fulfillment of required government labor; (4) common use of Western currency; or, (5) local recruitment of labor for German enterprises on other islands. Other aspects of the German administration did have an effect, such as the material relief and limited population removal to Ponape that followed the great typhoon of 1907, which devastated all of the Mortlock Islands.

At the end of German colonial administration in October 1914, when elements of the Japanese navy assumed control, the community on Etal had been thoroughly introduced to many items of Western manufacture and to the notion that Westerners were a new element to be contended with on a sporadic but continuing basis. Warfare had ended, and long-distance trading voyages were partially at an end. But island political organization, even with the introduction of the flag chief position, remained intact. Warfare aside, inter-island ties remained as before, even though there was now the added beneficial element of assistance from beyond the Mortlockese perimeter. The right of the Germans to demand that certain things be done on the island was accepted, but not with the expectation by the community that these things would, in fact, always be carried out should the traditional political leadership decide otherwise. In this curious way, an accommodation was made that served to maintain the autonomy of the island as a political unit effectively intact on a day-to-day, month-to-month basis. Primary on-going island affairs remained the political province of the island and its leaders. Just as traditional interisland assistance in times of disaster did not affect, and was not affected by, the scope or nature of political integration, so too the new potential of colonial government assistance did not seemingly alter island political integration in some larger sphere of action or concern.

The Japanese Colonial Period

With the advent of Japanese civil control, even the small outer islands like Etal were thrust into a period of general and pervasive cultural change, externally scrutinized and affected on a more frequent basis than ever before by an interested and powerful foreign rule. The League of Nations mandate given the Japanese did not obligate them to a program of political development, and they did not undertake such a program. At least in the beginning, their interest was in the economy of the region, as had been the case with the Germans. Yanaihara states that the rights of the natives were protected by laws instituted by the administration, particularly where land and labor were concerned (1939:154). This did not stop the promulgation of many ordinances directed at different facets of native life, including taxes, work, and even dress.

In 1922, the government appointed a village headman, or magistrate, on Etal. He was directly responsible to the Truk branch government and was given summary judicial authority for minor civil and criminal offenses. It was his duty to convey new laws and regulations, collect taxes, keep records of land transfers, trials, births and deaths, and transmit semiannual reports on local conditions or special events, such as epidemics or disasters. The Japanese did not wish to abrogate the traditional native authority system of clan and island chiefs, and apparently utilized members of the traditional system wherever practicable (*CAH* 1944:75). On Etal, the man who filled this role was selected by the paramount chief in a meeting with other clan chiefs. He was, in fact, himself a clan chief. His father, the "north" district chief, had been the first flag chief under the Germans. As before, little changed as a result of his appointment. He acted as the "messenger" between the clan chiefs and the Japanese. All decisions continued to be made by the paramount chief in meetings with the other clan chiefs and adult men. Some of the decisions reached in these meetings were, also as before, not always congruent with the wishes of the administration. This was particularly the case when matters such as dress or behavior were involved. On important issues that could not be avoided, such as the labor quotas of the late 1930s and early 1940s, the island leadership did not oppose the administration.

Customary law continued on the island, with trials remaining the duty of clan chiefs. Many of the stricter rules imposed were not enforced at all unless Japanese were present, which was rare because there were no permanent Japanese residents on the island throughout this period. Changes in other sectors of life, of course, were implemented. The yen became the only legal tender and was used, particularly when a local store was established on the island with a large stock of imported commodities. Long-distance voyaging was now at an end, although canoe travel between the Mortlock Islands continued. Government ships came at regular intervals now and provided not only a stable income from copra sales but also medical care and the opportunity, later to be a necessity, for men to go off-island for wage labor. During this period, over 70 percent of the island's adult men went to Truk, Ponape, or Palau to work for the government. But a part of most incomes was still regularly given to the clan chiefs as gifts of respect, just as large fish would have been in past days. At least some island men were subsidized for agricultural improvements. And, at least some of the younger people received a rudimentary Japanese education in a local Mortlock school.

Throughout this period new missionary activities began to strip away, or attempt to remove, many of the sanctions and prerogatives of island chiefs. A Catholic mission station had been established in the Mortlocks in 1921, and its occupant demanded the cessation of the interisland food exchange that ended mourning observances; native dancing; knot divining; and the clan-associated prohibition of some foods. He also attempted to stop many practices that were fundamental not only to clan organization itself but also to the position of clan chief, such as the right of a clan chief to taboo lands, receive respect gifts, or even first fruits. Each of these customs or beliefs was in some way directly or indirectly related to a belief in ghosts or spirits in the traditional religion. This missionary was not attempting to undermine the native authority system per se, and there is even good evidence that he wished to maintain it in order to work through its leaders. The people of Etal apparently did not wish to discard these practices that were considered by their chiefs and elders to be important to clan organization and political affairs. This is substantiated by the fact that many men were in fact excommunicated in the 1930s and that many of these customs did not cease until the 1950s.

Although clan chiefs had certainly not been divested of their influence and authority in island affairs, these religious demands were not without their impact. It now seems probable that they were among the important factors in the decision made by clan chiefs in 1933 or shortly thereafter to dissolve all clan-held lands, making them into individually owned parcels. This act, which would have been unthinkable in the precontact period, was undoubtedly made for many reasons, some other than religious. The Japanese had required, in 1930, that land shareholders divide income received from their lands (Tolerton and Rauch n.d.: 173). A great many men and some women had left the island, and their return was uncertain. The population, reduced in earlier days, was now only 255, and all had ample lands to work and were apathetic about clan lands. The government had disrupted some aspects of land ownership by declaring all land below the high tide mark to be government property, by seizing lands on neighboring islands for military purposes, and by stabilizing prices for land sales. Money was now more important than ever before and more readily accessible. Thus, though it is true that clan chiefs were in some danger of losing their authority through missionary attack, it seems more likely that Japanese influences acted as the primary agents. For whatever reasons, this action had remarkably little effect on the internal governance of the island.

By the end of the war, which itself did not involve Etal in any way, the leadership of the island remained in the hands of the paramount chief and his fellow clan chiefs. These men, and the island community, still considered Etal to be an essentially autonomous unit bounded by the continuous maintenance of customary laws and decision-making on internal activities. Although the community certainly did realize that they were a part of some greater governmental scheme, they were not integrated with it except in the somewhat abstract sense of being held accountable for regulations that were also being applied elsewhere. They clearly had no role in decision-making beyond their own island, but that itself remained a task that was regularly and preeminently theirs.

The American Administration

The first clear break with past political organization on Etal came only with the introduction of the American administration after World War II. The first agents of this administration, the navy, established local governments in 1947 on a democratic basis, directing that

> local civil affairs might be administered by either a magistrate or a council as the people preferred. The officials could be elected or appointed, depend-

> ing upon the wishes of the community. Magistrates could also be judges, especially in the small communities. (Richard 1957 3:310)

These local officials were paid by the government and enforced the rules and ordinances issued by the administration. Even though the directive cited above was to give the people the option of magistrate *or* council, elected *or* appointed, the people on Etal say that only the elected magistrate was suggested to them by visiting navy officers. In what was by now a familiar pattern, they duly "elected" a man to serve as island magistrate.

The new island magistrate was chosen by the paramount chief and other clan chiefs during a discussion that involved the adult men of the island. The chiefs suggested a man, and their choice was confirmed. The man selected was a close kinsman of the paramount chief, the stepson of another clan chief, and the son of still another clan chief. Through these connections and as a result of the earlier dissolution of clan lands, he was land wealthy and very influential. Although it was possible, the new magistrate did not exercise judiciary functions. All trials were instead carried out jointly by the magistrate and the clan chiefs. It is clear, however, that the magistrate was becoming increasingly important in island political affairs. This new man was forty-one years old, whereas the paramount chief and most of the clan chiefs were either approaching old age or already very advanced in years, many of them to die within the next half-decade. The magistrate would frequently initiate meetings, begin discussions, and conclude the meetings with a rendering of what appeared to him to be the concensus. Deference and attention was still paid to clan chiefs, especially the paramount chief, but the locus of political power for all non-food matters had begun to shift. The magistrate was no longer simply the "messenger" *qua* village headman of Japanese or German times.

Etal had become a separate and autonomous municipality, with the magistrate's duties including the levying, collection, and expenditure of local taxes, record-keeping for all court cases, census, and tax records. What was required of the island was essentially the same as by previous foreign administrations, with the difference that some things were now to be instituted by the people for their newly recognized island political unit. Whatever taxes were collected on the island were to be expended according to a budget prepared by the magistrate. In other ways, too, the island was becoming a stronger local entity, e.g., through the addition of its own dispensary and medical corpsman in 1947 and its own locally run school in the same year.

The shift from the navy military to navy civil administration in 1948 was the occasion of an administrative recommendation that each island municipality have a government consisting of a magistrate, secretary-treasurer, assistant magistrate, and island judge, who would be appointed by the government on Truk (USNA 1957 3:388–92). Etal, however, continued with only the magistrate and a newly elected secretary-treasurer and did not add any of these other offices to the island political scheme for several years. The one enduring alteration in native political affairs that did occur at this time was the "ship" island meeting. Each visit of the field-trip ship from Truk meant not only that copra would be exchanged for ship's stores but also that new regulations, suggestions, and other communications would be transmitted by administrative officers to the island. Occasionally, the topics so introduced required an immediate response by island leaders, in which case a hurried and informal meeting would take place. In most instances, however, a meeting to acquaint the community with these matters of concern would be regularly held following the departure of the ship. The holding of island meetings was not new, and the format followed the earlier scheme; but they were now expectable and regular occurrences at the time of each field trip. They also served to focus attention on the importance of the magistrate's position because he, rather than clan chiefs, invariably called such meetings. As a result of this, the influence of missionaries, and the loss of older clan chiefs, the authority of the clan chiefs by the early 1950s was primarily relegated to the enforcement of island work requested by the magistrate, the settlement of disputes, and participation as an advisory council to the magistrate in island or council meetings. The clan chiefs were still important in all food matters, but the magistrate would now be increasingly called upon to settle village and even clan disputes. At least some islanders had begun to lose respect for their clan chiefs, partially in the belief that the new administration had a certain way of doing things that only the magistrate could properly carry out. Although this process of authority shift would not be completed for several more years, the magistrate's position was now clearly an important and perhaps even vital one. Correspondingly, the community anticipated even now that the man filling the magistrate's position would be obligated to the same traditional behavior requirements and public stance that had always been required of clan chiefs.

All of the ordinances and organization promulgated by the navy were taken over intact with the arrival of the Department of the Interior administration in 1951. Unfortunately, logistics problems were also assumed intact and continued to plague districts like Truk, resulting in the continuation of an administrative gap between outer island communities like Etal and the district center administration, e.g., only one district administrator during the next eleven-year period actually visited the Mortlocks. By 1952, the new administration again suggested that each island have its own judge. A man on Etal became island judge that year and accordingly continued the process of authority displacement from the clan chiefs to foreign-introduced positions. This man was again selected by the clan chiefs and older men on the island, but this time with the magistrate. He had been to the Japanese school, was one of the leading elders in the local Catholic church group, and was the son of one of the last great clan chiefs of the island. Clan chiefs, now with the magistrate and island secretary, continued to participate in island trials and settlements, but with at least one critical difference. The new judge possessed the island land record book made during Japanese times, and this document became of equal or greater importance than the verbal testimonies of clan chiefs and other elder men in deciding all land disputes.

The same man who had been selected as magistrate during navy days continued in this capacity until 1958, but through elections held on the island. These were held at the behest of the district administration after 1952-53. The elections were relatively simple. Two or three men would be selected by consensus in both districts to vie for the magistrate's position. An island meeting would be held, and all island men would vote. Actually, the community seems to have merely gone through the motions, for it was tacitly assumed that the original magistrate should be kept because the administration had not signified any displeasure with him and he had acted responsibly and well. Until his retirement in 1958, this magistrate continued to operate with the clan chiefs as his council for deciding island matters.

In late 1952, the administration held a meeting on Moen, Truk, of all island magistrates in the district to discuss island problems and ways to solve them. The magistrates from Truk lagoon, the records indicate, dominated this and subsequent meetings, which were primarily oriented toward Truk lagoon problems. For the administration, the outer islands remained of relatively minor importance because of their inaccessibility, small size, and limited populations. The problems that received priority were those in Truk lagoon, where American-Micronesian relations were more patently put to the test. A general lack of administrative staff, time, and money complicated extensive contacts with the outers. If the outer islanders were not, during this period, participant in district political affairs, they were increasingly a part of district center economic activities. Increases in administration hiring prompted the start of what came to be called the "Mortlockese invasion" of Truk lagoon by the middle and late 1950s. Only a handful of people from Etal were a part of this emigration.

Meanwhile, an attempt to improve Mortlock-to-Truk communications through the placement of short-wave radios in the Mortlocks was effectively negated within a few months by a lack of trained personnel, equipment, and parts for repairs. In a further step to improve outer island participation in district affairs, the islands of Etal, Kutu, and Moch (the latter two in Satawan lagoon) were established as a voting precinct for the election of a representative to the Truk District Legislature, formed in 1957. The first representative chosen was from Kutu. Later representatives would continue to be from either Kutu or Moch. No Etal man apparently ever considered running for this position.

Regular interisland travel between Mortlock communities was maintained by canoe and missionary vessel. Similarly, local interisland ties remained important. Thus, when typhoon Phyllis devastated Namoluk in 1958, the little-damaged community on Etal rushed food to Namoluk and housed many Namoluk families for several months. These efforts were ordered by the paramount chief of Etal and implemented with the tacit approval of the magistrate, for it was still not the magistrate's domain to make important decisions involving island food. The administration provided USDA relief food to both islands.

In 1958, the island judge was elected to the magistrate's job, thereby combining judicial and executive authority as in early navy times. During the election meeting, a large number of the adult men urged the new magistrate to establish a council of elected men. This would mean an end to the informal council of clan chiefs that had exercised some degree of authority with the magistrate, and the new magistrate along with the paramount chief argued against such a move. Sentiment was strong, however, and the consensus such that a council of six men, three from each island district, was elected. The reasoning behind this change was apparently twofold. First, the new council would introduce some of the young Western-educated men into the operation of the municipal government, meaning that they could not only help run it but also keep a check on a magistrate if he were bad. Second, because councilmen, like magistrates, were compensated from district funds, the creation of the council would add four more paid positions to the island's foreign-derived income. Although clan chiefs would still have influence by participation in council meetings along with new councilmen, it is clear that at least part of the goal was to ensure that the island would benefit from the supposedly greater knowledge of the administration and its foreign personnel through the input of these young men with off-island experience.

In 1964, a new period of island politics began with the election of the island's third magistrate since the beginning of American administration. The new magistrate, like his predecessors, had considerable prestige on the island. Japanese-schooled and wealthy in land, he was related to the paramount chief and was the son of a late and influential clan chief. New councilmen were also elected at this time, and two new positions developed. The latter, two village bosses, were representatives of each island district to the magistrate and responsible for leading district men in island work as directed by the magistrate and council.

With the entry of the Peace Corps in 1966, the magistrates of each of the Mortlock Islands held a joint meeting to discuss what types of projects were most needed and should be requested. The coalition that resulted became formalized with the establishment of the Lower Mortlocks Advisory Council. Meeting several times each year, beginning in late 1965, the council discussed the development of projects for grant-in-aid applications. Each island wished to keep up with the improvements planned for any other island. The council also discussed other matters of mutual concern, such as a binding ceiling on canoe prices. This new level of political integration transformed the individual communities in the Mortlock Islands into a unit distinct from other islands or island groups in the district. Its integrity as a unit was demonstrated in 1968 when the advisory council itself submitted a plan for a new water system for all of the Mortlock communities, rather than each community making a separate request as had been done prior to this time.

This new development was also matched, by the late 1960s, with the virtual end of most aspects of clan chief authority. No longer were these men the recipients of respect gifts, first fruits, or even many signs of respect behavior. No longer did they taboo lands, settle disputes, or approve marriages. In the 1969 elections on the island, they endorsed no candidates and apparently did not influence voting for any particular man. They did not, on the whole, any longer consider themselves to be influential leaders of the community, at least by virtue of their positions as clan heads. The paramount chief of the island deferred his decision-making role on matters of island food to the "north" district chief, an older man with more esoteric traditional knowledge, and this man in turn usually deferred to the magistrate. As a result, the magistrate and councilmen, in island meetings, made all island decisions, including those dealing with food and feast matters.

As political authority shifted, so too were social and political obligations and responsibilities of leadership transferred. The magistrate, as the effective island paramount chief, now represented the island to the district administration and to the other Mortlock Islands. He now decided when feasts would be held and how they would be organized, inspected island households, and requested and then directed island work and island meetings. In all of these tasks he, as the councilmen, was expected to be working for the good of the island and was judged on this basis. Meetings were still aimed toward the goal of consensus. Council members were expected to behave as had traditional chiefs, simply and with no sign of haughtiness. Thus, though the foundations and recruitment of political leadership positions had radically changed, the essence of political responsibilities and obligations and duties associated with these positions had not.

Summary

Throughout the long history of island contacts with foreign administrations, one central theme of accommodation emerges. It seems clear from the interactions that have occurred that this was not a patently subservient form of accommodation but one continually directed toward certain key goals defined by the island itself. The objective of maintaining effective political autonomy stands out from the historical and contemporary record as the most important of these goals. Considering the difficulties inherent in attempting to deal with a succession of three different and increasingly active foreign governments, the pursuit of this key aim by the leaders of Etal has been eminently successful. From the outset, they have managed to retain overall control of decision-making on internal affairs. Accomplishing this task also occasioned radical changes in traditionally fundamental cultural features, clan organization, and leadership, which were replaced with a foreign organizational framework. Yet the essential qualities and elements of leadership as traditionally defined were continued intact.

It is also true that many aspects of island control over its own foreign affairs, such as warfare and inter-island reciprocity, were altered, thereby limiting the scope of action of island leaders. But this limitation did not alter the island's perspective of its own political space. The island continued to be concerned with, and responsive to, events in other communities in the Mortlock group, with whom regular and continuing contacts were maintained. Even the defunct traditional inter-island military alliance and aid systems were eventually replaced, in effect, by the Lower Mortlock Advisory Council. Thus, even the perceived essence of the island's defined political boundary was sustained through time and changes in administrations.

By the same token, the degree of political integration relevant to the island did not essentially change. The community had only been peripherally concerned with issues and problems beyond its own island boundary and that of the Mortlock group, a viewpoint that did not shift with the addition of a district magistrates' meeting or even the occasional emigration of its citizenry to the district center. This island remained basically inward-looking, most concerned with its own immediate and direct day-to-day affairs, little or not at all concerned with events beyond the close horizon. Certainly, the lack of district center and outer island communications has played a role in the island's retention of this confined and confining perspective. So, too, has the absence of any effective political education of the island community in district or territorial affairs, particularly in future political development. But these factors alone cannot serve as an adequate accounting. There remains the fact that this isolated, small, and relatively unimportant outer island community has developed through its years of interaction with foreign governments its own style and system of response as well as its own intimate and unchanging concern with itself.

There are undoubtedly many other outer island communities

where traditional chiefs and clan organization continue to be the dominant factors in local government, whether in a magistrate-council structure or not. Etal does have a democratized political structure and has been affected in other ways by foreign influence, especially in material culture, economics, and religion. The history of Etal Island's internal adaptations to outside contacts may be unique among outer islands in Micronesia. Yet if Etal is singular in the manner in which it has adapted to foreign political influences, it represents an even more striking case because its views of leadership roles and political space have remained not only traditional but what we could expect of any island that had retained clan chief governance. It is thus not a change in political structure that commands our attention so much as the nonchange in political behavior and perspective. This island's political stance has obvious importance in any consideration of the future political development of the territory. It represents a clear and present danger to any planning based on the premise that all concerned parties to the territory's future are equally able and willing to evaluate the issues and come thereby to a decision founded on knowledge of, or concern with, what is at stake. It may not be necessary to have equal political sophistication among the territory's communities in order to have reasonable and important political development. But this is a rather different matter than saying that an informed citizenry is, for whatever reasons of expendiency, history, education, or logistic difficulty, not a desirable goal. The very skill with which outer island communities such as Etal have dealt with political change in the past argues for their ability to continue to deal, if informed and willing, with further development. What is required for reasonable outer island participation is a significant change in the overall district, if not territorial, political scheme of the recent past. The minimum elements that are necessary if outer islands like Etal are to become functioning parts of the territory's polity are threefold. First, the community on an outer island must be given access to the necessary information and education that will give them a positive understanding of the general political system and how they can relate to it. Second, the community must actually have access to, or feel that they have access to, the general political system and its operations. And, third, the community must have the services of a general political leadership that, like their own local leadership, is attuned to, and actually responsive to, their own perceived problems and goals. Until these minimum conditions are met, it does not appear highly probable that the local communities of the outer islands will be either able or willing to actually participate in the reasonable development of the territory's political future.

1. The fieldwork on which this chapter is based was a general study of sociocultural change carried out from October 1968 to July 1969. The study included interviews and other research at the Truk district center as well as the intensive study on Etal Island. It was supported by Research Grant MH-11584-01 and Research Fellowship 1-F1-40578-01 from the National Institute of Mental Health, United States Public Health Service.

9

The Ossification of Local Politics: The Impact of Colonialism on a Marshall Islands Atoll

Michael A. Rynkiewich

> No system of succession is completely automatic, even setting on one side the recurrent possibility of dethronement, abdication or usurpation . . . some flexibility must exist or the dynasty will find itself out of power through inadequacy or incompetence. Secondly, where a large dynasty is involved in the military and civil government of a country, an element of ambiguity, of uncertainty, in the selection of a successor not only provides a spur to effort, but gives expression to the "corporate" character of the royal kin group.
>
> . . . Even in those systems we speak of as hereditary, some element of choice is always present, the extent of option varies greatly from next-in-line succession to "dynastic election." And despite the western idea that the automatic next-of-kin procedure is the normal type, dynastic election is in fact far more widespread. (Goody 1966:13)

The traditional political system of the Marshallese of Arno Atoll was based on a hereditary dynasty consisting of a particular matrilineage whose head was also paramount chief over all the other matrilineages of the atoll. The rules and procedures that governed succession to the political identity of paramount chief are not unusual for a matrilineal system, or of general interest in themselves, except insofar as their examination in connection with actual cases of succession will help clarify the meaning of flexibility as applied to such systems.

At least five variables contributed to flexibility in the processes of succession and leadership of the traditional political organization on Arno Atoll:

1. There was a clear tendency toward lineage fission provided in the first instance by the fertility of lineage females and spurred by an ideology of rivalry among lineage males who were classificatory siblings (matrilateral parallel cousins). Thus, the dynasty was constantly divided into opposing groups.

2. There was enough ambiguity in the rules to permit several candidates to interpret that they were the rightful successor to the deceased paramount chief.

3. In addition to the formal rules, succession depended on who could gain enough support to win the initial struggle, and leadership depended on the maintenance of support for the chief to exercise the prerogatives of office (see Goldman 1970:9; power resides in the office but it must be taken and developed in each case).

4. There were transferable commodities readily available for sanctions and rewards in order to gain support, namely the confiscation and allocation of rights in land.

5. There were a variety of strategies for elimination of candidates and usurpation of office, including assassination and warfare.

Following these variables, succession was indeterminate among the candidates selected by the formal rules. Any candidate's succession depended on his ability to build and maintain support among the populace. As a result, strong leader-follower ties were a necessary prerequisite to the process of succession, and a necessary adjunct to the process of leadership. This situation, one where structural contradictions that lead to conflict were built into the political system, and where that conflict actually contributed to the strength and perpetuation of the system, is not uncommon in the world. Max Gluckman has long maintained this position:

> To understand the structure of tribal society—or indeed of any society—it is essential to grasp that conflicts of organizing principles, expressed in disputes and quarrels, are not merely disruptive breakdowns in social organization but are attributes of society itself. Secondly, these are at work even within systems of authority (1963:141; see also 134-39).

This chapter will highlight the effects of colonialism on the structural contradictions and actual conflicts that combined to give flexibility to traditional Arno politics.[1] The colonial powers brought many changes. Among the most important in their effect on politics were the following: (1) demographic changes, including the introduction of diseases, increased mobility, an increasing birth rate, and eventually a decreasing death rate; (2) the suppression of traditional political strategies, i.e., warfare, assassination, and manipulation of land rights; (3) the introduction of a copra economy, which changed the relationship between chiefs and commoners with respect to the use of land rights; (4) the introduction of European and Asian legal systems, which led to the modification and codification of the rules for succession to chieftainship; and (5) the introduction of an appointed or elected local government that operated parallel to, or in place of, the chiefdom.

This chapter is about political change. Arno Atoll had a strong and effective political organization before the advent of colonialism. Colonial rule, both intentionally and unintentionally, brought about many drastic changes in Arno traditional politics. As a matter of official policy, the colonial powers perceived these changes as improvement. They call it development. I do not. I take the colonial policy of political development as a phenomenon for study. I do not use development as a concept in my framework for analysis. I am writing about political change by reconstructing the traditional political system, delineating the induced changes, and describing the decline of traditional politics through case analysis.

Arno Social Structure

The population under study, numbering 1,229 people in 1969, lives on a large atoll in the southern half of the eastern chain of the Marshall Islands. In contrast to the northern Marshalls, Arno is relatively lush and drought-free (see Tobin 1967 and Kiste 1968 for studies of northern atolls). Annual rainfall is 138 inches, and the temperature averages 80 degrees year around (U.S.D.C. 1969). Breadfruit, pandanus, coconut, arrowroot, and taro grow in abundance, though the latter two are now not cultivated or gathered by the majority of the population. The five square miles of land area is amply supplemented by eleven square miles of reef and one hundred and thirty-one square miles of lagoon area, which provide marine resources capable of supporting a much larger population (Hiatt and Strasburg 1950:13). Arno's rich environment has provided a necessary base for the support of a stratified polity (see Mason 1959:87–118 for a clear statement of this argument). Arno, like a few other atolls in the southern Marshalls is relatively rich in resources, large in population, and favored by climate.

The basic concepts of Arno Marshallese social structure revolved around the term *bwij* 'matrilineage'. Matrilineages are aggregated into named categories called *jou* 'matriclan'. Matriclans are noncorporate, their members dispersed. They function mainly for the regulation of marriage and for the provision of hospitality (for a discussion of clan exogamy, see Kiste and Rynkiewich n.d.). The matrilineage, on the other hand, is the land rights–holding unit. Matrilineages are not localized, do not reside or work together. They only control rights to certain estates, i.e., collections of land parcels. A child belongs to his mother's matrilineage, and his status relations within the matrilineage are determined at any given time by a recounting of the membership of the lineage starting with the ancestral female and including all branches of the lineage formed by the females in each generation. This recounting constitutes a genealogical continuum representative of the matrilineal descent construct (see Scheffler 1966:543).

There is a social identity named *alab* that includes singly or in combination the statuses of lineage head vis-à-vis all others, mother's brother vis-à-vis sister's sons, and land manager vis-à-vis all others. In the common case of matrilineage-held land, each of the statuses is appropriate for a single identity-holder. However, in other cases, a person may hold only one of the three statuses and still be named *alab* in that restricted sense.

Branches of matrilineages are ranked according to the birth order of the classificatory female siblings who founded them. Branches continue to ramify so that from any sibling set the sisters will produce "elder," "middle," and "younger" branches. The term for matrilineage is elastic in that it can be applied to the smallest branch of mother and child and to the largest lineage of seven or eight generations. Lineage fission occurs when the rights in the estate are divided among the lineage's branches.

The dominating principle in the Arno social structure is matrilineality. The second principle is patrifiliation. The patrifilial category of kinsmen is *batoktok* 'blood'. These are the children of the males of the lineage. While the lineage exists, the children of males may work on the lineage estate, even after their father's death, but they will never control rights in the estate. However, if the lineage members all die, then the children of the last or a recent lineage head are usually recruited as a patrifilial group to become the inheriting corporation. They replace the lineage on the land, unless the paramount chief vetoes the process. The inheriting sibling set then perpetuates itself according to the matrilineal principles. The children of the females of the sibling set will become the inheriting corporation.

All matrilineages fall into one of two classes, *iroij* 'aristocrats' or *kajur* 'commoners'. Only one matrilineage of one clan is entitled to be called aristocratic on Arno. Other matrilineages of that clan and all matrilineages of other clans are commoners. The head of the aristocratic lineage holds the identity of *iroij lablab* 'paramount chief'. Other lineage members are *iroij* 'aristocrats' or *iroij erik* 'lesser aristocrats'.

In addition to the two classes, which were once demarcated by differences in dress, adornment, respect, and food, there are other identities ascribed according to a combination of matrilineal descent and patrifiliation. All children of the females of the aristocratic matrilineage are aristocrats, but those whose father is also of an aristocratic matrilineage are ranked still higher. The father must, of course, come from the aristocratic lineage of a different atoll and be a member of a different clan. The children of the aristocratic males are not aristocrats, but they are ascribed an identity above commoners. They are *bwirak* 'nobility' (see Mason 1947:53–54). Finally, there was the achieved identity of *leatoktok* 'war leader', a man who organized males of the matrilineages in their control into fighting groups. Lesser aristocrats and nobles might also be leaders in war but not necessarily so. In the past, for the purposes of tribute collection, the paramount chief would appoint a 'feast maker' over certain of his matrilineages. Those recruited for this identity came from those holding titles as lesser aristocrats, nobles, and war leaders.

The traditional Arno political system was a redistributive chiefdom (see Tobin 1967:75–76). It was composed of a number of matrilineages that supported, through warfare and tribute, a single aristocratic matrilineage (see Sahlins 1963; but cf. Lambert 1966:155–72). The commoners depended on the chiefs for protection and for foodstuffs in hard times. The aristocrats depended on the commoners for support in war enterprises and in domestic and battlefield logistics.

The success of this system depended in large part on the development of strong ties of dependency and obligation between paramount chiefs and commoners. Without these, Arno would have been reduced to an unorganized satellite of another atoll chiefdom. If commoners had to accept paramount chiefs as they came along according to next-in-line succession, there would be no guarantee of mutual support. However, when each candidate for paramount chief had to build and maintain support among the commoners in order to succeed, then the ties of obligation were a natural outcome of the system. The principle of matrilineage fission, an ideology of rivalry among lineage branches, and the formal rules of succession all tended to put the chieftainship up for grabs among several candidates. This situation made the support of the commoners the crucial factor in succession.

The phrase used to symbolize succession is *binij jenkwan*, literally 'to cover his footprints'. Four principles guide succession:

1. Sex of the candidates
2. Relative ages of the candidates
3. Relative ranking of candidates' lineage branches
4. Relative generations of the candidates

First, only men were eligible for succession in pre-German times. The rationale, which is explicit, is that "Arno is a bellicose atoll," having been won and held only by warfare. Warfare was mainly the domain of males. Given the sexual division of labor, females would find it hard to build and maintain support.

Second, in any given sibling set, the siblings of one sex are ranked from oldest to youngest. Respect relations and special terminology characterize the ranking. The eldest male of the sibling set was first to succeed, and each of his brothers followed by order of birth.

Third, elder branches held precedent over younger branches. This is inherent in the phrase *bwij iman* 'the branch in front (will succeed first)'. Thus, when the last male of a generation dies, combining the three rules, the eldest son of the eldest female of that generation will succeed.

However, rule 4 runs counter to rule 3. It is *ebebin iman* 'the generation above (will succeed first)'. This rule indicates that if there are three branches to the lineage, then everyone in generation 1, regardless of the ranking of their branch, would succeed before anyone in the second generation. There is some indication, and Mason suggests the same (1947:57), that the elder branch is preeminent in the aristocratic lineage, whereas among commoner lineages, the generation principle is stronger in guiding succession to lineage head. However, the Arno data provide little chance to test the proposition because, in the aristocratic lineage, senior and junior branches were constantly being eliminated before any conflict could occur between a mother's brother and a sister's son when the latter was the elder. (See DeBrum and Rutz 1967 for cases of the lineage principle being used in chiefly succession.) The intensity of rivalry between classificatory siblings completely overshadowed any possible rivalry between mother's brother and sister's son.

In addition to these four formal principles, there were at least two implicit rules. First, and obviously, only the living could succeed. Second, only the mentally competent would be allowed to succeed.

Beyond these rules, conflict over succession involved the use of strategies and the selective use of ideology to gain support and dispose of opposition. These will become obvious in the case analyses. Conflict between branches of the lineage is expected and explicitly recognized as in the saying:

> Even though the chiefs are of one lineage they still do not love one another. They kill each other because they cannot live together on one atoll. They want to be alone and say "this whole atoll is mine only."

Precolonial Cases of Succession

I shall briefly recount the history of succession on Arno from about 1815 to 1970, setting off the trouble cases.

In Arno folk history, the aristocratic dynasty was founded by LaMari and his six siblings. The siblings came from Majuro Atoll, married people from Arno, and formed an alliance with some Arno matrilineages. Though Arno tradition never implies that LaMari had to take Arno by force, other traditions suggest that the dynasty made its base in the northern atolls and later returned to take Arno (see Krämer and Nevermann 1938:197–203 for accounts of LaMari's wars, and Mason 1947:153–54 for other traditions).

LaMari was succeeded in turn by each of his three younger brothers. The first two had short and uneventful reigns, but the last, LaKamo, reasserted the lineage's hegemony over the eastern chain and fought with peoples from the western chain.

Each of the three sisters had children, thus forming elder, middle, and younger branches of the lineage. Before LaKamo died, he divided the chiefdom by sending his younger sister, LiJibin, his only full sibling, to the northern atolls of the eastern chain.

These northern atolls were less desirable, but they were adequate. Perhaps LaKamo was trying to ensure his sister and her sons a place that they would probably not be able to attain if the chiefdom had remained unified and went entirely to the eldest son of his eldest sister. Thus, the youngest of the three branches was eliminated from the race for chieftaincy of the southern atolls, including Arno.

> *Case 1.* When LaKamo died about 1845, he was succeeded in the rich southern atolls by his eldest sister's eldest son, LaKamunmun. Immediately, the middle sister's eldest son, LaJete, engaged his classificatory sibling in a war over succession. After a few battles, LaJete won.

In this case, a male from the middle branch used the strategy of warfare to usurp the identity of paramount chief from his elder classificatory sibling. The effect of this action was to depose not only the elder sibling but also his entire branch, thus transforming the middle branch into the aristocratic lineage. The eldest branch was eliminated because they were *jibaukwe* 'disfranchised', i.e., defeated and disgraced in war. It is not clear whether the women were killed or not, but no one now remembers who the descendants of the elder branch were, if there were any.

> *Case 2.* When LaJete died, his eldest sister's son, LaBeliwa, succeeded him as paramount chief of Arno only. LaJete had four sisters. The two middle branches included no males, but the youngest branch had four. The eldest of these, LaJinlor, had LaBeliwa assassinated. For many years after that, LaBeliwa's own son, a noble, attempted to overthrow the aristocratic lineage, but it had too much support.

In this case, the youngest branch had more male members and had made marriage alliances with lineages noted for providing a series of war leaders. With this support and through ties outside the atoll, an assassin was imported, and the youngest sibling set was able to usurp the chieftaincy from their elder classificatory sibling, who had no male sibling support. However, it was not clear whether the elder three branches had been eliminated from candidacy since technically they had not been disfranchised by war.

> *Case 3.* When LaJinlor died, his only living younger brother, Rilung, succeeded him. When Rilung died, there were two claimants. The first

was LaKarik, a male from the eldest branch, the assassinated chief's sister's son. He claimed that the three elder branches were not disfranchised by the assassination. The other was Lekman, the eldest son of the eldest sister of LaJinlor, i.e., of the youngest branch, which contracted for the assassin. He claimed that the elder three branches had been eliminated.

The eldest branch had support from the descendants of the first paramount chief. The youngest had support from many war leaders and lineage heads.

LaKarik's mother's husband arranged a meeting whereby he sought to demonstrate support for LaKarik and settle the dispute. Lineage heads and lesser chiefs from all over the atoll gathered together, and a large square of preserved pandanus pudding was brought out. LaKarik's sponsor cut the square into five pieces, one for each of the four districts and one for Lekman. The intent was that the district representatives and Lekman should eat from LaKarik's store and thus show their submission.

The lineage heads all hung their heads, for they did not want to support LaKarik. Then one rose and, taking a bit of Lekman's share with his thumbnail, said, "Me, I'd rather eat with Lekman." LaKarik conceded the "election," and within a few weeks everyone had brought Lekman tribute, thus confirming his succession.

This case clearly shows the nature of flexibility in the traditional system. Two candidates considered themselves in line to succeed. They represent fission within the lineage. Each side had gained some support, but war was not imminent. The strategy used by LaKarik backfired, and the three elder branches were clearly eliminated, first by the assassination and then by the "election." Finally, it is clear that the source of power is the people. Indeed, the commoners were called *kajur*, which literally means 'strength'. Thus, to say *kajur an iroij* means both 'the commoners of the chief' and 'the strength of the chief'.

Case 4. During his reign, Rilung had made his eldest sister's children lesser chiefs in the western half of the atoll and his other sister's children lesser chiefs in the eastern half. Lekman then succeeded Rilung as recounted in Case 3. Near the end of his reign, the younger sibling set, led by Lijiwirak, attempted to usurp the chieftaincy. The trouble began ostensibly over a woman, but it also seems that the younger sibling set thought to depose the elder branch because they outnumbered Lekman five to one; and if the lineage principle was followed, they would have to defer in succession to Lekman's sister's son.

Each side was able to gather support from marriage and land-rights alliances, and a prolonged war ensued.

Lekman soon died, and his sister's son, Tawoj, prepared to flee the atoll in the face of strong opposition his classificatory mother's brothers in the junior branch had created. However, the people who had allied with Lekman against them were not willing to accept the loss of life and land that would result from Lijiwirak's succession. They persuaded Tawoj to stay and fight.

> Lijiwirak died, and was replaced by his younger brother LaRilang, and the war continued with the elder branch slowly losing. Then the German warship *Leipzig* steamed into the lagoon and put a stop to the fighting. The atoll was split into two halves, each contestant becoming paramount chief of his half and thus establishing two lines of succession.

This case again emphasizes the conflict between elder and younger branches of the lineage. Basic to the conflict are the facts of demography—the elder sibling set included one male, and the other had five. From this base were built the marriage and land-rights alliances that functioned to give or withhold support from candidates.

The precolonial dynasty included four generations. In the first generation, there were three females, each founding a branch. The youngest branch was eliminated without trouble and perhaps to protect it through the division of the chiefdom. The eldest branch was eliminated through warfare. That left the middle branch as the aristocratic lineage. In that branch, there were four females, each of whom founded branches. The three elder branches were eliminated by the younger one through the combination of an assassination and an "election." That left only the youngest branch as the aristocratic lineage, going into the third generation. In that branch, there were two females, each founding a branch. The younger branch began a war of usurpation but was not able to complete it before the Germans stopped the warfare. Thus, the atoll was split into two chiefdoms.

Instead of next-in-line succession there were intralineage intrigue and dynamics each time two female siblings founded branches. In each case, the candidate with the most support succeeded. Because support meant commoners who would follow, the chiefs had legitimacy and authority to rule, to redistribute goods and land, and to protect the chiefdom.

German Colonialism

The last war over succession was in progress when the Germans included the Marshalls in their protectorate of 1885. The German occupation brought changes. The atoll was split into two halves, with two chiefs and two lines of succession. Warfare and assassination were banned. A copra economy was introduced. The paramount chief functioned as local leader and copra producer in the German system of indirect rule. Finally, near the end of the German period, copra proceeds were divided by rank of land rights–holder instead of all the money being retained by the paramount chief. Some of the chief's prerogatives, particularly in war and physical sanctions, were stripped from him, but others were given to him with the authority of the German administration and the economy of the copra business as support. Thus, the tribute system continued relatively unhindered.

Case 5. The younger branch of Lijiwirak and LaRilang, which had successfully split the atoll by warfare, became extinct on the death of their younger brother Lejeken in 1912. They had had one sister, but she had been drowned before 1885 by a female from the eldest branch. Lejeken appointed a female in the youngest branch of the western aristocratic lineage as his successor. She, LiWaito, was a patrilateral as well as matrilineal kin of Lejeken.

The Arno Marshallese recognize two kinds of warfare, fighting and reproducing. The younger branch earlier had won half the atoll by warfare but lost the battle of reproduction. One branch may also affect another's fertility by killing the mother or making her barren through black magic (see Tobin 1958:3–4).

No one seemed to question a female's succession to chieftainship, in part because Lejeken had appointed her. Further, there were four lesser chiefs established in the east, each of whom had reasons for supporting LiWaito. None were in serious contention for the position themselves. With a female chief, they would be relatively free to control matters within their own lesser domains, especially since the threat of warfare was gone. And, in fact, LiWaito left the administration of the chiefdom to them.

The first major change in the political system, then, was the elimination of warfare as a political weapon and a raison d'être for the chiefdom.

Case 6. Tawoj was succeeded by his brothers in the western half of the atoll. Laelung reigned through the German period until 1913. On his death, his sisters and others in his generation but in junior branches were still alive. However, they all deferred to the eldest male in the eldest branch, although he belonged to the next descending generation.

Tobo received verbal opposition from the lesser chiefs in the eastern half of the atoll, but the support from his own branch, the support of his paternal kin among the chiefly lineage at Majuro, and the support of his commoners were enough for him to succeed. Throughout his reign, Tobo built his support until he was secure.

In this case, the lineage principle operated successfully. In the past, it is likely that Tobo would have had opposition from the junior branches and, being alone in his branch, might not have succeeded. But warfare was no more. In fact, those on his generation level did oppose him; but more important, one old warrior, Rakinmeto, supported him. Rakinmeto, who had found his glory in war, was old and ready to retire. He knew Tobo was more able in dealing with foreigners and that Tobo had the highest rank a chief could have, because his father had been paramount chief of Majuro Atoll. Rakinmeto was in a position to use the generation principle but deferred to the younger generation of the senior branch.

Changes brought about by the German administration affected two cases of succession between 1885 and 1914. First, the aristocratic lineages for the eastern half of the atoll became extinct with the death of the last surviving males. It would be expected that the chief of the elder lineage in the west would attempt through warfare to assert himself, and that he might be opposed by the lesser chiefs of the east. Instead, the dying chief appointed a low-ranking female aristocrat from the elder lineage to succeed him. She succeeded, but the lesser chiefs ruled for her. Thus, the eastern chiefdom had been weakened and its future made uncertain.

Second, on the death of the paramount chief of the west, his eldest sister's only child succeeded, but not without opposition. He was opposed by lesser chiefs and commoners from the east and by some members of the younger branches of his own lineage. However, he had enough support, especially among the commoners, to succeed. He spent many years after that building more support to consolidate his position and to increase the effectiveness of his leadership.

Japanese Colonialism

The Japanese took over peacefully in 1914, and the changes continued. There was an increased emphasis on the production of copra stimulated by a mandatory head tax and by the practice of dividing the copra proceeds so that the man who did the work got the largest share. Further, the traders divided the copra proceeds between the chief and the producer instead of giving them all to the chief and letting him divide. The legal recognition of the rights of the landholding matrilineages as against the paramount chief provided increased security so the people could go on unhindered with the work of providing copra for the South Seas Company. It also increased the autonomy of the matrilineage. The Japanese demanded an increase in commoner deference for the paramount chief, but continued to erode his power by the introduction of courts for the settlement of disputes, and by allowing cases between chief and commoner. (See also Kiste 1968:117 for an example of the emperor replacing the paramount chief.) There was a slow decrease in the use and importance of the tribute system as time and emphasis were placed on copra production and, near the end, on defense preparations. Finally, the introduction of the Japanese village system of government created a system parallel to the chiefdom. The chief continued to control most local affairs while the village government functioned for articulation with the Japanese administration (see Spoehr 1949:95–102).

In the western chiefdom, newly succeeded Tobo needed to build support in order to be a strong leader. Although certain methods of gaining support were forbidden him, he proved ingenious in using the resources at hand and built the last strong reign of a paramount chief on Arno.

Tobo needed a fund of rewards with which to gain support. The institution in late German times and Japanese times of four interests in copra proceeds (paramount chief, lesser chief, lineage head/land manager, and worker) meant that one new identity had been created with specific rights in land, i.e., lesser chief. Particularly in the other half of the atoll, this identity had already been taken by those who were nobles, feast makers and war leaders. However, in the western half, the lesser chief rights to only 15 percent of the land parcels had been allocated to, or claimed by, traditional chiefly subordinates. Tobo could then parcel out the remaining lesser chief rights to gain support.

Tobo gave lesser chief rights, implying specific administrative duties and rights to a share of the copra proceeds from certain pieces of land, to the remaining females and male (Rakinmeto) in the generation above him. He presented similar titles to his younger classificatory siblings, and to his paternal and his branch's affinal kin from the aristocratic lineage of Majuro. The support gained paid off almost immediately. In a dispute with the paramount chief of the east over the German-instituted division of the atoll, one of Tobo's cross-cousins from the Majuro lineage reportedly persuaded her husband, a Japanese, to bribe the Japanese court so Tobo could win.

Tobo also reinforced his position by serving two terms as the magistrate of Arno Atoll, an administrative position introduced by the Japanese. Thus, he combined what traditional and introduced authority he could garner to increase his base of support and legitimacy.

In the eastern half of the atoll, the chiefdom was not able to retain any strength.

> *Case* 7. LiWaito and her sister were without heirs. She had depended increasingly on one lesser chief, Joklur, who came from one of the branches deposed in an earlier assassination (see cases 2 and 3). She is reported to have appointed him her successor and raised him to paramount chieftaincy in his quarter of the eastern half. However, he died two years before she did. LiWaito died in 1932 without appointing another successor, leaving only the wish that no one should succeed without the support of her lesser chiefs and lineage heads.
>
> This statement was taken as a mandate to the people to choose a successor, a task at which they failed for twenty years. Each of the four lesser chiefs retired to his own domain.

Again infertility played a prominent part in changing the process of succession. LiWaito died without an heir. When the position was left vacant, the lesser chiefs preferred to share the prerogatives of the paramount chief with the Japanese government (each got half of the paramount chief's share of the copra proceeds), rather than select a new paramount chief.

In the Japanese colonial period, an astute chief of the western chiefdom was able to maintain leadership by combining aspects of traditional and introduced politics. Not the least of the reasons for his success was his luck in being able to distribute favors in the form of lesser chieftaincies, and his ability to manipulate commoner land rights without much interference since he combined the position of paramount chief with atoll magistrate and judge. However, things got worse in the east. The appointed paramount chief died, and no successor was found. The chiefdom was fragmented without even a titular head for twenty to twenty-five years.

American Colonialism

American armed forces took the Marshalls in 1944, and military and civil administration followed. American times have been characterized by new emphases. First, the administration and judiciary have been moved from Jaluit Atoll, the German and Japanese center, to Majuro Atoll, only fifteen miles from Arno. The American court is probably less sympathetic to the respect and legal status due the paramount chief than was the Japanese system. A series of court cases over a problem of succession has established the precedent of commoners successfully rejecting a candidate for paramount chief on the basis of their initial and sustained refusal to recognize him as such. This finding, recalling the necessity of gaining support in the traditional system, might have led to a new flexibility were not the special circumstances of the case such as to prohibit its use as a general precedent. Second, the American administration has not stressed copra production. Instead, its emphasis on the development of a district center at Majuro and a missile base at Kwajalein has led to a number of wage-paying jobs for Marshallese. Out-migration has changed the composition of the resident population on Arno. Many people in middle age are absent from the atoll, and the focus of activities for many people is not Arno but Majuro and Kwajalein. Finally, the Americans have introduced a local government council system of government. Supposedly, it replaces the chiefs in decision-making at the atoll level, but it has little legitimacy or authority. If a chief does not support or cooperate with the council on matters involving land use, then the council is powerless. Yet, the chiefs themselves are in no position to initiate community action.

Case 8. The eastern chiefdom had been without a paramount chief since the death of LiWaito in 1932. During World War II, a move was begun to gather support behind Jiwirak, a male of the eldest remaining viable branch of the royal lineage. His mother had been adopted by the former paramount chiefs of the east, and he was in line to succeed, patrifilially, to one of the lesser chief positions.

In 1944, as the American military government took over, an attempt was made to "elect" Jiwirak as paramount chief. Just when it seemed that support was sufficient, three of the lesser chiefs changed their minds. The patrifilial successor of Joklur, the lesser chief LiWaito had once appointed as her successor, claimed to be paramount chief of his domain. The lesser chief whom Jiwirak would eventually succeed patrifilially changed his mind when he found that he would not be able to increase his domain by Jiwirak's succession to the paramount chieftaincy. The third followed suit. Only the fourth lesser chief, descended from a line of war leaders, maintained her support for Jiwirak.

In the 1950s, Jiwirak succeeded to one of the lesser chief positions and began, with lineage head and other commoner support, a series of court cases that eventually netted him three-fourths of the original eastern domain as his paramount chiefdom. The successor of Joklur controlled the other one-fourth.

In the absence of candidates to which to apply the formal rules, the succession was based on the principles of right and recognition. The court found that, as a member of the aristocràtic matrilineage, Jiwirak was one of a class of people with the right to succeed. Further, the court ruled that those who had recognized him as paramount chief earlier could not change their minds. Thus, there was a partial return to the principle of gaining commoner support to succeed, but only because there was no clear successor.

The significance of the court's emphasis on right and recognition is seen in two court cases. In one, a female head of a weak lineage was able to reject Jiwirak as paramount chief on the basis that neither she nor her mother before her had ever recognized Jiwirak. Assuming that he had been successful, Jiwirak had moved onto her land and used the resources. The court took a dim view of this aggressiveness and ruled that the female's lineage and land would have no paramount chief until she recognized one.

With this case as a precedent, two lineage heads from the west attempted to reject Leben's succession to Tobo in 1957–58. However, the court ruled that because there was no question about the rightful successor in terms of genealogical rights, they had no choice about recognition. Thus, a ruling that might have injected some flexibility back into the system was limited in its application.

Another case demonstrates, however, that this further flexibility would lead to the demise of the system, because choice was returned to the people only after the reciprocal obligations between chiefs and commoners had been destroyed.

> *Case 9.* Jiwirak died in 1965. His elder sister assumed she would succeed him. However, those who had supported Jiwirak in his rise to power did not support her. Her only support came from close consanguineal and affinal kin, and then not all of them. She lost several court cases and the appeals.

The commoners claimed that because Jiwirak was an *iroij kunkuntok* 'a chief pulled in from somewhere else', his selection did not set up a line of succession. They claimed to retain the right of selection. Undoubtedly, the earlier series of court cases had made the impression that chiefs could be accepted or rejected. The ties between commoners and chiefs, the reciprocal needs, no longer existed. Given a choice, more and more commoners will decide to reject the idea of a chief and keep for themselves his share of the copra proceeds.

In the western half of the atoll, the chiefdom was also fast losing its support. Tobo died in 1957, and his branch was extinct. He was succeeded by Leben, from a younger branch and the only male left in Tobo's generation. There was still a branch older than Leben's, though there were only females in his generation. Some people suggest that a male, Jiwirak, from the next descending generation in this elder branch could have succeeded instead of Leben. However, Jiwirak chose to defer to his classificatory mother's brother. Jiwirak was attempting to succeed in the vacant chieftainship in the east, and perhaps thought he would succeed soon enough in the west at his mother's brother's death. However, Jiwirak preceded Leben in death.

> *Case 10.* In 1967 when Leben died, there were only females left in his generation and only one male in the descending generation. The male proceeded to assume the prerogatives of paramount chief, particularly in the collection of the chief's share of the copra proceeds. However, he failed to share the proceeds with his living classificatory mothers. One of them, who lived on Majuro Atoll, took him to court. The case ended when the male withdrew. A judgment was entered that the older woman was paramount chief.

The sex principle had been ignored. The principle of the primacy of the elder branch had been ignored. Further, the woman, old and sick, remained on Majuro and did not provide leadership on Arno.

Neither candidate had to gain support outside his lineage because the matter was handled on a strictly legal basis by a foreign court. Therefore, the tie with the commoners was very weak, and neither candidate developed leader-follower ties. In 1970, the eastern chiefdom no longer existed as a political organization, and the western chiefdom was weak and ineffectual.

Summary

At the beginning of the colonial era, there were four branches of the aristocratic lineage with rights to the western half of the atoll. Succession stayed with the first branch until it became extinct. In Generation 5, there were eleven females. Only three of those had female children; thus, in Generation 6 there are only three viable branches where there could have been eleven. Differential production of male and female children and infertility caused by sickness and venereal diseases eliminated potential branches where warfare could not. In the final instance of succession, the matter was decided by the court of the American administration on the basis of next-in-line succession without reference to the traditional criteria of sex and branch, and without reference to presence or absence of popular support.

The branch of the east began with five brothers and one sister who was drowned, thus eliminating the entire aristocratic dynasty for the east. The last chief appointed a successor from the youngest branch of the eastern dynasty, and she in turn died without an heir. After twenty-five years and a series of court cases, a male of the eastern dynasty was elected to the paramount chieftaincy of the lands in the eastern half of the atoll. The decisions were based on genealogical right and recognition by the commoners. The differential production of males and females and general infertility had led to a return to flexibility in the east, but it was at a time when the chieftaincy was becoming irrelevant so the commoners rejected further successions.

The preceding description and analysis suggests several observations. First, it is clear that the basic problem to be solved by the process of succession is to select a paramount chief from among several candidates, particularly among matrilateral parallel cousins. Second, there are limiting factors that give the problem a particular shape. These are differential fertility and differential mortality within the matrilineage. They are, in part, manipulable, and certainly quite capable of altering the complexion of the succession process at any time. Third, there are several determining factors that may be used to settle the question after the limiting factors have done their job. The determining factors, in early times, revolved around the processes of gaining support from consanguineal and affinal kin, from lesser chiefs, and from commoners for purposes of warfare, assassination, show of force, or "election." In later times, there was a shift in this process to securing legal title to the chieftaincy through court cases. Fourth, successive foreign administrations have changed the nature of succession, both the limiting and determining factors, such that the flexibility that derived from rivalry and competition for the support of lesser chiefs and commoners has slowly been lost to the legalistic next-in-line type of succession. The effect on the nature of leadership has been considerable. When a candidate had to fight for support, he had the basis for legitimacy and power. Now, when a candidate can be declared the successor by an American judge, he lacks a followership.

Following the first observation, both the ideology of descent and succession and the facts of demography contributed to the rivalry between parallel cousins. Lineage branches are ranked, but the primacy of the lineage or the generation principle is not clear enough, though there is an emphasis on the lineage principle among chiefs and the generation principle among commoners. This tendency is part of the reason for sibling unity in the face of parallel cousin rivalry. Table 1 distributes the twenty-one cases of succession or usurpation according to two variables, the successor and the opponent. Sibling unity is seen in that only one of the ten cases of sibling succession was opposed by a sibling. Seven of the ten cases went uncontested, making it the least troublesome type of succession.

TABLE 1

SUMMARY OF SUCCESSION AND USURPATION EVENTS

RELATION OF OPPONENT TO SUCCESSOR	RELATION OF SUCCESSOR OR USURPER TO PREVIOUS PARAMOUNT CHIEF				
	Sibling	Parallel Cousin	Sister's Child	Other	Total
(No opponent)	7	0	3	1*	11
Parallel cousin	0	3	1	0	4
Sibling	1	0	0	0	1
MZDS	1	0	0	0	1
Other chiefs and/or lineage heads	1	1	1	1†	4
Total	10	4	5	2	21

* Appointment of MZDD

† Mother was adopted by previous paramount chief

Three of the four cases of parallel cousin succeeding were in fact usurpations by the parallel cousin. In the other case, a parallel cousin opposed but could not prevent the succession of his cousin, who was sister's son to the last paramount chief. Clearly, much of the trouble, and flexibility, comes from parallel cousin rivalry.

Following the second and third observations, differential fertility between women provides the basic inequality of sibling sets that leads to struggle among candidates. First, infertile women leave gaps in the list of candidates. The infertility of the three youngest women in Generation 5, at a time when they might have succeeded because the lineage principle was being disregarded, eliminated younger successors of Leben and contributed to the dispute between his sister and classificatory sister's son. Had there been males younger than Leben, they would have succeeded.

Second, differential production of male and female children may affect the line of succession or the possibility of usurpation. Two women in Generation 2 failed to produce sons, and thus, the elder branches were not able to prevent LaJinlor's usurpation by assassination (Case 2). Similarly, in Generation 4, one of the reasons Lijiwirak thought to oppose Lekman and one of the reasons he was gaining the upper hand when the Germans put a stop to the war was that he had four brothers and Lekman had none (Case 4).

Finally, differential production of males and females affects the development potential of a lineage. The eldest eligible branch of the chiefly lineage subsequent to the German imposition became extinct in two generations because none produced female children. From Generation 5 down, fifteen women out of twenty-seven failed to have female children. In other words, thirteen potential branches, nearly half of the possible number in the chiefly lineage, failed to develop. Certainly, the picture would have been much more complex today and the problem of restricting the number of candidates more acute had these women succeeded in founding branches.

The effect of mortality on the line of succession is similar to that of infertility but has the added feature that it is capable of directing succession into a dead end. Thus, in Case 5 Lijiwirak and his brothers usurped power because of differential fertility in the previous generation; but when their sister was drowned before she could produce children, a branch that was successful in one generation became extinct in the next.

Also, the death of males removes them from candidacy. Seventeen males who would have been eligible were removed in this way, and nineteen males lived to succeed. Differential mortality by lineage branch may tend to keep the paramount chieftaincy within the elder branch, as in Generation 5, where the three males who served as chief all came from the eldest branch. Except for the case of Rakinmeto's refusal to succeed, this is due entirely to differential mortality.

After fertility and mortality have selected the candidates, other processes must determine who will be eligible and who will succeed. Methods of elimination, including infertility, some of which was forced by black magic, are shown in Table 2 according to their frequency. In the seven generations under consideration, forty-eight women were produced. Only twenty-two of these women produced branches that lasted past their own generation, that is, twenty-six were somehow eliminated. At least thirteen were eliminated by political action.

TABLE 2

FERTILITY, MORTALITY, WARFARE, AND ASSASSINATION

Generation	No. of females initially	No. of females with children	No. of females with female children	No. of females whose children remain eligible	Reason for elimination
G1	3	3	3	2	1 by division of chiefdom
G2	7	4	4	4	3 by disfranchisement by warfare
G3	10	4	4	2	8 by disfranchisement by assassination
G4	5	4	4	4	1 by drowning after fission
G5	11	4	3	4	7 by infertility
G6	5	4	3	4	1 by infertility
G7	7	2	2	2	5 by infertility
G8	6	2	1	2	(Not yet mature)
G9	1	0	0	0	(children)

Finally, following the fourth observation, it is clear that infertility is the only remaining method of eliminating branches and mortality the only method for eliminating candidates. That they are not easily manipulated attests to the loss of flexibility brought on by colonialists and their courts. During German and Japanese times, the chiefs still had to play the game of consolidating their power by gaining support and partly by manipulating the administrating power. Thus, Tobo solidified his position through gifts of lesser chieftainships in the west. In the east, no one was able to succeed to the chieftainship because the lesser chiefs wanted to retain half the power for themselves. The lesser chiefs were able to partially move into the power vacuum with local support, but no one was able to gain support for the entire eastern half.

In American times, a series of court cases finally established a paramount chief in the east. In this case, the court decision was based on recognition by the people and the right to succeed combined. The necessity of gaining support had once again become important, but it lacked two important attributes. First, no clear victory could be won permitting the full realization of powers. The battle had to be fought from court case to court case, with an occasional loss. Second, Jiwirak succeeded to only three-fourths of the realm and was rejected by at least one lineage head within that realm. Paramount chieftaincy became less a community issue, i.e., all accept or all reject, than one of each lineage choosing who will hold chiefly rights on their estate.

By 1970, Arno had become a political vacuum at the atoll level. Chiefs did not lead because they did not have support. They could not gain support because there were few prizes, sanctions, and rewards left to be manipulated in the local system. The loss of the ties of redistribution had made the people less dependent on the chief and the chief less dependent on the people. One candidate could not succeed because she could not gain support. The other paramount chief did not lead because she lived elsewhere and was disabled. Yet only the chief carried the traditional load of respect and authority to lead. Commoner magistrates did not wield power. Arno people said, "He is a commoner, the same as I am; I don't have to listen to him."

The local council was organized about 1960 as a part of a political affairs program emanating from the district center. Its institution was opposed by some aristocrats and commoners, and its functions were little understood by most. By 1970, it was clear that the council had gained little support from the people, even though the councilmen were chosen by popular election. The atoll council is not composed mainly of traditional lineage heads and lesser chiefs, so little support is received because of traditional ties. The council is mainly concerned with collecting taxes, preventing intoxication, acting as school board, and occasionally discussing matters of political or economic interest to the atoll. However, any important decision involves using the land and other resources of the atoll. Because the paramount and lesser chiefs still have rights in the land, nothing can be done without their full cooperation. There appear to be no means of coordinating the interests of the council with those of the chiefs. The only positive result is that divided resource rights have prevented the easy foreign exploitation of the Arno people's environment.

Colonial policies, often rationalized as development, led to the destruction of the Arno political system, mainly through the dissolution of ties of reciprocal obligation between chiefs and commoners. The suppression of violence, the repression of chiefly powers, and the introduction of courts that codified rules of succession, all functioned to rigidify the processes until in the western half of the atoll succession was strictly a legal matter that did not involve commoners and did not create leadership; and in the eastern half, due to a break in the line of succession, the commoners eventually chose not to have a paramount chief at all.

Local politics at the atoll level have been ossified. Neither chiefs nor the council can organize the whole atoll for any reason, even for community projects. Political strategies and rewards are phenomena of the Niti Jela (Marshall Islands Congress) and the Congress of Micronesia. They do not exist in the arena called Arno Atoll.

1. Fieldwork on Arno was carried out between June 1969 and December 1970 under a grant from the National Institutes of General Medical Sciences (GM 01164) administered by E. Adamson Hoebel and the Department of Anthropology at the University of Minnesota. Previous drafts of this chapter were read by Robert C. Kiste, Paul Schaefer, Leonard Mason, Jack Tobin, John Rybski, and Daniel Hughes, and I thank them for their helpful comments. The errors that remain are solely my responsibility.

10

The Role of the Traditional Chiefs on Ponape in the American Period

J. L. Fischer

Any recent visitor to the island of Ponape who has the chance to learn something of the daily life of the inhabitants will soon realize that there still are traditional chiefs who are important people. The purpose of this chapter is to describe something of the current functions of the chiefs and their sources of support, and to compare this with the position of the chiefs in earlier times.

In the period before extensive contact[1] with modern nations, Ponape had five independent states or chiefdoms, each ruled by an elaborate hierarchy of titled chiefs, headed by one called by early Europeans the "king" (Ponapean *nahnmwareki* 'paramount chief'), who in turn was assisted by another who had more direct contact with the general populace and has sometimes been compared to a "prime minister" (Ponapean *nahniken* 'minister'). The occupants of these and other lesser offices were chosen partly for their membership and birth order in certain matrilineal clans and lineages, partly for their father's rank, and partly for their own personal achievements, including service to the preceding high chiefs and to the state generally. Typically, a man who ultimately became a 'paramount chief' or a 'minister' would pass through a number of increasingly higher titles as he grew older. On reaching the highest rank in either the royal or ministerial line (or perhaps also in the priestly line, which is reported to have been amalgamated with the other

..wo after conversion to Christianity in the mid-nineteenth century), a chief was supported mostly by food, goods, and services contributed by his subjects in an annual cycle of feasts as well as in special levies when needed. In theory, at least, the paramount chief owned all the land in his state and gave it out to loyal subjects, who became the chiefs of the *kousapw* 'sections' of the chiefdom. Each section was composed of a number of farmsteads inhabited by extended families who owed service to the section chief, somewhat as the section chief himself owed service to the paramount chief. Each section had also a number of lesser titles, awarded by the section chief to residents of the section. Some of the larger sections, such as Awak in the state of U, were in effect semi-independent, but nominally all owed allegiance to one of the five paramount chiefs.

In aboriginal times, the paramount chiefs had the power of life and death over their subjects, although in fact they probably exercised it only rarely. More common punishments were to remove a man's title or, more seriously, to burn down his house, destroy his gardens, and exile him to another part of the island. The paramount chief and his court were principally occupied with certain public works—feast houses, canoe houses, boat channels, religious structures—and with administering the flow of tribute from the people and ensuring respect for the paramount chief's person and property. The settlement of disputes between commoners was mostly left to the parties concerned and sometimes involved feuds between kin groups both owing allegiance to the same chief. The paramount chiefs appear to have intervened in such disputes only when requested, and many commoners apparently preferred to handle these matters privately.

After contact with large nations in the nineteenth century, Ponape continued to be independent until the visit of a Spanish warship in July 1886, whose captain demanded and received the submission of the chiefs. There is little evidence for major change in the position of the chiefs in the period of independence before Spanish rule. Possibly, the position of the chiefs was strengthened by the introduction of firearms, for the chiefs tended to control contact with traders, who in turn welcomed the protection of the chiefs. At the same time, however, this was a period of depopulation due to venereal disease and various introduced epidemics, including most notably a disastrous smallpox epidemic in 1854. Accordingly, the chiefs had fewer subjects to serve them than before; and missionary observers reported a growing independence on the part of the common people, for if their current chief did not like them, another chief would be happy to have them move to his part of the island.

The Spaniards seem to have taken over active possession of Ponape and the rest of the Carolines mainly as a matter of national pride, following up their initial discovery of them in the sixteenth century. They had little economic interest in the islands, but they did sponsor the introduction of Catholic missionaries, partly to counteract the effect of earlier American Protestant missionaries, some of whom were known to favor U.S. annexation of the islands. In general, the Spanish regime operated through the traditional chiefs insofar as it operated at all. Partly as a result of the aggressive tactics of some of the Spanish missionaries and military, the Ponapeans engaged in periodic open warfare with the Spaniards, who failed to bring peace to the entire island before they sold it along with the rest of the Carolines to Germany after the Spanish-American War.

The German regime made the first major attempt to change the role of the chiefs. Like the Spaniards, the Germans also recognized the traditional chiefs as the local rulers. They explicitly limited their authority to punish their subjects, reserving all serious offenses for disposition by the German authorities. After an effectively suppressed rebellion in the state of Sokehs (also spelled Jokaj, among other variants), the German administration proclaimed a land reform in which title to family farmsteads was given to the senior occupant and the chief's rights in the land were terminated. In exchange for yielding the land, the German certificates specified that the landowner owed the paramount chief an "honor feast" once a year, to which he should contribute one (large) yam, one animal (pig or dog), and beverage (kava). The rest of the annual cycle of food contributions to the chief was declared to be no longer required. The German government was very interested in turning its new subjects into peasant cultivators of cash crops (principally copra), and the numerous traditional feasts interfered with making copra and other economically useful work.

Shortly after the German land reform, the Japanese took over the Carolines, along with the Marianas and the Marshalls, at the beginning of World War I. In the peace treaty, they were given a League of Nations mandate over the area. Initially, the Japanese recognized the traditional chiefs as local rulers; but eventually, in response to the conditions of the mandate, they introduced the *sonchō*, an elected local 'headman', and other officials. They developed a system that continued to recognize the traditional paramount chief as nominal head of the community under the title *sōsonchō* 'supreme village head', but the actual administrative work from the Japanese point of view was done by the 'headman'. The Japanese, like the Germans, were concerned with the economic development of the island and were opposed to the traditional feasts. They made attempts to abolish the "honor feasts" prescribed by the Germans and instituted a system in which anyone wanting to hold a feast was required to obtain a permit from the local Japanese "policemaster." The presence of the "policemaster" in each state or "village," as the Japanese termed them, had the effect of reducing the power of the traditional chiefs as compared with the German period. However, at the same time, the responsibility of the traditional chiefs for making their people conform to the goals of the foreign administration was lessened. Although the Japanese continued to recognize the traditional paramount chiefs as nominal heads of the community, the role of the chiefs toward the Japanese became more that of spokesmen for the people. To the extent that they fulfilled this role and were freed both of administrative duties and judicial powers, it is my impression that popular sentiment in support of the chiefs tended to grow during the Japanese period.

Ponape was occupied by the American navy after World War II, and all Japanese, military and civilians, were rapidly repatriated. Ponape has been economically insignificant for the United States, and it has also been militarily insignificant, although this country holds Ponape and the rest of the former Japanese mandate as the world's only "strategic trust territory" under a United Nations trusteeship. The attitude of the American government toward Ponape and most of the Trust Territory has been something like the former attitude of the Spanish government: the island is basically of little value to the United States, but it is thought by many to be a matter of national honor for us to hold on to it because we conquered it in World War II. (We also conquered Japan, Italy, half of Germany, and so on, but they are perhaps too big to hope to digest.) A bewildering succession of new high commissioners, district administrators, and other American officials has briefly attempted to solve the problems of Ponape and the Trust Territory, and the frequent vacillation in policy has resulted in many fine promises but much less in the way of permanent accomplishment. All these officials have been characterized by initial ignorance of unique local conditions. If some remain long enough to become familiar with the local cultures, they generally leave soon after.

American attitudes toward the traditional chiefs have been ambiguous. On the one hand, there have been some officials who have thought of the American regime as liberating the Ponapeans from the oppression of the Japanese to resume their traditional ways; and if these include semihereditary chiefs, so be it. On the other hand, there have been those who consider it their duty to make Ponapeans into members of the fifty-first state and try to oppose or ignore the traditional chiefs as undemocratic. On balance, however, the American government has officially ignored the traditional chiefs, but has given them considerable informal recognition from time to time. The government has on two occasions become involved in settling disputes about succession to the title of paramount chief, which presumably might have been settled by military force in precolonial days. The most recent instance of this involved the succession to the position of paramount chief of the state of U. In lieu of a battle, an election was ordered, and the present incumbent received a clear majority. The paramount chiefs as well as the local elected officials are often invited to ceremonies for meeting visiting dignitaries and other official ceremonial occasions.

Concerning customary feasts, the American government has generally taken the position that the people are free to make whatever feasts they want but are not compelled to make any feast, including the "honor feast" prescribed by the Germans. In fact, it is my impression that the Ponapeans have been reviving customary feasting in the American period and that this revival may still be gradually growing. The principal reason for the persistence and revival of the customary feasting seems to be the traditional title system. Titles are very widely used in address in preference to personal names, especially in public situations and toward persons of higher social position or non-intimate acquaintances. Nearly all adult Ponapeans hold some kind of traditional title. In a recent survey of over 1,200 adult Ponapeans aged 20–60 years, including many residents of Kolonia, the island capital, only a very few claimed they had no traditional title, and these were almost all young women who had not yet married. Anyone who receives a title owes a title confirmation feast to the paramount chief who gave him the title, and it is further understood that he is expected to continue making at least some of the customary annual feasts for this chief as long as he holds the title. If he grossly fails to do so without good excuse, his title will eventually be taken back and given to someone else. Even this is done rather rarely, although it is highly unlikely that such a delinquent would be promoted to a higher title for which he might otherwise be considered; and this is well understood and approved by nearly everyone. There is currently no other clear sanction supporting participation in feasts. Some people have a feeling that if they offend a paramount chief his ancestral or clan spirits may punish them, but this does not appear to be a very prominent explanation for misfortune nowadays. Nonparticipants are in safe possession of life, limb, and property, and are not even subject to much direct criticism or censure. However, a Ponapean without a title is much like a professor without a Ph.D.: there can be such people, but it is likely to be awkward and embarrassing for most.

In addition to the annual cycle of feasts, the paramount chiefs are also invited to life cycle feasts for individual subjects, which they try to attend. They usually attend funeral feasts for anyone in their state and also may attend marriage feasts, first birthday feasts, farewell and welcome feasts for travelers such as college students, and so on. If a chief is present, it will often be announced that one of the regular calendrical feasts is being combined with the private occasion. Because the population of Ponape has increased substantially in the last twenty years, there are more life cycle feasts for the chiefs to attend, apart from whatever increase there may be in feast activity per capita.

The traditional food to be presented at feasts included some kind of starch food (mostly tropical yams or breadfruit), some kind of protein food (especially dog or pig), and kava plants for preparing the beverage. Local handicrafts such as sennit twine, mats, and textiles were also sometimes offered. At present, traditional food is usually offered at the scheduled periodic feasts, but canned food, rice, bread, and other imported products are often added at certain other feasts, such as housewarmings, funeral feasts (to which the paramount chiefs are invited), and title confirmation feasts.

Contributions to a feast often include more than is necessary for feeding the participants. It is expected that there will be extra food for the participants to take home, but money and goods other than food are often contributed. In one way or another, the paramount chiefs can now receive substantial cash income from feast contributions. At one recent feast that was a combination housewarming and title confirmation, for instance, it is reported that the holder of the feast presented his high chief with a "money tree," a large branch to which several hundred one-dollar bills had been attached. Paramount chiefs who receive more trade goods or live pigs than they and their families need sometimes sell these for cash through stores in which they have an interest. There are complaints from some of their subjects that contributions of money and trade goods are not traditional. Although this is true in a narrow sense, it is also true that chiefs traditionally received a variety of goods other than food and that the modern gifts, unlike the earlier ones, are supported only by the desire of the donors for high traditional titles, not by the threat of police action.

The traditional title system has actually expanded in recent years. In precolonial times, even the five petty states were internally split by local jealousies between neighborhoods, and the larger neighborhoods were at times nearly self-sufficient communities. Men of low rank especially might be taunted or attacked if they visited another hostile neighborhood in their own state. Under these circumstances, the local (neighborhood) titles were probably the only ones held by many men, and they regarded these as important. With the freer travel under the imposed colonial peace, the local titles appear to have declined in importance in most parts of the island, and the state titles have gained in importance. Probably the greater freedom of movement resulting from the widespread adoption of outboard motors on boats and canoes has even further broken down neighborhood ties, as has the centralized distribution of homestead land by the American government.

Currently, in most parts of the island, most people hold state titles, although they may also hold a minor section title that they make little use of. The paramount chiefs and their advisers have created or "discovered" additional titles, so that there will be enough titles for all. Some of these new titles are actually known from tradition and myths but had not been awarded for a long time until recently. Others appear to have been created by recombining elements in existing titles. A Ponapean title has typically two parts, the title proper, which in theory says something about the duties of the titleholder, and a place name, which gives the particular locality within the state in which the titleholder is supposed to operate. Traditionally, certain titles have been paired with certain places, e.g., *Nahmadau* ("Lord-of-the-Sea"?) of Idehd (an island in Nan Matol, the former capital of all Ponape, where an important turtle sacrifice used to be held before the advent of Christianity on the island). However, because there are a few dozen other basic titles, the number of titles for the site of Idehd or any other place can be multiplied by combining each of these with traditional place names. Thus, there might also be a *Kiroun* of Idehd, a *Kehlahk* of Idehd, a *Koaroahm* of Idehd, and so on. Some of these combinations sound unfamiliar to the Ponapean ear because no one has held the titles in recent times. Regardless of what the chief awarding a title might proclaim about its importance, people generally appreciate more a title that has previously been held by a well-known and admired person. The paramount chiefs explain this policy of creating new titles as a way of spreading the pleasures and glories of the title system to all their deserving subjects. Some of the subjects complain that the proliferation of titles simply makes the chiefs rich and reduces the value of all titles; but as noted above, practically all Ponapeans accept at least the first title offered to them.

Another recent development in the title system is the increase in high-level titles. Traditionally, the titles vary in rank according to the word used for "food" when announcing distribution at feasts. Originally, the word *koanoat* was used for the paramount chief and perhaps a few other high titleholders. *Koanoat* titles were announced in order of precedence before all other titles in distributing food. In the last decade or so, dozens of titles have been elevated to *koanoat* level, so many, in fact, that there is no generally recognized order of precedence among them. A recipient of a *koanoat* title has an obligation to make a greater repayment feast and is more obligated to contribute to the annual cycle and special projects of the high chief, e.g., sponsorship of local athletic teams, building a state feast house, and so on. In return, he is entitled to a good portion of the feast contributions when they are redistributed and also to certain marks of respect. In fact, the increase in public deference to most holders of the new royal titles is minimal, although the recipients are usually middle-aged men of substance and therefore entitled to a certain amount of deference even before they receive their royalty-level titles.

There is some suggestion that the rate of promotion in the title system has increased. Each new title that a man receives is satisfying to him as public recognition of his achievement. It also brings in additional wealth to the paramount chief in the form of the title confirmation feast. A greater turnover in the titles can make more people happy. Recently, the paramount chief of the state of Matolenim has introduced the innovation of allowing his subjects to accumulate multiple titles as rewards for public services. (In the past, whenever anyone got a new title from a chief, he automatically relinquished any old title received from the same chief.) Under this system, when a man has accumulated five ordinary state titles, he is eligible for appointment to a royalty-level title. Matolenim is the senior-ranking state for ceremonial purposes, and past innovations in its title system have often been adopted by the other states. It remains to be seen whether this one will also spread.

The title of paramount chief and others in the line leading up to it are still largely reserved for members of the chiefly matriclan. However, the claim of the second-ranking clan to titles of the minister's line has been weakening. It is still felt desirable to give high titles in this line to sons of paramount chiefs or of high-ranking members of the paramount chief's matriclan, but it is no longer considered so important for men of the paramount chief's clan to marry women of the second-ranking clan. The new wide distribution of royalty-level titles is not extended to members of the clan of the paramount chief himself. Junior members of this clan can be placed in the line of succession for the position of paramount chief, but as in olden times, they cannot be considered as royal in the presence of the paramount chief himself. Formerly, there was a tendency to consider that titles vacated by death (outside of the two main lines of titles) should be awarded to a matrilineage mate of the deceased if possible. This tendency has declined, and it is my impression that a son of the deceased might have a better chance than a matrilineage mate.

Along with the decline in the importance of hereditary rank as a qualification for titles has come an increase in the importance of public service outside the traditional culture. Government officials, ministers and priests, and successful businessmen are likely to be offered titles and are likely to accept them. The transactions in titles between the traditional chiefs and the leaders of the imported culture are a kind of expression of solidarity and coöperation between the traditional and modern spheres.

There are some residents of Ponape who speak Ponapean as their first language but do not currently possess a Ponapean title. Most of these people live in the island capital of Kolonia, situated in what was originally a part of the state of Net. However, as implied above, even many residents of Kolonia have received a Ponapean title and have acknowledged this by making a title payment feast. A friend of mine told me how he had received his title. He had bought a piece of land in another part of the island. The chief said, "Because you now own land here, you need a title." My friend replied that because he had bought the land with his own earnings, he did not expect to make an honor feast for it and therefore should not have a title. The chief noted further that my friend was married into the community because his wife came from there. My friend replied that he disliked traditional customs of feasting and did not believe in the institution of chieftainship. Nevertheless, the chief publicly conferred the title on him, and my friend made a title payment feast. This may sound as though the chief was exploiting my friend. On the other hand, a good Ponapean is expected to make some protestations of his unworthiness to receive a title even when he might want it very much, and it could be argued that the chief was generously honoring my friend in spite of his strong resistance. Also, although I did not ask, I suspect my friend's wife wanted him to have a title, which she would share.

In the Marshalls, in contrast to Ponape, the traditional land rights of the chiefs have received formal legal recognition to some degree, and it has been argued plausibly that the continued importance of the traditional chiefs in the Marshalls is based in large part on their land rights. When an earlier version of this chapter was presented orally, a member of the audience suggested that perhaps the continued importance of the chiefs on Ponape is in some way related to a feeling that they really still own the land. Possibly there still is some vague feeling to this effect among the older people; but if so, it is much less prominent than the concern over promotion in the traditional title system. Ponapeans have sold land and transmitted it to heirs by written wills since the Japanese regime. The chiefs have at times been informed as witnesses to these transactions, as provided by the German land certificates, but most Ponapeans would deny that the chief's permission is sought or needed on these occasions.

The relative prosperity of the Ponapeans as compared with most other Micronesians has allowed them more freedom to hold on to their traditional culture. Until recently, Ponapeans had enough good land per capita to provide the basic necessities of life and some luxuries with a few hours of work per day, leaving plenty of time for feasting, recreation, social activity, and religion.

The reassignment of formal governmental responsibilities to elected and appointed officials since Japanese times has made the high chiefs practically immune to interference by higher authority, and at the same time has placed them in a position where they can maintain their influence principally by seeking popular favor. Although the precolonial chiefs undoubtedly had greater authority than the modern chiefs, and they received greater deference and tribute from their subjects, even in the old days the paramount chiefs' position was not purely hereditary; the chiefs were selected and maintained in office by their adroitness in diplomatically balancing conflicting interests and appealing for general support. The flexibility built into the traditional Ponapean political system is, then, probably one reason why important parts of it have continued to flourish up to the present.

Some of the traditional attitude toward the person of the paramount chief as sacred still persists. Although many former customs of respect are no longer observed, people still treat the chief with special respect. They use honorific speech toward him or speak very little if they do not feel skilled enough. They avoid assuming physically higher positions than the chief in public places. A paramount chief could probably stop any brawl between Ponapeans today if he chose to intervene. This is a kind of authority the modern police do not possess, as is shown by the shooting of two policemen in the summer of 1971 when they tried to disarm a reportedly drunk man who was carrying a firearm.

Ponapeans complain about their chiefs a lot behind their backs, but are generally polite to them to their faces. Private grumbling about the chiefs is recognized as an ancient custom in the proverbial phrase *pilen pahn mweli soupeidi* "water under the boulders–the chiefs."[2] In this phrase, private grumbling about the chiefs is compared to the soft sound of flowing water under the boulders at the foot of a cliff: it is not very loud and has no visible effects. The complaints are often about the way titles and food at feasts are distributed, but much less often about the basic desirability of having titles and feasts.

The traditional chiefs provide the Ponapeans with a symbol of continuity and security in a world of rotating foreign bureaucrats, visiting investigative teams, and changing administrative policies. The feast and title systems that the chiefs administer validate one's status as a respected adult in the society. In addition, the chiefs serve as informal spokesmen for community interests. Perhaps just because popular support for the chiefs is now basically voluntary, their influence cannot be easily altered by governmental policy.

1. For the traditional culture of Ponape, Bascom (1965) and Riesenberg (1968) give good descriptions that take into account earlier work. A briefer summary is given in Fischer (1957).

2. This proverb has previously been reported in Riesenberg and Fischer (1955), which also contains a number of other proverbs exemplifying traditional values about the chiefs and other matters.

11

Political Development at the Municipal Level: Kiti, Ponape

Paul A. Dahlquist

As noted by Hughes in chapter 6, the American administration of Micronesia has more profoundly affected Ponapean political organization than any of the three previous colonial regimes. Only the people of Ponape themselves can decide whether the changes that have occurred have been worthwhile, but they have been undeniably important. The area of political organization is, of course, not the only area of Ponapean culture in which important changes have occurred. The major thrust of the American administration, however, has been directed toward political change—political change specifically in the direction of democratization on an American model. Also, many of the changes in areas other than political organization are closely related to changes in political organization.

The traditional political organization of Ponape (outlined in the General Introduction to this volume) was not incorporated beyond the level of the *wehi* 'chiefdom' ('municipality' in current American usage). At that time, there was no structure tying the five chiefdoms together, nor was there any structure linking the island of Ponape with other Micronesian islands. Beyond the level of the chiefdom, then, there was no traditional form of political organization to contrast with that introduced by the American administration. On the chiefdom, or municipal, level, however, the introduced democratic forms come into direct interplay with the traditional forms.

Past studies (Hughes 1970) have shown that a new elite is being formed on Ponape. Lingenfelter (1971) has shown that the process of formation of new elites is also found more generally in Micronesia. At the same time, however, the traditional leaders in Ponapean society have retained a great deal of power (see Fischer, chapter 10). The new elite on Ponape is largely composed of leaders who are not in the traditional noble class, but who have been elected to political office primarily on the basis of their formal education, fluency in English, and experience with the American administration (Hughes 1970). On the territorial and district levels of government in Micronesia, this new elite is generally unchallenged by the traditional Ponapean chiefs. It is the local level—chiefdom or municipality—that exhibits the most direct contact between new elite and traditional chiefs, and it is there the possibilities for confrontation or adapation, or both, are strongest.

This chapter undertakes to examine the problem of what can happen when two sets of leaders—the new elite and the traditional chiefs—come into close contact on the local level. Some aspects of the adaptations made between the two sets of leaders in the Ponapean chiefdom of Kiti are discussed. The focus is upon the *nahnmwareki* 'paramount chief' of Kiti and the moves he made in response to the creation of the new elite. The paramount chief was elected to the office of magistrate of the municipality, thereby establishing a nontraditional as well as a traditional claim to authority in his chiefdom. The paramount chief has also distributed important traditional titles liberally to the new elite, thereby binding them in personal ties to himself.

The Research

For ten months in 1970 and 1971, I carried out a participant-observation research project in the Wene area of Ponape.[1] Through participation in the life of the community, observation of ongoing events, and interviewing, data were gatherered on many aspects of the life of the people of Wene. My main objective was to describe and analyze changes in the food complex during the twenty-five years of the American administration of Ponape, but I was also involved in observations and interviews concerning the political organization of Kiti, both traditional and new.

Past studies of the political organization of Ponape (see especially

Hughes 1970 and Riesenberg 1968) have been island-wide studies. My own study, which concentrates on a particular municipality, adds a new dimension to the literature concerning political change on Ponape.

Background

The Wene area is a part of the chiefdom of Kiti, located at the extreme south of Ponape island. Kiti, the largest of the five chiefdoms on Ponape, stretches from the Wene area on up the southwest side of the island to the border with the chiefdom of Sokehs. Ponape has only one town, Kolonia, located on the north end of the island. At no point is Kiti (or Wene, of course) connected with Kolonia, the seat of greatest acculturative pressure from Americans. Very few Americans other than some Peace Corps volunteers and a Catholic priest live in Kiti, for most Americans remain in Kolonia. Kolonia is the district center of Ponape District and as such is the site of the district government, the Ponape District Legislature, Ponape airport, and a majority of the commercial undertakings on the island. The Wene area, and all of the chiefdom of Kiti, stand in contrast to Kolonia.

The distinction between the Micronesia of the district centers and the Micronesia outside of the district centers is clearly made by Mason (1971). This is an important distinction to make when examining political change in Micronesia. Mason estimates that only 35 percent of the Micronesian peoples are "directly involved in urban-like environments," the other 65 percent being located outside of the district centers. Much of what has been written of the present and future political status of Micronesia seems to take into account only the district centers. The outer island areas are often treated as little more than attached appendages that somehow follow the district centers. For the island of Ponape, the district center (Kolonia municipality) is in many ways distinct from the rest of the island. Developmental programs, though not limited to Kolonia, are clearly centered there. Opportunities to earn money are severely limited outside of Kolonia. The democratic political structure is also clearly centered in Kolonia. Nason in chapter 8 shows that in the Mortlocks, as elsewhere in Micronesia, failure to look beyond the district centers has been a serious oversight.

Mason's basic distinction is between district centers and the rest of Micronesia, but he also makes an important distinction between "semi-urbanized" areas and "traditional rural" areas outside of the district center. Semi-urbanized areas are those areas, such as Wene and the rest of Kiti, that fall outside of the district centers, but are close enough that regular contact with the district center is maintained. The chiefdom of Kiti clearly falls into the semi-urbanized category. Despite some difficulties encountered on walking trails, the island of Ponape is not so big that people cannot walk from any point to Kolonia. Unless they live quite close to Kolonia, however, few people walk; most travel by boat. Although paddle-powered canoes are still used, most boats are now powered by outboard motor. Even Wene, at the opposite end of the island from Kolonia, may be reached by boat in only one and one-half hours (unfavorable tide conditions, however, can more than triple this time). Another important tie to Kolonia is the transistor radio. Most households have a radio that is left tuned to the Kolonia station for much of the day.

The chiefdom of Kiti, then, though distinct from the district center of Kolonia, still has many important and regular ties to Kolonia. Kolonia, it must be noted, is no longer part of any traditional chiefdom, having been separated from the chiefdom of Net and made a separate municipality. Thus, the traditional political organization of Ponape does not function in Kolonia in the same manner it does in the five traditional chiefdoms. As a result, the study of the interplay between traditional leaders and the new elite is better done in a traditional chiefdom such as Kiti rather than in Kolonia.

Chapter 1, chapter 6 by Hughes, and chapter 10 by Fischer, contain the necessary background material on the form of both the traditional political organization and the newly introduced democratic political organization.

The New Elite

One of the major effects of the introduced democratic political system has been the creation of a new and different type of elite based on different criteria than those for the traditional elite. Closely involved in the formation of this new elite has been the increasing monetization of the Ponapean economy. The major source of money throughout Micronesia is the American government, and the great majority of opportunities for gaining access to money come through governmental channels—either by working for the Trust Territory government or by being elected to political office.

As Lingenfelter (1971) has noted, the formation of new elites is a common pattern of change in colonial contexts. The American administration has had political development as its major goal in Micronesia, concentrating on this goal to the detriment of economic development. Political development has specifically meant the introduction of democratically elected officials and the creation of a corps of bureaucrats performing many governmental functions. On Ponape, the process of democratic elections has usually meant that individuals of low title in the traditional system could effectively gain prestige and power by moving outside of the traditional system into the democratic hierarchy. In fact, as Hughes (1970) has demonstrated, criteria such as fluency in English and formal education have vastly outweighed rank in the traditional system as a qualification for office in the democratic system. Once an individual is elected to office, or gains a position in the Trust Territory bureaucracy, a number of avenues to gain money are opened, and the individual's prestige is further enhanced. Thus, a new hierarchy has been set up, a hierarchy based upon one's position in the introduced governmental system or position in the money economy, or both.

Demonstration that a new hierarchy has been created does not automatically lead to demonstration of a new political elite. Hughes (1970) has shown that, particularly beyond the municipal level, traditional leaders have not generally attained public office in the new system; and even on the municipal level, public offices are not usually held by traditional chiefs. This exclusion has often been based upon the choice of the traditional chiefs themselves—they have not run for office in many cases—but also by choice of the electorate, who have been developing new conceptions of leadership qualifications for the elective offices. In general, then, there is a clear distinction between the personnel of the traditional political system and the personnel of the introduced political system. Ponapeans themselves try to differentiate between traditional affairs (the province of traditional chiefs) such as feasting and the title system, and nontraditional affairs (the province of officials in the newly introduced system) such as taxation and the promulgation of laws (Hughes 1970).

Thus, leaders in the democratic system are separated both in terms of personnel and function from the traditional chiefs. They are also increasingly separated in terms of their position in the monetary economy. New political leaders in most cases have salaries that place them far above the average income level of even the highest traditional chiefs. Their positions as leaders in the new political system also afford them an inside track to many other money-making propositions. For example, out of three hotels in Kolonia in 1971, one was owned by a man who had formerly operated the hotel for the government, one was owned by a legislator in the Ponape District Legislature, and one was owned by a storekeeper who was formerly an elected political leader. In addition, a fourth hotel was being built by a man who was a member of the Congress of Micronesia. It is clear that a new elite has been created on Ponape, that this new elite is distinct from the traditional leadership in many ways, and that the introduced political system has been a major instrument in the creation of the new elite.

The new elite is, in many ways, a threat to the traditional leaders and the traditional political system, particularly on the local level, where traditional leaders and the new elite come into direct confrontation. One way in which the new elite is a threat to the traditional leaders is that the new system offers a means for individuals to gain great prestige even though they lack the traditional qualifications for office. The highest titles in the traditional Ponapean system are gained primarily through ascriptive processes. Competition plays an increasingly larger part in gaining titles as one is further from the noble titles, but even for the highest titles, there is some element of competition. Descent-group membership is, thus, the major criterion for access to the highest titles. Other criteria for access to titles at all levels include successful competition at feasts (this means bringing more and larger contributions of goods), first fruits offerings, and other service to the chiefs. Thus, in order to gain prestige in the traditional system, one has to compete with others in making offerings and giving service to the chiefs. To gain prestige in the new system, however, new criteria come into play allowing people to advance their prestige without giving corresponding service to the chiefs. It is theoretically possible, then, for an individual to drop out of the traditional system of competition entirely and yet still gain high prestige by successfully competing in the new political and economic system.

Another threat the new elite poses for the traditional leaders is the usurpation of power. The power of the traditional leaders to rule their people is severely curtailed by the new political system. The curtailment of the power of the chiefs is not new to the American period, but in the American period a significant number of Ponapeans are being placed in legislative and decision-making positions. This threat is most direct at the chiefdom or municipal level. With no political organization traditionally found beyond the level of the chiefdom, district and territory-wide political positions have no direct counterparts in the traditional Ponapean polity. Municipal officials, however, have direct counterparts in the traditional polity. Even those officials beyond the level of the chiefdom, however, pose a threat to the chiefs in that under the traditional system the chiefs had full control over their chiefdoms. Now the Ponape District Legislature and the Congress of Micronesia have significant law-making functions that can heavily affect people on the local level. The passage in 1971 of an income tax by the Congress of Micronesia is but one important example.

Democratization through the creation of a new elite has posed some important problems of adaptation and survival for the traditional leadership of Ponape. A closer look at the chiefdom of Kiti will provide an illuminating example of how this adaptation can be made.

Paramount Chief/Magistrate

One of the important moves made by the paramount chief of Kiti to adapt to the new political system was to be elected to the office of magistrate. With the combination of the positions of paramount chief and magistrate in one man, the chiefdom of Kiti was once again united under the rule of one individual. Only in the case of laws passed by governmental bodies above the local level was Kiti not governed by its paramount chief.

In 1966, when Hughes carried out his research on political changes on Ponape, the then paramount chief of Kiti was not also magistrate. In 1968, upon the death of the former paramount chief, a new man, Albert Domsin, became paramount chief. In 1969, the new paramount chief successfully stood for election to the office of magistrate. Two reasons seem to have influenced his decision to run for office.

The first reason centers on the fact that the paramount chief was not of the proper sub-clan. By birth, Ponapeans are assigned membership in both a clan and a sub-clan (the descent rule is matrilineal). In order to be eligible for the office of paramount chief (and other of the high noble positions), membership in the proper clan and sub-clan was a theoretical prior qualification. Genealogies are very important because of this, and I was approached by a number of people who claimed eligibility to the office of paramount chief and carefully explained their genealogies in support of their claim. At the time of the death in 1968 of the former paramount chief, there were two major claimants to the position. One, who became second in the line of the paramount chief, was of correct clan and sub-clan. The other, who became paramount chief, was of the proper clan, but not of the sub-clan that has controlled this title in recent years. Through a complex series of maneuvers, partly engineered by Catholic priests in order to prevent actual fighting between the families of the claimants, the dispute was settled. The man lacking proper sub-clan credentials became paramount chief. His chief rival became the second noble in that line, and the chief rival's brother became the third in line. At the same time, the brother of the paramount chief was only allowed to move as high as sixth in line. The end result is that the brother of the present paramount chief is unlikely to ever succeed to his brother's position. Either of the men now second in line and third in line, or perhaps both in turn, will become the next paramount chief.[2] At any rate, it is important to note that the paramount chief is recognized as being of the wrong sub-clan.

Genealogical difficulty in a hotly contested ascension to the position of paramount chief was probably a major reason for the paramount chief having stood for election to the office of magistrate as well. Given the Ponapean system of prestige competition (see Bascom 1948), it is likely that lack of the complete set of genealogical credentials led to feelings of insecurity on the part of the paramount chief. In fact, he has publicly proclaimed that sub-clan membership is not really important, but what is of importance is that "we are all of the same clan." By becoming magistrate and thus becoming the sole ruler of the chiefdom, the paramount chief solidified his position in the eyes of his people.

The second reason for the paramount chief wanting to become magistrate partially overlaps with the first. By becoming sole ruler of the chiefdom, some of the tensions created by having two rulers over somewhat arbitrarily separated spheres of influence—traditional affairs and nontraditional affairs—are reduced. The paramount chief, by holding these two roles, holds sway over the entire chiefdom in both traditional and nontraditional matters. The chiefdom, then, has only one leader, the situation of the traditional political organization of Ponape.

Election of the Paramount Chief

The election of the paramount chief of Kiti as magistrate contains a paradox. Even though many people recognize difficulties in having the same man perform both roles, the people of Kiti overwhelmingly reelected their paramount chief to the office of magistrate in 1971.

I arrived on Ponape early in November of 1970, just prior to the holding of biennial elections. For reasons explained only as "an administrative mix-up" (bureaucratese is universal, apparently), the municipality of Kiti was the only one in Ponape District that did not hold municipal elections. Kiti participated in the elections for district legislators and Micronesian congressmen, but did not hold municipal elections. Special elections were finally held in June of 1971 for municipal councilmen, and in December of 1971—more than one year after the scheduled elections—for magistrate. Interestingly, I did not learn of the missed municipal elections until five or six months afterward. Not until the special election for municipal councilmen was imminent did people start to talk of municipal government. No municipal council meetings were held from November of 1970 until after the special election the following summer. The magistrate—also the paramount chief—continued to act as magistrate in many administrative functions with the approval of the district administrator. For example, I saw a lease for land where a new dispensary was to be built signed by the paramount chief acting in his position as magistrate.

It would probably be difficult for the people of a chiefdom to vote against their paramount chief in any election. The office and person of the paramount chief retain great prestige and power today, as shown by Fischer in chapter 10. People are careful not to "break the honor" of the paramount chief, and they act with great deference toward him. The great respect people hold for the paramount chief is one of the reasons people, paradoxically, recognize difficulties in having the paramount chief also perform the role of magistrate. My informants often asked me, and Hughes (1970) reported the same thing, "How can we speak against our paramount chief?" To speak against a paramount chief would be tantamount to insulting him, an offense that few people would wish to risk. The paramount chief is recognized to hold sway over traditional affairs, such as feasting ritual, and people do not speak directly against him on these matters. Municipal affairs, however, are conceived of as operating under different rules. Although respect forms of behavior are used toward magistrates (Hughes 1969b:281), municipal councilmen are expected to speak out against proposals they do not agree with; and people of the municipality are also expected to do so, although they may do this through a third party rather than directly. Yet if the magistrate is also the paramount chief, people say that they are very hesitant to speak against him for fear of "breaking his honor." At the same time, the fact that paramount chiefs can be elected to office is a sign of the continuing secularization of traditional leadership positions, a process that began under the German administration and continues today.[3]

In the only municipal meeting I know of during the ten months of my stay, the paramount chief/magistrate came to the Wene area to discuss the special elections to be held for municipal councilmen. Had he been acting in the role of paramount chief solely, it is likely that he would have stayed overnight. Even though a low tide caused some transportation inconvenience, the paramount chief did not stay overnight for the explicit reason that his position as such would have required a large feast to be made for him by the people of Wene. An attempt was made, then, to separate the roles of paramount chief and magistrate, a separation that in many ways was impossible to fully accomplish.

Despite the fact that people recognize difficulties inherent in having the same man perform parallel roles within both the traditional and the introduced political structures, the special election for magistrate held in December of 1971 resulted in an overwhelming victory for the incumbent. During the summer of 1971, two men from the Wene area were publicly discussing the possibility of running against the paramount chief. These two men were close relatives and of very high rank in the traditional system although not in the direct line of either the paramount chief or the minister. Because of the high rank these two men held, they could realistically consider running against the paramount chief. It seems clear that a man of low rank would not consider running against a paramount chief unless he possessed truly outstanding qualifications for nontraditional leadership positions. The older of the two men, holder of the title *souruko* (one of the most prestigious titles of Wene when Wene was an independent chiefdom), did run against the incumbent, only to lose by more than a seven-to-one margin.

It is evident that the people of Kiti chiefdom find it most difficult to act against their paramount chief. Traditional rank on the level of the chiefdom can still hold sway over other considerations in the election of municipal leaders.

Titles and the New Elite

The traditional chiefs have responded to the growing power of the new elite in other ways than by running for office themselves. A practice that has grown considerably in Kiti in recent years is the bestowal of high traditional titles on new political and economic leaders. Acceptance of such titles binds the new leaders into socioeconomic relations with the traditional chiefs.

Virtually all adult males have a title, and married females have the equivalent title of their husbands. A few women also have titles in their own right. All titles are ranked, but for purposes of this chapter, five types will be distinguished:

(1) Noble titles, or the top twelve titles in the titular lines of the paramount chief and minister

(2) High honorific titles (*koanoat*), or titles of very high prestige but not part of either noble line

(3) Chiefdom titles, or titles that carry less prestige than the titles in the first two categories but, like those two categories, pertain to the entire chiefdom

(4) Section chief titles, or titles given to the leader of each section

(5) Section titles, or titles pertaining only to particular sections

Attainment of a noble title is primarily an ascriptive process, although competition and political maneuvering also play important parts. Attainment of other types of titles is based upon achievement, although ascriptive criteria are also important.

In the traditional title system, most men held only section titles, but at present most hold chiefdom titles or high honorific titles. The American period, in particular, has seen great proliferation of the prestigeful chiefdom and high honorific titles.

Why the proliferation of prestigeful titles? One highly important dimension of the answer lies in the confrontation of the traditional political system with the rising power of the new elite. The case of high honorific titles will be considered here because I am best aware of this situation, but the case of chiefdom titles is similar.

Traditionally, there were only three high honorific titles in the chiefdom of Kiti, and all three were given to the paramount chief. In 1971, I collected a list of ninety-four high honorific titles. All section chiefs had also been given these titles, so I estimate that there are at least one hundred twenty-five high honorific titles currently in use in Kiti.

By far the most common rationale put forth by my informants concerning the proliferation of prestigeful titles was that the title system had become like a business. People said that if the paramount chief saw someone with a good job or a store that made money, he would often give that person a high honorific title so that a title repayment feast would be made. These informants were viewing the title system as a system in which people in essence bought their titles. Other informants noted that many people seemed more interested in making money than in working hard in the traditional manner, and that high honorific titles were given to such people so they would work within the traditional system. In other words, once they had a high honorific title they would then work within the traditional system or be highly embarrassed socially.

The preceding rationale is closely connected to the rise of the new elite if only because the new elite, through salaries or other access to money-making ventures, were just those people described. In the list of high honorific titles that I collected, a number of elected political officials and government bureaucrats appear. These people were making money far above the income of the average person, and even plain money has been accepted in place of the traditional goods at title repayment feasts (see Fischer, chapter 10).

Money, however, is not the only reason for giving high titles to members of the new elite. Once a title has been accepted—and given the continued power of the title system today, very few men would refuse a proferred prestigeful title—the holder has certain obligations to the paramount chief and other traditional leaders. In this sense, the traditional leaders, by awarding high titles to members of the new elite, are recognizing new gambits in an old game—the prestige competition. They approve new avenues to success with traditional rewards, and thus bind the new elite into the complex of traditional socioeconomic ties and political subordination. The advantage for the new elite is that award of high titles gives great prestige and legitimizes their endeavors in the traditional system. For the traditional leaders, the award of high titles to the new elite is a major means of retaining control over all members of the chiefdom. The decision of the paramount chief of Kiti to award high honorific titles to all of the section chiefs so that they would not be outranked in their own sections was an attempt to insure that both old and new leaders were seen as important.

Conclusions

The traditional chiefs and a rapidly rising new elite are engaged in a confrontation between two different political systems on Ponape. The introduced democratic system that allows people not qualified for leadership in the traditional system to gain positions of power presents a threat to the traditional leaders. They and the new elite vie for power more directly on the local, or chiefdom, level than on other levels of government. The way in which the paramount chief of Kiti has been able to dominate the democratic system (via election to the office of magistrate) as well as the traditional system in recent years shows clearly that the traditional leaders retain great authority on the local level, even in the introduced democratic system.

In the chiefdom of Kiti, the paramount chief has reacted to the rise of the new elite in two major ways. First, he ran successfully for election to the office of magistrate. In 1971, he was overwhelmingly reelected to this position. By becoming magistrate, the paramount chief was able to solidify his control over his chiefdom in both traditional and nontraditional affairs. Second, highly prestigeful titles have been given out to many members of the new elite, thus binding the title recipients to the traditional leaders in a complex set of socioeconomic obligations.

The directions taken in Kiti and other Ponapean chiefdoms as the traditional leaders attempt to adapt to the rising new elite will in part determine the direction of economic and political development seen on Ponape. It will also determine in part how much Ponape will remain Ponapean rather than just a dim echo of the United States. The traditional system and its leaders still retain much power and are a vital force on Ponape. Whether they continue to be a vital force, and even whether the people of Ponape desire them to remain such, are questions that can be answered only in the future. This chapter has shown that thus far the traditional system has been flexible enough to make adjustments to the changing political conditions on Ponape and in Micronesia generally.

1. The research on which this chapter is based was partially financed by a faculty fellowship from Ohio Wesleyan University made possible by a College Science Improvement Program grant from the National Science Foundation.

2. In the fall of 1972, the paramount chief of Kiti unfortunately died. At that time, his former chief rival moved from the number two spot to the position of paramount chief.

3. Traditionally, the paramount chief was so cloistered and sacred that the minister was largely responsible for the running of the chiefdom. The German administration started to bring the paramount chief into active leadership of the chiefdom. The minister has lost much of his power, and the paramount chief has lost some of his sacredness.

4. When the paramount chief/magistrate died, new elections were held for magistrate, and the brother of the deceased was elected. The new magistrate is now third in the titular line of the paramount chief. Kiti once again has two men in the top offices of the chiefdom. The new magistrate is, however, a very-high-ranking chief.

PART THREE

The Future: Integration or Disintegration?

12

Introduction to Part Three

The future of the U.S. Trust Territory of the Pacific Islands poses a series of problems and questions so complex that they almost defy analysis, much less resolution. The attempt to create a nation from such widely scattered and culturally diverse peoples as the Micronesians would under most circumstances be considered sheer folly. The gulfs of communication created by the diverse languages and the vast expanses of water between island groups are so great that the contact between ethnic groups necessary for breaking down boundaries is nearly impossible.

One of the long-range objectives of the U.S. administration has been to unify the Trust Territory into a nation-state with strong ideological and permanent political links to the United States. Toward this aim, the government has invested its greatest resources in political development and education.

As this volume is being written, negotiators from the Congress of Micronesia and the U.S. government are forging a new agreement for the future political status of that territory. Regardless of what form the final agreement takes, certain issues have emerged that are critical not only to Micronesians but to every nation that shares the waters of the Pacific. The final chapters in this volume address themselves to the potential "national" and international outcomes for these "future political status" negotiations.

Political Development in Micronesia

"National" Perspectives

The current political situation of the Trust Territory is a classic case of ethnic pluralism created by colonial rule. From early Spanish rule to the present, successive colonial governments have imposed unified rule over the medley of peoples and cultures indigenous to the area. Only the United States, however, has attempted to forge this conglomeration of cultures into a plural society or nation-state. The concept of pluralism, referring to the situation in which people from different backgrounds interact in varying degrees (Cohen and Middleton 1970:9), is certainly applicable to the current situation in the Trust Territory. In the district centers and at the capital in Saipan, members from each district and ethnic group interact on a daily basis. Yet one is hard-pressed to give adequate justification for calling the Trust Territory a nation-state, or for that matter, even a plural society.

In order to better understand the nature of pan–Trust Territory society, it is useful to digress briefly and define the concept of integration as applied in the analysis of African nation-states. Integration is generally defined as the processes of interaction between diverse groups that produce a viable political system. Cohen and Middleton (1970:6–7) identify three measures useful for testing the nature and degree of integration in a nation-state: transactional flow, functional interdependency, and congruence of values.

Transactional flow refers to the amount and nature of interaction over geographical space between the various segments of the population in question. For the Trust Territory, this applies to interaction between the separate districts as well as within the districts. The concept implies reciprocal relationships occurring over time and assumes that the more frequently interaction occurs, the greater the resulting integration.

Functional interdependency is derived from Durkheim's notion of organic solidarity and has traditionally referred to the dependent relationships between the different parts of a system that must be maintained to meet the requirements both of the separate parts and of the whole. With reference to the Trust Territory, the concept is more useful if applied in the context of an open "field" as opposed to a closed "system" and expanded to encompass both relationships within the territory and relationships beyond. Interdependence is particularly relevant to economic and political fields that are premised on wider networks of relationship than social systems. It identifies a distinctive type of transactional relationship that may override the fragmenting tendencies of pluralism. It is therefore especially pertinent to the question of whether the Trust Territory is indeed a society or nation.

The third criterion, congruence of values, refers to a sense of common identity and outlook on life that hold people together. The difficulty in applying this concept lies in determining which values are most crucial for integration, and with what degree of intensity they are shared. Perhaps the most plausible method for measuring congruence of values is cluster analysis, collecting lists of values from a sample of informants from each ethnic group and identifying the recurrent clusters that emerge from these lists.

Julian Steward (1955:43–69) has supplied a useful analytical framework for investigating these measures of integration as they apply to the Trust Territory. Steward suggests that national entities may be broken down into sociocultural segments and formal institutions. The sociocultural segments furnish the context for noneconomic daily activities, and the formal institutions supply the framework within which these activities occur.

Steward divides the sociocultural segments into two principal types: "vertical cleavages" in the larger society such as household and community, and "horizontal cleavages" such as occupation, class, or special interest. The horizontal cleavages tend to fall into hierarchial arrangements forming social classes.

Formal institutions include government, legal system, political parties, labor unions, schools, international trade, banking, and mass media. Generally, these institutions permeate the sociocultural segments to such an extent that they cannot be functionally separated from them. Rather, they are manifest in two ways, at the formal, institutionalized level and the behavioral level of specific community representations.

With regard to the problem of transactional flow and integration in the Trust Territory, horizontal cleavages and formal institutions are directly applicable. In contrast, vertical cleavages provide ethnic identity and the framework and integration for the various traditional societies. The traditional political systems are pyramidal in structure without significant horizontal ties to entities beyond the boundaries of the local structure. Interisland, interethnic trade was the only formal institution bringing diverse island groups into persistent contact, and represents a very minimal amount of precolonial transactional flow.

The horizontal cleavages of society that span the Trust Territory today are all colonial innovations. Of these, the only extensive occupational structure is found in the colonial bureaucracy. This does, however, represent a significant number, who, in the higher group levels of responsibility, travel periodically to other districts for formal interaction with officials having similar rank and responsibility.

Schoolteachers form the only group that might potentially create a labor organization. In 1970, teachers walked out of classes in Saipan, striking for higher salaries. Shortly thereafter, teachers in Palau followed suit. These groups had no formal connections, but the communication network between them worked rapidly enough to cause a bandwagon-type reaction.

Another, much smaller, group exhibiting a similar degree of transactional flow are the entrepreneurs. Businessmen from all districts travel from time to time to Guam and even to other districts on personal business. Successful entrepreneurs frequently establish contact and meet for business or for social purposes when the occasion permits. These men are very small in number, but generally powerful in their home districts.

The only clear-cut horizontal class spanning all of the ethnic groups is that of the new educated elite. In chapter 5, Singleton suggested that the boarding school situation in the early years of territorial education served to select the most promising students from the diverse districts, to integrate them through common knowledge and skills, and to set them apart from the masses lacking their experience. This process has continued with the increasing importance of a college education. Students travel to Guam, Hawaii, or the United States mainland, where they have long-term associations with students from other districts. These contacts are often renewed in later years at administrative conferences or when these individuals assume elected offices and assemble for congress. Without question, the highly educated enjoy an elevated status at home and share common ground with their fellow students from other districts.

Transactional flow is greatest in the district centers of the territory due to the process of interdistrict migration. A small minority of Micronesians from each district have migrated to other districts for one reason or another. Many go in search of wage work or business opportunities. Others are sent by the government to fill specific administrative positions. The most numerous migrants in the territory are the Palauans and the outer islanders of Truk and Ponape districts. The Palauans constitute a significant minority group in Yap and Mariana districts. These mobile people form a horizontal ethnic class and greatly increase transactional flow in each district center. Palauans and the migrants from other districts maintain a steady, but small, force for greater integration.

Air transportation is the second most important process for transactional flow. All the district centers are serviced by at least three weekly flights to and from the district. Students travel to and from boarding schools, government officials and congressmen travel on business, entrepreneurs travel to establish contacts, relatives visit, and Micronesian tourists travel to see the bright lights of Guam, Hawaii, and even Japan.

The Trust Territory is replete with formal institutions, all colonial in origin, that attempt to integrate the territory into a nation-state. The missions and the schools have been indoctrinating the populace for over twenty-five years. Since the mid-sixties, radio stations have broadcast music and district, territorial, and world news. This in itself is extremely important. One of the authors has observed households in Yap where the 8:00 P.M. news in the vernacular brought all activities to a halt and provided topics for conversation for an hour afterward.

The most important of colonial instiutions are the governmental structures. Although the bureaucracy supplies the administrative framework of the territory, the most important units for integration are the Congress of Micronesia and the district legislatures. In their formal characteristics, the congress and the legislatures furnish the only significant functionally interdependent units in the territory. The congress is empowered to charter the legislatures, define their scope of powers, and share tax revenue. The legislatures make local appropriation of funds and give input on issues of importance to the Territory and the districts. In chapter 13, Mason suggests that any future unity of the Trust Territory is entirely contingent upon the leadership of the congress and upon the interaction and interdependence of the congress and the district legislatures. Without their mutual cooperation, the hope for a Micronesian nation-state appears dim indeed.

From evidence available, it appears that such cooperation is not only possible but probable. In each district of the territory, members of the congress and legislature have formed coalitions and incipient or functioning political parties. Meller notes in chapter 14 that these parties have not achieved territory-wide influence, and therefore do not yet fill an integrating function. However, they do assure continuing interdependence between congressmen and legislators.

Meller does suggest that the use of English as a common language in the congress and in the administration facilitates integration and the growth of a national identity. He does not feel, however, that this influence is strong enough to offset the problems of pluralism.

The greatest single deficiency in U.S. plans for a Micronesian nation-state is the lack of economic development, particularly development utilizing local markets and establishing functional interdependency between the various island districts. The tons of fish, rice, and sugar imported each year from Japan, Australia, and the United States might just as easily be produced and marketed within the Territory itself. The sad fact is that almost nothing is produced within the Territory for marketing in the other districts. The only major economic activity currently requiring dependent cooperation is transportation by air and by ship. Successful import and export trade is, of course, premised upon the continuation of this transportation system, and ensures continual need for interdistrict cooperation.

The final area for consideration is that of congruence of values. Micronesians today share many wants and values common to their experiences with the colonial administration. One need only look at the records of annual legislative appropriations to see the importance of roads, water supply, and now even electricity to the people. The list of wants could be greatly expanded, and includes everything from automobiles to needles and thread. These new items, however important, do not identify the core of values that might further integrate Micronesians into a nation or at least into a plural society.

Some very key values do appear to be common to Micronesians. Perhaps most basic is the universal concern for land. Due to limitations of land area in the Territory, threats to Micronesian sovereignty over land spur a united protective response. The strategic needs of the United States or any other world power for land in the Territory supplies an issue around which all Micronesians will rally.

A number of other values may be listed that elicit less emotion, but are central to a Micronesian identity. Micronesians share common regard for persons who exhibit the attributes of respect, kindness, generosity, modesty, and personal restraint. They place high value on cooperation and group solidarity. Perhaps most compelling are the traditional personal desires for wealth, prestige, and new experience. The colonial unity of the Territory has opened many new avenues for obtaining these desires. Individuals who have tried these ways and succeeded may be expected to press on for expanded opportunities. These people, the leaders, the new political and economic elite, share traditional and new values and motivations that supply the core for a new Micronesian identity.

Whether the Trust Territory will become a nation-state is a question impossible to answer. The decisions surrounding the termination of trusteeship status will influence, but not close, the issues. Forces both from within and without the Territory will influence the directions of change for many years to come. In chapter 13, Mason takes a closer look at the internal forces at work in the Territory and at their implications for the future status of Micronesia.

International Perspectives

The problems facing Micronesians are not unique in the Pacific. The international unpopularity of colonialism has everywhere provoked colonial governments to reconsider their policies and move their dependent territories toward self-government and independence. Among these Pacific territories, nascent nationalism appears everywhere. In chapter 14, Meller compares the programs for self-government throughout the Pacific and finds many parallels to events in the U.S. Trust Territory.

The problems of emerging nations in the Pacific are not unique. They are first of all concerned with protecting their own interests and revising colonial forms of government to meet their own values and needs. Beyond these immediate concerns, they invariably turn to economic development, to world trade, and to consideration of the strategic interests of world powers in their new nation.

The concluding two chapters in the volume address themselves to the problems of Pacific islands in general and the Trust Territory in particular with regard to international politics. Moos, in chapter 15, examines the historical role of the Japanese in the area and their contemporary economic influence in Micronesia. He suggests that Japan's presence in the Pacific is once again expanding and that its economic foothold will be translated into strategic power in the future. His chapter then considers the implications of Japan's economic expansion for the future political status of the Territory.

In chapter 16, Mihaly projects one step further to what he perceives as an inevitable arms race in the Pacific. He suggests that competing world powers will attempt to woo newly independent nations to permit the building of naval bases on their lands. Because these nations have only land to offer, they will become pawns of the super-powers and subject to severe economic and social dislocation. Mihaly proposes, then, an international policy of neutralization for Pacific islands, including the U.S. Trust Territory, and suggests how current negotiations between Micronesians and the United States might further such a goal.

13

Unity and Disunity in Micronesia: Internal Problems and Future Status

Leonard Mason

Whatever semblance of unity exists for the more than two thousand islands officially known as the Trust Territory of the Pacific Islands must be credited to three centuries of colonial dominance by a succession of foreign powers. The last of these, the United States, has for a quarter of a century administered the area on behalf of the United Nations. It now appears possible that colonialism in Micronesia, as the area is more commonly referred to in modern political parlance, will come to an end within the next three or four years at the request and urging of the United Nations Trusteeship Council.

In negotiations begun in 1969, the Micronesian leadership, represented by the Congress of Micronesia's Joint Committee on Future Status, has consistently sought from the United States government a guarantee of Micronesian autonomy, at least with regard to internal affairs. Such agreement would be spelled out in a Compact of Free Association with the United States and could lead eventually, if so desired, to the complete independence of Micronesians. In August 1972, the Congress of Micronesia directed its Status Committee to initiate negotiations with the United States concerning the immediate establishment of Micronesia as an independent nation and, at the same time, to continue the talks based on the free association principle. The new strategy, reasoned the congressmen, would provide the Micronesian people with a more realistic choice between the two alternatives in a plebiscite planned as a precondition to final review and approval by the United Nations.

Whether the people's preference turns out to be immediate independence or free association with the United States, several troublesome questions for the future arise. Until late in 1972 these questions had received but little serious consideration in Micronesian councils. For example, what promise can Micronesians hope for, in actuality, to continue as a unitary state after termination of trusteeship? Will the existing territory fragment into a series of smaller, separate states, possibly in loose confederation (or none at all) for dealing politically and economically with other countries in the Pacific basin? What internal forces may be expected to confront the Micronesian leadership as it seeks to develop and maintain a viable unity—if that be the official goal?[1]

The Packaging of Micronesia

Hundreds of books and articles both technical and popular describe and analyze Micronesia in the twentieth century. In these publications, Micronesia usually comprises the Marshall, the Caroline, and the Mariana islands (except Guam). This practice coincides understandably with the delimitation of the territory governed as a single entity by Germany after 1899, by Japan between the two World Wars, and by the United States since 1945. A series of treaties, agreements, public laws, and executive orders clearly delineate the legal status of the Trust Territory. From that fact have issued generalizations about the islands, their peoples and cultures, and the accommodation to modernizing influences. It is unfortunate when such statements tend to portray Micronesia as far more integrated than the facts of anthropology, geography, or history will testify. The illusion of unity easily translates into the presumption of unity. This chapter will examine the validity of that presumption in the light of recent rapid changes in Micronesia and implications for the future ordering of internal Micronesian relations.

Compare modern Micronesia in its manifest unity to a package of assorted goods—all wrapped, tied, and ready for delivery. The wrappings and tie cords are the means of holding the package together. Should the wrappings be torn and the cords parted in delivery, nothing could prevent the goods from spilling out and being lost. The package would be delivered in sadly damaged condition, if at all. In applying this analogy to the present course and future status of Micronesia, the following discussion aims to identify the principal assorted goods, ties, and wrappings, and to suggest the outcome when the packaging comes undone.

First, consider the assortment of goods contained in the package. About twenty-one hundred individual islands in ninety-six inhabited groups total in land area just over seven hundred square miles. Some are high volcanic islands, others are only tiny coral islets. Reasonably fertile land exists on the larger islands, but the sandy soils of coral atolls support only a modicum of plant forms. Mineral deposits are almost completely absent. Much the same is true of land mammals other than those introduced in historic times. Marine resources, on the other hand, present a striking contrast. In reef shallows, lagoons, and deeper offshore waters, a wonderfully rich and varied marine fauna abounds. Certain high islands and atoll lagoons offer excellent anchorage for ocean shipping. Other islands, lacking safe passages through the fringing reefs, remain relatively inaccessible.

Additional goods in the package exist in the variety of Micronesia's human and culutural resources. Nearly one hundred and fifteen thousand people hold residence as natives in the islands. They live in a wide spectrum of communities ranging from district center aggregations of five thousand or more to outer island villages and hamlets of less than fifty persons. Collectively they command nine—some say eleven—mutually unintelligible indigenous languages. Similarly, diversity persists in their traditional customs—in local technologies, economic systems, art styles, family arrangements, religious practices, and political institutions. In historic times, differing degrees of foreign influence in different parts of Micronesia compounded or overlaid these traditional commitments as the aftermath of contacts with missionaries, traders, merchants, colonists, administrators, and military occupation forces during the successive Spanish, German, Japanese, and American regimes. In recent years, one can discern a new quality of acculturation in the semiurbanized concentrations of islanders attracted to district and subdistrict centers in contrast with the more traditional communities in islands and atolls of Micronesia's hinterland.

Unifying Ties

If, for the sake of argument, one admits the packaging of Micronesia, as a product of colonialism, what tie cords and wrappings secure the package in the islands' present state of development, thus serving in some degree to unify Micronesia's disparate parts?

Controls from outside Micronesia

The most visible bonds are those imposed from outside Micronesia, continuing the colonialist tradition formally initiated by Germany at the close of the nineteenth century. They stem from the international and national commitments of the United States government as administering authority in the Trust Territory of the Pacific Islands. The Trusteeship Agreement between the United States and the United Nations Security Council came into effect on 18 July 1947. The former Japanese-mandated islands thereby passed from military government by the United States Navy to a form of civil administration under the same agency. By presidential executive order on 1 July 1951 the Department of the Interior succeeded the navy in administration of the trust islands. A single basic order by the secretary of the interior on 27 December 1968 brought into one document previous secretarial orders concerning the Trust Territory government, and spelled out the executive authority of the high commissioner, the legislative authority of the Congress of Micronesia, and the judicial authority of the high court and other courts in the Territory. The Trust Territory Code of 1 January 1971 and amendments, a compilation of laws and regulations based on precedents in the United States civil and criminal codes, applies equally throughout the Territory.

The high commissioner's staff at headquarters on Saipan directs territory-wide programs in education, finance, health services, personnel, public affairs, public works, resources and development, and transportation and communications. In each of the six administrative districts (Marianas, Marshalls, Palau, Ponape, Truk, and Yap), the district administrator acts for the high commissioner and supervises officers and departments paralleling those of the headquarters staff. Although the administration's objective is to fill every Trust Territory government position with a Micronesian, the top policy-making appointments at headquarters continue to be assigned mainly to American expatriates. Principal funding of the Trust Territory administration depends on annual review and approval of the budget by the United States Congress. In fiscal year 1972, this commitment amounted to approximately sixty million dollars from federal tax monies.

Wants and Needs of Micronesians

The second principal set of tie cords or bonds, in contrast with the set discussed above, finds its basis within the Micronesian people. Likely to be important in shaping individual preferences for future status, these ties are implicit in new wants and needs derived from islanders' past and present accculturative experiences. Just within the last decade, the United States government's increase of 350 percent in annual dollar subsidy has notably heightened Micronesian expectations, particularly in the areas of education, health services, living standards, and social awareness. The maintenance of present levels in each of these areas would seem to depend on continuing support from outside Micronesia.

The reference here to wants and needs follows the terminological usage suggested by Goodenough (1963:49-60). Wants are the "desired states of affairs," ultimately the "feeling states" within individuals with which they are "content." Needs are the "effective means for achieving or maintaining" wants. They are "felt" needs in that they may, or may not, be realistic means of achieving or maintaining desired ends. Nor do they necessarily coincide with "real" needs an "omniscient observer" from outside might select to achieve the community's wants. Wants and needs will rarely be expressed unanimously within a community because of the wide ranges of difference in individual experience as the latter departs from tradition in favor of introduced goods, ideas, and practices. With these qualifications, the following exposition represents an estimate, based on recent observations and interviews, of the inclination of many Micronesians, especially in the district and subdistrict centers, to support whatever degree of territorial unity is judged essential to continue the status quo.

Education. Micronesian wants and needs in the area of education ostensibly focus on formal schooling in English language and other skills sufficient to gain employment or other participation in a society more and more oriented toward political and economic involvement in the world at large. This statement requires some qualification in that Micronesian leaders argue increasingly of late for curricular materials more relevant to traditional cultures and values and more responsive to the self-expressed wants and needs of the Micronesian community.

The administration's education program stresses universal schooling from grades one through eight. A similar goal exists for the four years of secondary schooling, but public facilities and staff fall far short of the existing demand. Curricula at both levels are based primarily on materials in the English language, mathematics, science, and social studies developed outside Micronesia. In fiscal year 1972, some 208 public elementary schools in the Territory served 26,974 boys and girls (19 private schools enrolled an additional 2,943), and nine public secondary schools served 5,093 students (nine private high schools registered 1,408 other students). In the same year, 778 Micronesians studied at institutions of higher learning outside the Trust Territory. Of these, 46 percent received Trust Territory government aid through scholarships. In addition, the administration operates a Community College of Micronesia on Ponape, a Micronesian Occupational Center in Palau, and a Micronesian Maritime Center in Truk. Government expenditures on education for fiscal year 1972 totaled approximately 13.5 million dollars, of which 20 percent went into new construction (U.S. Department of State 1973:328-50).

Health services. In the area of health services, Micronesians have come to expect freedom from most diseases and direct access to hospital care in preference to help from traditional practitioners. Because private medical services are almost nonexistent, Micronesians are dependent on the administration's public health offerings. Six general hospitals in the district centers and three field hospitals in subdistrict locations, with a total capacity of over five hundred beds for inpatient care, directly serve a government-estimated 78 percent of the Territory's population. For islanders with less immediate access to district center facilities, health aides in 153 outer island dispensaries provide outpatient care (U.S. Department of State 1973:115). Most hospitals support dental clinics and maternal and child care clinics. Services to Micronesians are either free or available at modest rates appropriate to the patient's ability to pay. Supplemental programs deal with environmental sanitation, immunization, health education, and family planning. Physical facilities in most hospitals and nearly all dispensaries are sorely in need of modernization or replacement, and a capital improvements program now under way promises to remedy the situation by 1975. In fiscal year 1972, the Department of Health Services employed a total of 1,140 persons of whom 1,086 were Micronesians. Besides health aides, nurse aides, and service workers, the latter figure included 56 medical and dental officers many of whom trained at the Fiji School of Medicine in Suva, and 157 nurses of whom 97 percent graduated from the Trust Territory School of Nursing. The departmental budget for that year totaled 7.4 million dollars, with 67 percent applied to direct support of hospitals and outer island services (U.S. Department of State 1973:312–16).

Living standards. More than a century of trading with foreigners revolutionized island living standards with regard to wants and needs for material things. Local consumer demands mounted through the years for those commodities ordinarily considered essential to life in an industrial society. Micronesians today import incredible quantities of flour, sugar, rice, canned foods, beverages of all sorts, tobacco and cigarettes, clothing, textiles, building materials, home appliances, petroleum products, machinery, and vehicles. In return, they export principally copra, fish, handicrafts, vegetables, beef, fruits, shells, and scrap metal from the wrecks of World War II.

Limited world markets for island products together with rising consumer needs create a critical imbalance that seems unlikely to abate. The estimated value of Micronesian exports fluctuated at about 3 million dollars in fiscal years 1968 to 1972, while imports climbed steadily from 13.6 to 26.3 million dollars during the same period (U.S. Department of State 1973:271). Local purchasing power to surmount this disparity comes primarily from wage labor concentrated in the district centers. Of 13,913 indigenous wage earners reported for fiscal year 1972, approximately 66 percent worked for the Trust Territory administration or other government-funded activities. Those in private employment, to a large extent serving the needs of Micronesians in government and of Americans in the administration, were associated mainly with merchandising, transportation, stevedoring, construction, food and drink services, and transient lodging (U.S. Department of State 1973:307–8).

The Trusteeship Council in 1971 cautioned the United States in its administration of the trust islands that the "excessive dependence on external assistance prevents the establishment of a solid financial base within the Territory" (U.S. Department of State 1972:167). Yet the United States Congress approved an administration request for a 20 percent increase in the 1972 budget, for a peak figure of 60 million dollars. The Congress of Micronesia, seeking to generate more territorial revenue, passed a 3 percent tax on all earned income over $1,000. This went into effect 1 July 1971, and was expected to bring in 1.46 million dollars in fiscal year 1972, of which possibly as much as 79 percent would represent tax levies on earnings of non-Micronesians, especially Americans employed at the Kwajalein

Missile Range (U.S. Department of State 1972:263–64). (The annual report for fiscal year 1972 fails to include the actual amount collected from this income tax.) This illustrates again Micronesia's dependence on external resources.

In general, Micronesia reflects a distressing shortage of capital, managerial skills, and trained labor for developing local capabilities to meet indigenous expectations of material prosperity. Most of the capital required by Micronesian businessmen, corporations, and cooperatives for undertaking new enterprises or for expanding existing ones now comes in the form of direct loans from the administration's Economic Development Loan Fund. Some forty credit unions and American banking facilities in the Territory afford additional though restricted financial assistance. Further developments in agriculture, fishing, and tourism—commonly regarded as the most promising areas for generating local inputs to increase the per capita gross national product—appear unlikely to produce more than moderate returns without continued subsidization from outside sources.

Social awareness. The foregoing discussion has identified several unifying ties stemming from modified indigenous wants and needs in education, health services, and living standards. Other ties in this set are implicit in the widening horizons of social awareness indicated by the current behavior of many islanders. Modern Micronesians want to know about happenings in the other districts and in other countries. They want to visit those places whenever their personal finances or employment permit. Admittedly, district center inhabitants display this tendency more than do dwellers in the hinterland. Development of communications and transportation networks, notably within the last decade, has broadened the scope of the islander's social awareness both by heightening the intensity of his wants and by providing the opportunity to satisfy those wants, if not yet adequately, at least to a significant degree.

Although the geographic mobility of high islanders was fairly restricted in traditional times to their home shores, the seafaring propensities of atoll peoples in the west-central Carolines and the Marshalls often took the latter far afield. Today, however, the outrigger voyaging canoe is fast becoming an anomaly. Sophisticated sea and air transportation is vitally needed to link the modernizing island economies, which are spread over three million square miles of ocean. The Trust Territory government, attempting to provide reasonably regular and frequent passenger and cargo service among the outer islands, district centers, and Japan and the United States, administers a complex network of transpacific and interisland shipping by direct operation, chartering, and private carrier agreement. In fiscal year 1971, field trip vessels alone carried 13,120 passengers within the districts. Of that number, at least 79 percent, who traveled as deck (not cabin) passengers, were Micronesian and represented an increase of about 50 percent over the number of deck passengers reported only two years earlier (U.S. Department of State 1972:292). (Comparable figures for fiscal year 1972 are not available.) Statistics such as these reflect to some extent the growing desire of the islanders to travel to the limits of available surface transportation.

With Air Micronesia's assumption of responsibility in 1968 for air service in the Territory, flight schedules linking the six districts, Hawaii, and Okinawa improved to the point where traffic increased 350 percent in four years to nearly 118,000 passengers annually (U.S. Department of State 1973:298). A good deal of this traffic represented American and Micronesian government officials on priority business. In order to meet the growing space demands of private and commercial Micronesian travelers, Air Micronesia by late 1972 had added new equipment and was scheduling more flights each week. Although the expanding money economy in the Territory today enables more Micronesians to finance their personal travel by sea and by air to places away from home, they will of necessity continue to depend on the territorial government's subsidy of that mobility through constant upgrading of airports, harbors, and navigational aids required to assure maximum operating security and efficiency.

Although government control of information transmissions in the trust area may leave something to be desired in a free world, all Micronesians have greater access than ever before to knowledge of what goes on and what is available to them beyond the shores of their home islands. The Trust Territory government maintains an extensive communications network, primarily for its own use although private parties may use the facilities on a commercial basis. Radiotelephone and teletype services link all districts to a relay and control station on Saipan and through it to the world outside. Secondary government stations supply two-way radio communication between some ninety outer islands and their respective district centers. Amateur radio operators provide supplemental communication and assistance in emergencies. The administration owns and operates an AM broadcast station in each district center, with programs of news and other information beamed to an estimated 50,000 transistorized receivers owned privately even in the outermost atolls. A private television service operates on Saipan (U.S. Department of State 1973:296).

In recent years independent newspapers in the Marianas and the Marshalls have brought to Micronesian readers a more critical reporting of territorial, United States, and world news. In each district, at least one federal post office represents the extension of United States mail service into the Trust Territory. Micronesians, highly literate in their own languages if not in English, are prodigious letter writers. In fiscal year 1971 (comparable figures are not available for fiscal year 1972), these eleven postal stations handled approximately 1.7 million pounds of outgoing mail and 1.5 million pounds of incoming mail, of which an unreported amount was government correspondence (U.S. Department of State 1972:289).

Congress of Micronesia

Whereas the first set of unifying ties discussed in this section reflects the century-long imposition of colonialist controls from outside Micronesia and the second set identifies certain less tangible though incipiently integrative wants and needs that motivate many Micronesians from within, the third set is inherent in the structure and responsibilities of the Congress of Micronesia. In evaluating the prospects for a unified Micronesia in years to come, this last set may well be the most instructive of all.

An Interior Department secretarial order, dated 28 September 1964, created the Congress of Micronesia to succeed the purely advisory Council of Micronesia. First elections to the new bicameral legislature were held the following January, and the First Congress convened on Saipan on 12 July 1965. Two of the twelve members of the Senate are elected at large from each of the six administrative districts. They serve four-year terms. The twenty-one members of the House of Representatives are elected for two-year terms from single-member voting districts apportioned to represent approximately equal numbers of the population. For this reason, the size of the six district delegations varies: Truk has five representatives, Ponape and the Marshalls have four each, Palau and the Marianas have three each, and Yap has two. In even-numbered years, citizens of the Trust Territory of both sexes eighteen years and older vote by secret ballot for congressional candidates. Except in Palau and the Marianas where political parties and party platforms have been formalized, voter preference depends more on demonstrated ability of the candidate, his position in the community, and traditional ties of authority and kinship. However, when members of the Congress are compared with members of the district legislatures, it appears that the voting public conceptualizes congressional roles as much further removed from local, traditional social systems and that, therefore, these roles tend to be filled by persons who are more fluent in English, well traveled, at least high school- and usually college-educated, and previously experienced in district or territorial administration or in a district legislature (Meller 1969:275–90). It is this younger, educated, outer-oriented Micronesian elite that represents the vanguard of indigenous political aspirations in the early 1970s.

Within the Congress of Micronesia lies the single, most effective concentration of indigenous power vis-à-vis the American-controlled Trust Territory administration and the Washington-initiated policies of the United States government. The Congress appropriates and disburses revenue monies raised within the Territory, and reviews and recommends priorities in the high commissioner's budget proposal prior to its submission to the Department of the Interior and subsequent action by the United States Congress. Any appropriate legislation may be enacted, except as may conflict with laws, treaties, or international agreements of the United States, presidential or secretarial orders, or stated sections of the Trust Territory Code. Although the high commissioner may veto legislation, his veto may be overridden subject to review by the Interior Department secretary. The Congress meets in regular session at the beginning of each year and in special sessions convened by the high commissioner. Congressmen work full time and receive annual salaries from appropriated territorial funds. They travel widely to explain their work to Micronesian constituents and to update their understanding of grass roots opinion on critical issues. In both houses, standing committees on education and social affairs, judiciary and government operations, resources and development, and health matters work between sessions, as do special committees established by the Congress for specific purposes. Each year, a member of the House and a member of the Senate are elected by their colleagues to accompany the high commissioner to New York as special advisers, where they may give independent testimony before the United Nations Trusteeship Council.

District legislatures. No direct ties link the six district legislatures, chartered by the Trust Territory government, with the Congress of Micronesia. However, their comparable legislative function and electoral basis suggest a contributing role in uniting Micronesia's widely dispersed populations within each district that complements the role of the Congress at the territorial level. The cultural diversity and geographic isolation manifested within most districts are to some degree alleviated by the shared participation of island delegates in the legislative sessions that convene once or twice a year in the district centers. Legislators represent designated electoral precincts within each district, except in the Palau and Marshalls legislatures, where some seats are reserved for traditional chiefly titleholders. Bills passed on matters of common concern, including the levying of district taxes, become law when approved by the district administrator. As already remarked, these district assemblies fulfill yet another function as proving grounds for many of those Micronesians ambitious to serve in the territorial congress.

Joint Committee on Future Status. Unilateral action by the Congress of Micronesia on 8 August 1967 initiated a new and critical phase in American-Micronesian relations when both houses adopted Senate Joint Resolution No. 25. The act, in establishing the Future Political Status Commission as an arm of the Congress, sparked the onset of Micronesia's decolonization. The group of six congressmen appointed to represent the six districts were mandated to study the issues involved and to recommend future political options open to Micronesia. After extensive research and consultation, the commission in July 1968, in an interim report, reviewed the experience of other Pacific territories that had achieved self-government or independence, or were in the process of so doing, and outlined tentatively a number of possibilities judged applicable to Micronesia's situation. The Congress granted the commission's request for more time to observe those states at firsthand and to inquire into the viability of their governance. The commission submitted its final report to the Congress in July 1969, a "statement of intent" that will certainly stand as a landmark display of Micronesian unity. Commission members recommended: (1) that Micronesia be constituted as a self-governing state with indigenous control in all three branches of its government; (2) that it negotiate an agreement with the United States based on the principle of free association; and (3) that, failing such agreement, it choose independence as the only other realistic alternative for Micronesians.

In acting on the commission's final report, the Congress created the Micronesian Political Status Delegation, composed of five members from each house, and responded to Interior Secretary Walter J. Hickel's invitation made three months before to explore together possible legislation concerning future American-Micronesian relations. Further, preferring neither to reject nor to endorse the commission's recommended priority for free association with the United States, the Congress authorized the delegation to study steps that would anticipate independence as well as free association. In the first round of talks, convened in Washington in September 1969, the ten-member delegation met informally with Interior, State, and Defense Department officials, and presented for discussion a list of eleven subject categories, including immigration, customs, postal services, courts, postwar damage claims, eminent domain, defense, foreign affairs, financial aid, and a constitution for Micronesia.

The second round of negotiations, held on Saipan in May 1970, ended in impasse. The seven-member American delegation, drawn from Interior, State, and Defense Department offices in Washington and headed by the Interior Department's Assistant Secretary for Public Land Management Harrison Loesch, proposed a commonwealth status for Micronesians, an irrevocable association with the United States modeled closely on that of Puerto Rico. The Micronesian delegation, under cochairmen Senator Lazarus Salii (Palau) and Representative Ekpap Silk (Marshalls), found the offer to be completely unsatisfactory, especially with regard to Micronesian options to administer their own lands and laws and to change the association in future.

The Status delegation, reporting to the Congress of Micronesia in July 1970, defined four "basic principles and legal rights" developed in connection with the Saipan talks and considered to be nonnegotiable in any proposed association with the United States. These are the rights of sovereignty and of self-determination, the right to structure a Micronesian government and constitution, and the right to terminate the compact of association unilaterally. Each principle emphasizes the desire and need for a unified Micronesia. Together they constitute a kind of charter for pooling Micronesian efforts and resources in support of shared goals. These guidelines for future negotiating, as delineated in House Joint Resolution No. 87, received overwhelming approval in both houses of the Congress. Then, in House Joint Resolution No. 102, the Congress established the Joint Committee on Future Status, enlarged to two members from each of the six districts, to continue negotiating for as long as required on the terms mandated by HJR 87, and to study the economic implications of free association and independence and conduct a political education program throughout the Trust Territory. Senator Salii and Representative Silk continued to serve as cochairmen of the new committee.

Ocean Expanse and Geographic Location

In concluding this section, the discussion returns to the analogy of Micronesia as a package bound with tie cords and wrappings. Three principal sets of tie cords have been identified. The first set referred to controls imposed from outside Micronesia. The second reflected the changing wants and needs of Micronesians from within, with particular attention to education, health services, living standards, and social awareness. The third focused on the Congress of Micronesia and its agent the Joint Committee on Future Status. Together these have served to create and to maintain whatever unity prevails in modern Micronesia.

If it does not strain the analogy too much, one may go further and identify two other factors, each being a wrapping of sorts, more generalized than a tie cord and contributing in a different way to the packaging of Micronesia. Each of these factors carries a potential for enclosing or enveloping the disparate parts of Micronesia. Certain of the more specific tie cords already described complete the packaging and ensure more security to the contents within. The wrappings referred to are the ocean expanse and the geographic location of Micronesia.

The Trust Territory of the Pacific Islands encompasses three million square miles of Pacific Ocean, an area approximating that of the continental United States. Conjecture about Micronesia's future understandably concentrates scrutiny on the islands and their populations, and the surrounding waters are less thoughtfully either taken for granted or accepted as an isolating medium. This tends to divert even more attention to the islands and their habitants apart from the ocean in which they are located. The expanse of open sea, conceived as a wrapping around the package, affords a practicable means of bringing closer together into a single collectivity the widely dispersed Micronesians, whose island shores are all washed by tides of the same ocean. To adopt this more positive view of the Micronesian sea depends very much, of course, upon applying the more specific tie cord of ocean shipping before the ocean's value as a highway can be fully realized. Traditionally, navigators from the atolls sailed their seagoing outrigger canoes long distances from home, and thereby converted the watery medium from an isolating barrier to an integrative asset. Modern transport systems in the Trust Territory, noted earlier in this section, continue to translate the ocean's potential for bringing island peoples together in closer concert, just as new technologies of travel and transport throughout the world are capitalizing on the existence of oceans (and the air space above them) to reduce the barriers of distance between inhabited landforms. In this sense, then, the Micronesian sea is emphasized as a noteworthy resource to be utilized even more than at present in the creation of one nation, if that be the will of the Micronesian people.

Geographic location is the second factor suggested above as a generalized wrapping in the packaging of Micronesia. The islands achieve a certain strategic value in the international politicking of nations in both the East and the West by reason of their central location within the Pacific basin. Historically, German activities in the area were economically oriented for the most part. Japan maintained a strong economic investment but also initiated a determined military buildup throughout the islands. The United States has shown remarkably little concern for the Territory's economic development. However, its assessment of Micronesia's strategic value became evident in 1946 when the United States proposed the islands as a *strategic* area trusteeship, the only one in the United Nations system. Future land requirements for use by the military, outlined by the United States during the fourth round of talks with the Micronesians in April 1972, are limited to sites in the Marshalls, Marianas, and Palau districts. These would be secured by negotiated grant or lease to complement the permanent major military base on Guam. Beyond that, it must be emphasized, the United States requires that no part of the Territory be available for military purposes to any third nation, and thus would apply the concept of strategic denial in all six districts to such foreign powers as China, Japan, and the Soviet Union. Recent military withdrawals by the United States have occurred, and others appear likely to occur in the future, from Southeast Asia, Taiwan, the Philippines, Okinawa, and Japan. If a corresponding escalation of American missile, air, submarine, and surface fleet bases and support facilities takes place within the Trust Territory, the strategic value attached to its geographic location will inevitably perpetuate the image of Micronesia as a single entity in the United States' view.

Terminating the Trusteeship

Does the present illusion of unity in the Trust Territory presume a unity that in fact does not exist at all? This question is one of several posed at the start of this chapter. Rather than affirm or deny outright the questioned unity of Micronesia as other observers have done with varying degrees of documentation, it will be instructive here to examine the packaging of Micronesia in the light of anticipated termination of trusteeship and its eventual realization. What happens to the package when existing tie cords and wrappings are removed or weakened? Will others replace them and hold the package intact? Or will the packaging be so altered that goods contained inside are separated or lost? In other words, can the presumed unity of Micronesians survive the termination of trusteeship and become an unquestioned reality?

The United Nations Trusteeship Council has on several occasions affirmed support of its 1970 Visiting Mission's recommendation that, considering the particular situation of the trust area and its problems, it would be desirable to reach a decision on future status sooner rather than later. Observers in general guess that present negotiations and transition to a new government cannot be completed before the end of 1974, or even 1975, at the earliest. But many, both Micronesians and Americans, are more pessimistic, and for good reason, too, in view of all that needs to be done prior to formal termination regardless of what future status is finally agreed upon.

The four basic principles for a unified and autonomous Micronesia, accepted by the Congress in July 1970, ensured the requisite common ground for reasonable cooperation within the Congress of Micronesia and the Joint Committee on Future Status during the next two years of legislative deliberations on future status and the next four rounds of American-Micronesian negotiations. Nevertheless, there did emerge during this period two dissenting views from the joint committee's continuing priority for free association. The Marianas District leadership from the beginning had favored a closer relationship with the United States, either through a commonwealth status or by merger with the American Territory of Guam. In April 1972, Marianas members of the joint committee applied successfully to the United States delegation to undertake future status talks with the latter separate from the other Trust Territory districts. At the other end of the political spectrum, a coalition of congressmen rallied about a position favored by Truk District delegates demanding that steps be taken toward immediate independence for Micronesia.

Meanwhile, President Nixon, in March 1972, had appointed Franklin Haydn Williams, head of the Asia Foundation, to be his personal representative with the rank of ambassador to lead the United States delegation. A permanent Office for Micronesian Status Negotiations opened in Washington. Negotiations resumed at Hana, Maui, Hawaii, in October 1971. They continued at Koror, Palau, in April 1972, in Washington in July, and at Barbers Point, Oahu, Hawaii, in September. In the course of these talks, the United States did modify its prior stand to accord with most of the basic principles adopted by the Micronesian Congress. A compact of free association began to take shape for application to all of the Trust Territory excepting the Marianas District.

When the Washington talks ended in July 1972, a joint drafting committee of the two delegations had reached preliminary accord on sections dealing with internal and foreign affairs and defense. Other sections on finance, trade and commerce, nationality, and conditions for terminating the compact remained to be drafted and agreed upon in later sessions. However, when the Congress of Micronesia in special session that August reviewed finished portions of the draft compact, considerable debate and some doubts ensued about the specifics emerging from application of the free association concept to district situations. Senate Joint Resolution No. 117 reflected this critical concern and modified the joint committee's mandate so that the independence topic would be explored at the same time as drafting of the compact of free association continued. In the latter months of 1973, the United States delegation had not yet agreed to adopt the two-track approach in future negotiations. Neither had the Congress of Micronesia moved affirmatively on the joint committee's proposal to call a constitutional convention in the immediate future to determine the organization of a new Micronesian government, an action required by the United States before any negotiated compact could be put into force.

The whole negotiated agreement on Micronesian future status must be submitted by the two delegations to their respective Congresses for review. Hopefully approval by that time would be given, but either or both of these assemblies could conceivably demand revisions that would necessitate return of the document to the negotiating table. One must point out here also a very real difference in membership and accountability of the two teams, for this has already created some problems in understanding each other's role. The United States delegation is a creature of the executive branch of government (Interior, State, and Defense departments), its chairman reports directly to the White House, and it presents a united front based on national policy established at the highest administrative level. Any agreement negotiated by the American delegation must be acceptable as well to the legislative branch of government, i.e., the United States Congress, particularly if Micronesia's future status will require continued federal funding. On the other hand, the Micronesian delegation is made up of legislators to begin with. Although the Joint Committee on Future Status represents both houses of the Congress of Micronesia, it lacks any authority to commit that body. The United States delegation expects that when the jointly negotiated status agreement is presented to the Congress by the joint committee, the latter will endorse and defend the document as a unanimous membership. However, each committee member is at the same time a Congressman. As such, he is obligated to act individually in expressing his personal judgment and that of his constituents when the full Congress moves toward a decision on the draft agreement.

When congressional approval is finally given on both sides, the compact (and any other agreement that may have been produced concurrently, e.g., for the immediate independence of Micronesia) must be submitted to the people in a Territory-wide plebiscite. Only after the will of the populace has been freely expressed will termination of trusteeship be considered in the several chambers of the United Nations that are party to the issue. A complicating development, which at the end of 1972 appeared more than likely, is that the product of a separate series of negotiations may be channeled through the reviewing pipeline at or about the same time, namely, the creation of a commonwealth status binding the Marianas District in a closer relationship with the United States.

Consequences of Termination

Anticipating the termination of trusteeship, we have reviewed certain developments and requirements in the ongoing process of revising the islands' political status. Questions were posed about the future packaging of Micronesia should the existing tie cords be removed or weakened as a consequence of termination. We now move directly to consider the changing condition of those bonds depending on whether they are eliminated, preserved, or altered in some degree.

Elimination of ties

Immediately upon termination, of course, the trusteeship status of the islands is eliminated, and with it any international supervision of the area as a single entity, such as the United Nations and the Trusteeship Council have exercised since 1947. No matter which of the several options now under consideration is finally approved, the present American-controlled administration will give way to a Micronesian government (or governments, if any separatism prevails) with autonomy in domestic affairs at the very least. Micronesians will replace American employees of the present administration, unless the new government chooses to retain some of them as expatriate advisers or technicians. Finally, with the conclusion of American-Micronesian negotiations on future status, the common bond evoked by having to confront the United States, which to date contributes to some semblance of unity among Micronesian leaders, will no longer exist. The package that is now Micronesia will be vulnerable in the future to outside pressures if the bindings implicit in international supervision, American administration, and Micronesian confrontation of the United States in negotiation fail to be replaced by other ties as strong or stronger,

Preservation of ties

The indigenous power concentrated in the Congress of Micronesia has been cited here as the single most effective force for unification emanating from within Micronesia. The Congress can be expected to preserve that role in the future if forces for fission that began to surface in 1972 do not erode its strength. A second basis for cooperation among islanders is their increased commitment to acquired wants and needs in education, health services, living standards, and social awareness of other peoples and places, which promises to persist especially in the more populous district centers. A third factor in favor of continued unity of action at the territorial level is a realization that the several districts must pool their differences in human and natural resources if the goal of maximizing economic self-sufficiency for all Micronesian groups is to be achieved. These three bonding elements constitute the principal foundation available to Micronesians for building a future political union. Without such tie cords to preserve the package whole, the islanders would face inordinate difficulties in creating and developing a Micronesian nation, regardless of assurances of external assistance.

However, a fourth element may turn out to be the most decisive of all in containing the islands of Micronesia as a single, bounded totality, whether they be politically unified or not. What is at issue here is the position of the United States government that no change in the territory's political status will be acceptable that opens up the waters and lands of Micronesia to other world powers, or in any way restricts options by the United States to construct or retain military installations in its western defense perimeter.

Alteration of Ties

In order to assess the impact of tie cords altered by termination of trusteeship, one must consider the critical financial problem of providing support for the new Micronesian government and maintaining satisfactory levels of want and need gratification among the populace. An essential aspect of this problem relates to the degree of American involvement in future Micronesian affairs, whether in the commonwealth arrangement projected for the Marianas District, or a form of free association with the United States controlling defense and international affairs, or complete and immediate independence of the islands that would admit the United States into Micronesia for military purposes by negotiation only. The continued inflow of American tax dollars understandably might be maximized in the closer relationship of commonwealth and minimized if Micronesians opt for independence.

Under Micronesian authority, government expenditures could probably be pared considerably with the removal of high-salaried Americans from territorial employment and the reduction of the costly infrastructure required to maintain their residence in the islands. However, this might still leave Micronesians with a more expensive government than they could afford without appreciable aid from the United States. To attempt further attrition among Micronesians in civil service and cutbacks in capital improvement projects, which provide jobs for Micronesians in construction work, would result in lowered per capita income and tax revenues. Correspondingly it would restrict buying power among Micronesian consumers of goods and services, provision of which now keeps many island entrepreneurs, cooperatives, and corporations in profitable business. Micronesians, as human beings with personally defined wants and needs, could hardly be faulted if they decide to compromise their commitments to ideals of freedom and independence with their desires to preserve the satisfying economic status quo.

Another aspect of the central problem noted above is a corollary of the first. If financial aid from the United States is not available, or is not desired for political reasons, to what extent can a more effective exploitation of the island resources be achieved as a principal source of tax revenue and the means to an acceptable Gross National Product? Many observers, both in and out of Micronesia, are convinced that increased attention to the development of commercial agriculture, fishing, and tourism can provide the necessary foundation for a viable Micronesian economy. These are areas that have in general been neglected by the present government. Others theorize that though such improvements have merit and should certainly be pursued, the end results will not be adequate to the nation's needs. Some look more to the potential of what they regard as a dependable source of income and revenue, that which derives from negotiated leases and various other forms of compensation by the United States government for military use of restricted land and water locations and for the right to deny access to the islands to other Pacific powers for military purposes.

Up to this point, we have viewed the continuance of American financial aid as an important bonding element for support of Micronesian unity and reinforcement of the common tie implicit in the acquired wants and needs depending on a free-flowing dollar economy. If termination results in reduction of American aid, two alternatives might still allow gratification of these wants and needs, namely, the curtailment of government spending by eliminating the American bureaucratic component and/or the creation of new local revenue and income by accelerated development of Micronesian resources. Failure in these alternatives will force the Micronesian people to take a hard look at their list of wants and needs. They must then determine, in a competition of values, whether to compromise the dream of political freedom in favor of an arrangement with the United States that guarantees the necessary inflow of American dollars, or to cut back on existing wants and needs in education, health services, living standards, and social awareness. Disagreement on these issues could well lead to political fragmentation when Micronesians make differing assessments of the need to compromise.

What sorts of accommodation are possible, or sacrifices necessary, if Micronesians are compelled to retreat from present levels of wants and needs? For example, if new state goals for education were to place more emphasis on attaining a close fit with island cultures and environments, and less on preparation for life in a modern technological world, the present costs of elaborate facilities and specialized staffs maintained in schools in the district centers could be lowered dramatically. In matters of health, the relative freedom from illness and disease insured by access to modern medical services may now be too deeply ingrained in Micronesian custom for islanders to give it up easily if required to do so for reasons of governmental economy.

To give another example, where living standards in the district centers have accelerated markedly in recent years, any accommodation could be made only at considerable personal sacrifice. Outer islanders by comparison face almost no problem in cutting back, because their living standards are already minimal by any contemporary measure. It is the infrastructure created by the American administration that has attracted Micronesians in large numbers from the outer islands. If opportunities for employment and business profits in the district centers decline as a result of reduced American spending, many Micronesians there have no choice but to return to their home islands or atolls and resume the simpler way of life. The addiction of Micronesians to travel, in the context of extended social awareness or as adjunct to official employment, may evaporate with little strain if present needs for travel decline (to economize in government) or if passenger rates increase (owing to lessened per capita use of airline and shipping services, or without current subsidies). Travel and communication in general would then be more reasonably responsive to the requirements of everyday living.

In sum, the alteration of tie cords based upon the islanders' current wants and needs is contingent on the resolution of certain financial issues. Such alterations as do develop could well lead to dissolution of the package that is now Micronesia, insofar as island groups fail to agree on options open to them. To the extent that agreement is forthcoming, whatever the rationale of that agreement, the chances of preserving the Micronesian package whole will have increased.

Opposing Identities

The packaging of Micronesia has been portrayed here as a loosely bound containment of disparate island groups, an artificiality born of colonialism and vulnerable to dissolution now that the end of colonial dependency is near. Centripetal forces working for unification have been identified and their efficacy assessed as the tie cords and wrappings that at present maintain the package intact. Anticipation of termination is moving the islanders, amidst the turmoil of rapidly changing circumstances, to reconsider their relationships with one another. In the "many faces of Micronesia" (Mason 1971) reviewed below, social identities are reflected that if placed in opposition become potentially centrifugal forces quite capable of preventing, or at least hindering, formation of a new state of Micronesia.

Behind the present facade of unity, peoples of the Trust Territory display a welter of opposing identities deeply rooted in Micronesia's geography, traditional cultures, and history of contact with the rest of the world. Only in recent years, when confronting the United States on political and economic issues, have some islanders come to regard themselves keenly as "Micronesians," employing a label that symbolizes their status as territorial citizens seeking emancipation. Otherwise, individuals will on occasion identify themselves as residents of a certain district—as Ponapean, Marshallese, or Palauan—but such denotations generally lack strong feeling and commitment to other members of the named reference group. In the face-to-face interaction of daily life, identities are colored with a greater emotion and sense of belonging to social groups that are distinctive in beliefs, sentiments, and behaviors. Examples are island villages, clans, lineages, kindreds, classes, and collectivities based on shared language, religion, occupation, or proprietary rights.

Such primary identifications, if set in opposition, are capable of producing friction and open conflict that can fragment by factionalism less-established, large-scale organizations such as the district and the territory. The latter, as foreign-imposed constructs, have little credence and not much promise as building blocks for Micronesian nationhood without a more intensive education of the populace. This is not to say that the ingrained identities at a community level have to be eliminated before popular allegiance to the larger organizations can be achieved. However, Micronesian leaders, when they devise a constitution for the new Micronesian state, will do well to fashion a system that in its implementation will be flexible enough to accommodate the identity requirements of the "many faces" of Micronesia until the people are ready to accept more inclusive identities.

Language

Language differences continue to pose problems in communication and identity. At least nine mutually unintelligible indigenous languages are known in the Territory, plus a number of dialects some of which further research may determine to be additional languages. They constitute the primary means of communication in most island homes and, of necessity, in the lower grades of many public schools. All belong to the widespread family of Austronesian (Malayo-Polynesian) languages. In each district a single language prevails because its speakers represent a majority of the district population. Chamorro is the major language of the Marianas. Palauan, Yapese, Trukese, Ponapean, and Marshallese are the principal languages in the remaining districts. Woleai-Ulithian, a group of dialects used in the Outer Islands of the Yap District, is also spoken by a minority of the Marianas population whose ancestors migrated there in the nineteenth century. In Ponape District, Kusaien is the speech of Kusaie Island, and the people on Nukuoro and Kapingamarangi atolls speak Polynesian languages.

English is the language of instruction in school and of communication in official government matters. Possibly 40 percent of Micronesians past the age of five speak English with some fluency. Most of these fall within the age group 10–25 who have received instruction in school since World War II. Although this group grows in numbers each year, it does not yet provide a very firm linguistic basis for developing Micronesian identity and unity. Micronesians learned to speak Japanese under the previous administration, both in school and in daily communication with Japanese colonials and officials. Today, probably less than half of the age group 45 and older still remember much Japanese, and most of these live in Palau and the Marianas, where Japanese influence was strongest. Official and popular views both regard English as the only answer to the need for a common language in Micronesia's future.

The administration since 1967 has emphasized a coordinated English language program in all elementary and high schools of the Territory (U.S. Department of State 1973:135–36). With strong urging from the Congress of Micronesia, a bilingual research and instructional program has also been inaugurated. The latter aims to establish linguistically appropriate orthographies for writing all Micronesian languages, develop reference grammars and bilingual dictionaries, and train Micronesians as linguists to direct indigenous language instruction in the schools (U.S. Department of State 1973: 149–51). This two-track approach in utilizing both English and vernacular speech in the educational system promises to prepare the school child to participate effectively in two cultures, his own and that of the Territory and the world beyond. Fluency in English is being urged as a shared investment in creating a common Micronesian identity. At the same time, however, every indigenous speech community is encouraged to preserve its own traditional identity. Unless the bicultural approach with regard to language is coordinated with other learning experiences, both in school and out, the end product could well provoke more of conflict than of resolution in the Micronesian dilemma of social identity.

Social and Cultural Practices

Casual tourists visiting the principal places in the Trust Territory may well leave with an impression of the essential sameness of Micronesian social and cultural practices. Nothing could be further from the truth. Factors such as age, sex, residence, kinship, and world view provide structure and priority for the many social groupings that Micronesians identify with. These intangibles are more difficult for outsiders to perceive as compared with housing, food, clothing, and other technological culture. The sociocultural diversity characteristic of traditional Micronesia is more evident in island communities that are distant from the places commonly listed on a tourist's schedule. Furthermore, traditional differences today are obscured, even in the outermost islands, by the cultural overlays established in varying degree by the social and political interaction of Micronesians with the successive tenures of Spanish, German, Japanese, and American authority systems.

When enumerating the differences in traditional practices from one part of Micronesia to another, it must be remembered that a few underlying similarities do link the island cultures of Micronesia and also indicate their affinities with other parts of Oceania. This suggests that in prehistory they shared a common heritage, made similar adaptations to island settings, and experienced widespread diffusion of customs through long-distance voyaging. Some of these regularities are readily observed in island technologies where foreign imports have not completely replaced traditional artifacts. Other resemblances are revealed in regard to land tenure, unilinear descent, economic cooperation, social competition, ranking, and stratification (Alkire 1972:45–48).

The centuries-old influence of Spanish rule in the Mariana Islands changed the people physically and culturally to a degree that nowadays they find it difficult to relate with Micronesians in the other five districts. Deeply embedded Hispanic and Catholic customs were compounded in later years by German commercialism, Japanese colonization, and, finally, by an American paternalism motivated by militaristic self-interest.

In Palau District, thousands of Japanese colonists changed the face of Koror Island, center of Japan's administration of the mandated islands. Palauans labored in the Angaur phosphate mines, learned new trades in specialist schools, provided goods and services for the Japanese in town, and relinquished traditional landholdings on official demand. Unlike the Chamorros in the Spanish-dominated Marianas, Palauans under the Japanese managed to retain their traditional identities and fundamental customs in spite of the strongly acculturative forces at work. The most traditional and conservative of all Micronesian areas, however, proved to be Yap and the Outer Islands in Yap District. Under German rule, Yap was a primary administrative center, but even in successive regimes the people never interacted much with foreigners. Islanders in the Truk District were affected to some degree by German and Japanese official policies concerning land and local authority and by Christian mission work in a few islands. Generally, Trukese populations were too dispersed and lacking in organization above the community level to be unduly disrupted by the foreigners' presence.

In Ponape District, Kusaie Island was subjected to compelling acculturative impact by American whalers and missionaries during the nineteenth century, when much of the island custom was altered or completely destroyed. On Ponape Island, German and Japanese officials enforced rules that significantly modified indigenous institutions of land tenure, rank, and titled authority. Other Ponapean customs survived reasonably well. In the Marshall Islands, Protestant missionaries from New England wrought notable changes in religion and morals, and German and Japanese agencies extended the commercial production of copra from coconuts to provide a major source of money income for the island producers. After 1945, American military forces carried on numerous weapons-testing operations in the atolls. All of these activities had extensive repercussions in the life styles of the Marshallese.

Acculturative changes have made each of the districts somewhat unique in the principal orientations, motivations, and expectations of their respective populations. Behind these historical modifications, however, are striking distinctions in the sociocultural institutions rooted in tradition that further contrast one part of Micronesia with another. This is particularly true in Palau, Yap, Ponape, and the Marshalls, where systems of rank and class privilege had been developed prior to European contact and continue to be remarkably viable in the modern scene. Within this realm of social and cultural associations, whether they be founded in prehistory or altered by history, centrifugal forces pose a constant problem for those attempting to unite Micronesian groups within larger-scale organizations such as the district and the territory.

District Centers and Outer Islands

Micronesians and Americans alike recognize that today there are two worlds of Micronesia—the district center and the outer islands. The life style, orientation, satisfactions, and problems of the one are not at all the same as those of the other. Herein lies a stumbling block for those observers who try to generalize about modern Micronesia. In this verity also is a potentially divisive power to confound those aspiring to unify the island populations under one banner symbolic of a nation with identical promise for all Micronesians. What could that future promise, when two very different worlds of Micronesia have to be satisfied?

The world of the district center comprehends all of those more-urbanized islanders who reside regularly in the capital of each district, about 35 to 40 percent of the Territory's population. These congregations are found in the administrative complex (Darrit-Uliga-Dalap) on Majuro Atoll in the Marshalls, Kolonia Municipality on Ponape Island, Moen Island in Truk District, Colonia (Donguch) in Yap, Koror Island in Palau District, and Saipan in the Marianas. Also qualifying in urban life style though not a district center is Ebeye Island, home for several hundred Marshallese commuters who work daily at the Kwajalein missile-testing site. Less urbanized communities, adjacent to or within easy travel distance of the district centers, account for another 25 to 30 percent of Micronesians. Owing to their nearness, these islanders may participate to a significant degree in the district center world although they are not part of it. The remainder of Micronesians, maybe up to 40 percent of the territorial population, live and work in the outer islands. These are the rural, more traditional areas in the hinterland of Micronesia, which have benefited little from American trusteeship over the past twenty-five years. The proportion of each of these segments of Micronesian society varies much from one district to another. In the Marianas, for instance, possibly 80 percent of the people fall into the more urbanized category. A comparable figure for the Palau and Marshalls districts is about 45 percent in each case. Only 12 to 18 percent of residents in each of the remaining districts—Yap, Truk, and Ponape—are living in the district centers (Mason 1971).

To characterize life in the district centers is, first of all, to list some elements of the physical infrastructure, such as, administration offices, hospitals, missions, high schools, banks, stores and supermarkets, water and electric services, airfields, harbors and docks, roads and buses, hotels, restaurants, clubs, and movie houses. Here lies the locus of Trust Territory administration away from headquarters on Saipan. In just the last ten years or so, the district centers have received more attention in master planning and federally funded development projects. Inflated living standards based on wage employment are creating a feeling of prosperity that is deceptively pleasing. A majority of working residents are on the government payroll. To a large extent, those in private business operate to serve the needs of this labor force.

Yet another aspect of district center living that cannot be left unmentioned is the intense crowding of people and their attendant problems of housing, sanitation, noise, waste and pollution, vehicular traffic, unemployment, juvenile delinquency, alcoholism, and crime. Graduates of high schools, trained more in a liberal arts tradition than in vocational education, compete for government scholarships to go on for higher education outside the Territory, or scramble for increasingly scarce job opportunities within the administration. Dropouts and other youths who fail to locate desirable employment have a choice of returning to their conservative outer island homes and the difficulties of readjustment encountered there, or of remaining in the district centers with little to keep them occupied but to roam about undirected and too often uncontrolled.

In spite of such deterrent factors as those mentioned above, islanders continue to regard the district center as an exciting and challenging place. Some view high school education and government employment as advantageous channels to success. Others go into business and build careers on the profits they can make in the populous district center. Here is a training ground for would-be politicians who hope one day to be elected to legislative office on reputations established in business or administration. Respected district center residents may seek to gain a seat in the Congress of Micronesia, an elective office representing to many island people the acme of social mobility in modern times.

District centers are like hinges between the outer island hinterlands and the world beyond the district boundaries. Airlines and shipping services bring a constant flow of strangers to the centers and provide a means for local residents to leave in order to explore the outside world. Movies, radio broadcasts, and government and independent newspapers in the district centers introduce inhabitants to a smorgasbord of novelty and excitement about the happenings and personages reported on daily. For most Micronesians the initial move from the outer islands to the district centers was an exhilarating experience. The possibility, always present, of moving on again, from the district center to someplace in the world, holds for many individuals enough promise to keep them from returning to their outer island homes ever again to stay.

One cannot overemphasize the striking contrast in this decade between the district centers and the outer islands. In almost every way, the latter represent the opposite of what is described for the district centers. From one end of the Trust Territory to the other, the centers hold more in common in their respective life styles than is the case between any one center and other islands in the same district. As noted previously, the out-islanders epitomize the conservative and the traditional. Change occurs but slowly in the hinterland. This is the "unspoiled" portion of modern Micronesia. Its communities are isolated most of the year, visited only by field trip vessels bringing trade goods, administrative services, and news from outside, in return for copra, handicrafts, and the few other local products still possessing export value.

In these small islands, surrounded by expanses of open ocean, man's relationship with nature is direct and intimate. Gaining quiet fulfillment from daily routines, out-islanders display a stubborn pride in their self-sufficiency, which is rooted in enduring custom.

The demanding physical labor of producing food from the land and the sea is mixed with cooperative sociability, ignoring the distinction between work and play observed so slavishly in Western cultures. In the past decade, however, gaps in the generation of middle-aged men and women, caused by migration to the district centers, are leaving critical social roles unfilled at home. By necessity, the responsibilities for providing sustenance from fishing and agriculture are, more and more, being taken over by the old people and children who have remained in the outer islands.

Outer island peoples live always close to the margins of survival. Their interest is small on questions about future political status or the economic and social issues proliferating in the district centers. Instead, they devote their primary efforts to ensuring the basic necessities of life and to making the best of declining markets for their export products. The present, not the future, must continue to be their principal concern. These people who live on the peripheries of Micronesia have been ignored and neglected by a succession of foreign colonial powers. In one sense, this was probably a blessing, for it held to a minimum disruption of their island life. But as conditions changed in the islands at large, the survival powers of out-islanders came to depend on events beyond their control. They watch, now, to see if the trend of history will continue. They remark that their relatives who have settled in the district centers tend to forget about them. They interpret actions of the Congress of Micronesia as giving priority to needs of the district center communities. Although outer island populations number barely more than a third of all Micronesians, their voices surely must be heard if unification of all island groups is ever to become reality.

Natural Resources

The islands and atolls possess an ecological diversity that causes Micronesian populations to experience serious inequities in their respective access to natural resources. The Territory has been portrayed as a mixture of high islands born of volcanic origin in ages past and of low coralline islands perched atop winding atoll reefs. The Marianas group uniquely represents the first category, and the Marshalls are exclusively of the latter type. Advantages in land size, soil quality, groundwater supply, plant speciation, and zonal variety support *land*-oriented cultures in the high islands. Reef, lagoon, and deep sea ecologies predispose a *sea*-oriented way of life in the low islands. Both environments are present in the Caroline Islands archipelago. Here, the high islands are Palau, Yap, Truk, Ponape, and Kusaie; most of the atoll formations are strung out in the Ulithi-Woleai area between Truk and Yap. Abundant rainfall favors all of the islands except the northernmost Marianas and Marshalls. Typhoons set a ceiling on agricultural production in the western portion of the Territory, as does an occasional drouth in islands nearest the equator.

Throughout Micronesia, the dire scarcity of land is a primary concern, aggravated during the twentieth century by a rapidly increasing population. Aboriginal Micronesians in their subsistence economies appear to have made reasonably satisfactory adaptations to local ecologies. After foreigners began to arrive on the scene to exploit the islands, Micronesians found it necessary to make new adjustments to the changing circumstances. However, the fact of environmental diversity still favors some island groups more than others in opportunities to convert Micronesia's limited natural wealth to contemporary economic advantage.

Spain's selection of Guam in the sixteenth century as a watering place for ships sailing between Mexico and the Philippines marked the start of foreign exploitation in Micronesia. Three centuries after, American whaling vessels were wintering at Kusaie and elsewhere in eastern Micronesia, and German commercialists had initiated trade in coconut oil and copra in the Marshalls and eastern Carolines. The Germans also recruited native labor in the western Carolines to mine phosphate on Palau's Angaur Island. A cable station was erected on Yap in 1905 linking German communications with an international network in the Pacific basin.

Between World Wars I and II, Japanese corporations with government subsidy undertook the most extensive development of Micronesian resources ever known, either before or since. Enlistment of the islands' economic assets, limited though they were, contributed importantly to Japan's dream of empire. Cultivation of sugar cane soon covered most of the Marianas. Phosphate and bauxite extraction complemented profitable bonito and tuna fisheries in Palau. Expansion of the existent copra industry benefited Micronesian producers throughout the Marshalls and Carolines. Commercial adaptations of pearl shell, trochus shell, corals, and sponges were initiated. Thousands of Japanese colonists came to settle in towns on Saipan, Tinian, Rota, Koror, and Ponape. The government improved roads and harbors and aided air and shipping lines to incorporate all of the islands into a commercial network with the home country. Considerable land acreage, much of it allegedly unused by Micronesian owners at the time, was acquired for public and private development. The islands' strategic worth, quite properly an important Micronesian resource, gained special attention in the late 1930s when Japanese military agencies built new and enlarged naval and air bases for support of the 1941 assault on enemy holdings in the Pacific. Following American occupation of the former Japanese mandate in 1944–45, Micronesia's strategic value continued to receive first priority in the United States' retention of the entire territory as a strategic area trusteeship, the only one to be approved by the new United Nations organization.

Statistically, in 1972, the total land area of the Trust Territory equalled approximately four acres to every one of nearly 115,000 Micronesian inhabitants. Yet for single districts and islands, such a statement is vastly misleading. For example, Truk District, which is numerically the most heavily populated, accounted for 28 percent of all Micronesians and only 7 percent of the land. The Marshalls District was little better off. The Palau and Marianas districts showed to advantage, each with about 11 percent of the total population and 25 percent of the total acreage. The atolls, by comparison with the high islands, are very much overpopulated. Pressure has been relieved in several instances by planned resettlement in homesteading programs on the high islands. Other atoll residents on their own initiative have sought escape through wage employment at the district centers. But, once more, this fails to represent an accurate view of the situation, because most land in the Territory is not in the hands of Micronesians.

Title to properties acquired from Micronesians by foreign nationals and governments during the German and Japanese administrations continues to be recognized as non-Micronesian under existing United States policies. Only 41 percent of all land in the Territory is clearly established as Micronesian, either privately owned or held in homesteading rights. An additional one-half of one percent is registered in the names of foreign nationals or religious missions. The remainder falls into the category of "public lands," amounting to 58 percent of all acreage in the Territory. This last includes areas occupied by government facilities, leased for public use by special agreement, or otherwise regarded as public domain. About three-fourths of so-called public land is classified as arable, grazing, or forest land, although rarely is any of it put to such use. The other one-fourth is described as "rocks, swamps, bushland, built-up land, highways, airports, quarries, etc." (U.S. Department of State 1973: 285).

When one considers only indigenous land, the per capita holding in the Territory reduces from 3.9 acres, cited above as approximately four, to barely 1.6 acres—an obviously considerable difference. More important for this discussion, however, is the fact that deduction of public land acreage from district totals significantly alters the situation outlined above in regard to inequities prevailing between districts. That is to say, a very high proportion of public land exists in some districts while in others it is very low. The greatest losses of indigenous lands took place in those same districts that were most actively developed under foreign administrations. By 1972, for example, 80 percent of the Marianas District area was classed as public land. A comparable figure for Palau District was 73 percent, and for Ponape District it was 64 percent (U.S. Department of State 1973:289). The advantages suggested earlier as being implicit in the ratio of population to total land area for the Marianas and Palau districts disappear in this recalculation. By either measure, Truk is the district most critically in need of land to sustain its island populations. Yap remains the only district with a definitely favorable man-to-land proportion based on lands held in native title.

As for contemporary resources other than land, imbalances continue to favor one district or island group over another and vary with the resource in question. Copra, dried meat of the coconut, has always been the largest commodity export item and the only cash crop of any significance. Official estimates of coconut production assign 90 to 95 percent of the Territory's total to the Marshalls, Truk, and Ponape districts (U.S. Department of State 1973:290). About half of that amount consistently comes from the Marshalls where coconuts grow well in the atoll environment. With the decline in recent years of copra values on the world market, island production has dropped in favor of more remunerative wage employment in the more urbanized island centers. The unusually low export of copra from the Palau Islands is the result of extensive damage to coconut palms for a number of years by the rhinoceros beetle (*Oryctes rhinoceros*), though control measures have successfully confined the pest to the Palau District. The highly acculturated population of the Marianas District has for some time abandoned copra production except in the outlying islands to the north. Throughout the Territory, other agricultural activity is directed primarily toward local consumption. Principal crops are taro, breadfruit, bananas, yams, sweet potatoes, cassava, and pandanus. Small amounts of Micronesian fruits and vegetables are exported to the American Territory of Guam, mainly from the neighboring Marianas District. On Ponape Island the Agriculture Extension Service is experimenting with local farmers in producing potential cash crops, such as black and white pepper, cacao, and white rice. A modest beginning has been made in the export of black spice pepper.

Utilization of marine resources has been accorded only secondary attention by the United States administration in Micronesia's commerical development. Some progress is reported in the production and processing of tuna and other fishes, crabs and lobsters, and trochus shell for export to Japan or the United States. The Marshalls District is king in copra production, and Palau District holds top title in commercial fisheries. As already noted, Japan had established Palau as the center of marine exploitation before World War II. Since then, American business interests have supported a fishing, freezing, storing, and shipping operation based on the availability of skipjack tuna in Palauan waters. Palauan fishermen and plant employees are being trained by experienced Okinawans imported for that purpose. Exploration of like prospects for Truk, Ponape, and Majuro has resulted to date only in small-scale, locally controlled fisheries in the first two locations. Crabs and lobsters are abundant in Palau, Yap, and Truk districts, but only Palau has sufficient surplus for export to the Guam market. Trochus shell for export to Japan has been coming almost entirely from the Palau Islands in the last few years (U.S. Department of State 1973:292).

Swine and poultry production in all districts is for local consumption, though beef cattle in Marianas District are raised for marketing on Guam. Of lands used for grazing cattle in the Trust Territory, an estimated 82 percent lies in the Marianas and most of the remander is in Ponape District. In 1972, the Marianas claimed 96 percent of all cattle reported in the Territory and produced 99 percent of all beef marketed (U.S. Department of State 1973:291). Limited lumbering was conducted on Ponape Island during German and Japanese administrations and also in Palau by the Japanese. Today locally cut timber, including a large amount of mangrove, is used for native housing, handicraft, and charcoal production. In all districts, the continuing needs for lumber require that extensive quantities be imported from outside the Territory (pp. 78–79; 292). In the small islands that are characteristic of Micronesia, forest land has greater value as "wildland" in the retention of water reserves. Although the Japanese mined phosphate, bauxite, and some manganese in Palau District, present mineral resources in the Territory are judged insufficient to warrant further exploitation (pp. 79–80; 293).

The recent growth of tourism in Micronesia has moved this industry into first place ahead of copra and marine production as primary sources of the territorial gross product. An "invisible" export, tourism capitalizes on Micronesia's tropical climate, unique environmental features, and island cultures. In fiscal year 1972, visitors from the United States, including Guam, comprised 59 percent of all who entered the Trust Territory, compared with 33 percent from Japan, the only other principal country of origin. Tourists preferred to vacation in Marianas District, which recorded 68 percent of all entries. Other districts, though far behind, were achieving recognition in about equal amounts, that is, 8 percent in Truk District, 7 percent each in Palau and Ponape districts, and 5 percent each in Yap and Marshalls districts (U.S. Department of State 1973:48).

Marianas District with its hotels, restaurants, and recreational assets is the best equipped to please tourists. It is favored by Japanese visitors because of its prewar and wartime associations with Japan and its easy access from Guam, terminal point for flights from Japan. Palau's "rock islands" of raised reef limestone and a "story-board" art form in carved wood are special attractions in this district. Truk Lagoon has gained worldwide recognition among scuba divers for its spectacular underwater views of reef corals and sunken Japanese war vessels. Ponape, the "garden of Micronesia," advertises extensive ruins of a 700-year-old ceremonial complex at Nan Madol. Yap manifests an aboriginal charm as the most conservative of all districts, and the Marshalls boast the best beaches and shell-collecting opportunities. Islanders in all districts have adapted time-honored craft techniques and materials in their cottage-type manufacture of articles congruent with tourist tastes. Every district specializes in certain types of craftwork for local sale, but some of this is also shipped to handicraft shops in other districts, Guam, and Hawaii. Even though each island group presents unusual items of interest to beguile the discriminating tourist, visitor destination still depends very much on the relative advantages offered by each district in terms of direct access by air (or ship) and the suitability of accommodations upon arrival.

Finally, in this review of the differential access to natural resources that distinguishes the six districts from one another, it is necessary to consider the strategic worth of each island area. The United States, as administering authority of the strategic area trusteeship, is concerned that there be no essential change in existing guarantees relating to the country's national defense needs in the Pacific and its self-imposed responsibilities for maintaining international peace and security. The military requirements of the United States were outlined in the third round of negotiations on the future political status of Micronesia in October 1971, at Hana, Maui, Hawaii (Williams 1971:31–37). They were further defined in the Draft Compact of Free Association, Title III (Defense) and Annex B, prepared jointly by representatives of the United States and the Congress of Micronesia during the fifth round of talks in July 1972, in Washington, D.C. (*Highlights*, 15 August 1972, pp. 5-6), and in separate talks with delegates from Marianas District in May–June 1973, on Saipan (*Highlights*, 7 June 1973, p. 6). According to these statements, only the Marianas, Marshalls, and Palau districts would be directly involved. No military need for land was envisioned for Ponape, Truk, and Yap districts.

The United States' view of its defense posture in Micronesia is twofold. The first part is a policy of strategic denial to any third nation, namely, that "no country other than the United States shall enjoy the right to conduct military activities or to establish and maintain military facilities and areas within the territory of Micronesia at any time" (Title III (Defense), Section 304 (A), *Draft Compact of Free Association*). The second part is more specific and refers to authority to use certain areas for military purposes in the three districts first named above. In the Marshalls, the United States requires continuation of existing use rights to certain lands and waters in Kwajalein, Bikini, and Eniwetok atolls. In Palau District, it is considered essential to have access and anchorage rights to Malakal Harbor for a naval support facility and, on Babelthuap Island, to have rights to the exclusive use of 2,000 acres for storage facilities, the nonexclusive use of 30,000 acres for intermittent ground force training and maneuvers, and the joint use of an airfield capable of supporting military jet aircraft (Annex B, *Draft Compact of Free Association*). In the Marianas, the United States military has plans for the immediate buildup of Tinian Island, either wholly or in greater part, as a major operational base in the western Pacific, and certain lesser requirements relating to other islands in the district (*Highlights*, 7 June 1973, p. 6).

These military proposals for future use of Micronesian land resources have yet to be negotiated in greater detail, but their realization promises both advantages and disadvantages for Micronesians resident in the three named districts. Indeed, the same applies to those living in the other three districts where the United States apparently has no local military requirements. Increased American activity, by its very presence in a given district, must be regarded as a mixed blessing. On the one hand, it will certainly bring about changes in the local economy and society, some of them desirable and others not. It will provide new sources of income for a few Micronesian landowners through leases or other negotiated arrangements. And it will mean, in some cases, the loss of lands critical to future Micronesian occupancy and development. The other side of the coin, the absence of military programs in Ponape, Truk, and Yap, will also be interpreted in terms of loss or gain for those districts. The excitement and the augmented personal income and government revenue associated with a new foreign activity will be wanting. At the same time, of course, island practices and life styles will be less subject to disruption. What one considers to be a blessing, in the final analysis, must depend upon each islander's private assessment of his own wants and needs.

Power, Authority, and Influence

In this section on opposing identities, attention has been directed to potentially divisive forces represented in language, social and cultural practices, district center and outer island living, and exploitation of natural resources. One other area of psychological investment calls for comment, namely, the juxtaposition of certain spheres of Micronesian power, authority, and influence. The ongoing controversy in the islands about Micronesia's future has evoked an increasingly vigorous and open competition among spokesmen from these spheres of participation who claim a right to speak on behalf of Micronesians regarding the direction, pace, and manner of moving to a new political status.

The primary locus of indigenous power vested in the Congress of Micronesia and its negotiating arm, the Joint Committee on Future Status, has been remarked upon repeatedly in this chapter. Since the first session in 1965, the Congress's principal preoccupation has been, almost by definition, to confront the authority and power of the American-controlled executive branch of the Trust Territory government. Gradually, if not grudgingly, the high commissioner has responded to pressures from the Congress to expand the latter's powers and to widen its range of activities, for example, in the congressional review of executive appointments, advice on federal budgetary matters, and participation in program planning by investigative congressional commissions. Yet, as measured by aspirations of the impatient fledgling legislature, these limited gains have fallen far short of its ultimate goals for self-government. Senator Andon Amaraich of Truk District in June 1973, dramatically summarized the relationship between the Congress and the administration, when he addressed the annual meeting of the United Nations Trusteeship Council in New York City as Congress representative and special adviser to the United States delegation:

> In general, I believe that it is accurate to say that the only significant steps which Micronesia has taken toward self-government are those which have been initiated by the Congress of Micronesia, and have somehow survived the restrictive scrutiny of the Administering Authority. The Administering Authority, it would seem, continued to maintain a negative attitude toward many needed and far-reaching reforms in our political and economic structure which have been proposed by the Congress; rather than suggest ways in which a stated objective can be accomplished, the Administration on many occasions simply rejects out of hand the methods which the Congress has chosen. As a result, progress toward achieving our goals remains painfully slow at a time when we cannot afford delay any longer. (*Highlights*, 1 July 1973, Special Section, p. 11)

The compulsion felt by congressmen to concentrate their efforts upon equalizing legislative and executive powers at the territorial level of government has inevitably detracted from their obligations to maintain close communication with Micronesian constituents in the districts. Here, at the grass roots of Micronesian opinion, organizations and pressure groups have become more outspoken in seeking a greater visibility in the political status debate, which congressmen have tended to monopolize. These include the district legislatures, Micronesians in the territorial civil service, traditional chiefs and other community leadership, local chambers of commerce, religious groups, and the independent press. The past year or so has seen the emergence of a ground swell of public opinion that is questioning the exclusive right of the Micronesian Congress and its joint committee to negotiate with the United States about the islands' future status. Micronesians everywhere in the Territory are demanding more information from their congressional representatives about the progress of the status talks. They also evidence an urgent need for some program of political education that will translate the ideological rhetoric of the several status options into realistic appraisals of what changes will be required of Micronesians in the routine of everyday living.

District administrators, meeting in semiannual conference late in 1971, recommended to their superior officer, High Commissioner Edward E. Johnston, that "the composition of the political status delegation be changed to allow for participation from Micronesians other than those of the legislative branch." The district heads, all of them Micronesians, hoped that "the Congress will explore the possibility of including Micronesian members of the executive branch, the district legislatures, and from other areas of the community in the status talks—at least as observers, if not as actual participants" (*Highlights*, 1 December 1971, p. 3). Just one year earlier, a group of thirty-three Micronesians in the executive branch, including the six district administrators, had been invited to the nation's capitol for a week-long conference on the budgetary process, federal agency activities in the Territory, and a briefing on the political status talks to date. The group, oddly enough its membership identical in number to that of the Congress, had asked at that time if the negotiating delegation for Micronesia might be "more representative" and include others than congressmen. To this, Washington officials had replied that the Congress possessed the mandate to negotiate and any change would have to be made by it. Later in Majuro, in response to the same question, Senate President Amata Kabua remarked that the Congress is the only rightful party to negotiate. "The people give us this unique right when they elect us," he said. "They do not elect members of the other branches of the government" (*Micronitor*, 5 December 1970, p. 3). The United Nations Visiting Mission, while in Ponape District in February 1973, listened to the mayor of Kolonia Town voice his opinion that since the Congress had been established to formulate laws and not to engage in negotiations, Micronesians who were not members of Congress should also participate in the talks on future status (U.N. Visiting Mission 1973:14). Nowhere in its subsequent report to the Trusteeship Council did the mission question either the composition of the joint committee or the right of the Congress to negotiate on behalf of Micronesians.

Traditional leaders on Ponape Island in that same month convened to discuss the progress of negotiations with the United States. In a public announcement, they expressed "deep concern" about the proceedings and noted their desire to be kept fully informed on all matters relating to the future political status of Micronesia (*Highlights*, 15 February 1973, p. 7). In Palau District, traditional leaders and elected officials, dismayed at the direction taken in the negotiations, assembled on Koror Island in November 1972 to assess the implications of United States military needs as defined in the Draft Compact of Free Association. They publicly addressed the Congress in a "Declaration of the Leaders of Palau," signed by fifty-two persons "representing the entire people of Palau," stating "that we are unequivocally opposed to the use of land in Palau by the United States Military; and we further declare that the Joint Committee on Future Status of the Congress of Micronesia is hereby respectfully requested to implement this declaration" (*Friends of Micronesia Newsletter*, vol. 3, no. 1 [Winter 1973], p. 10).

The Joint Committee on Future Status, responding to such pressures for more information and involvement by other Micronesians, named two subcommittees to hold hearings with local groups in the western and eastern districts during the summer of 1973. Thus, one subcommittee was told by a group of schoolteachers in Yap District that "the present negotiations should be terminated immediately, until such time as the economy and the level of political awareness of the people is brought to a point where an intelligent decision can be made in a plebiscite" (*Micronitor*, 16 July 1973, p. 14). Earlier in the day, a meeting with members of the Yap Islands Council demonstrated the latter's awareness of underlying issues in the status talks. Although councilmen avowed general support of the joint committee's work in implementing the mandate for free association, they were very much concerned with details about the need for land by the United States military and the bargaining for financial assistance from the United States government.

During a meeting with members of the Ponape District Legislature, the other subcommittee listened to Speaker Itor Harris question the propriety of congressional negotiations on matters directly affecting the people of Ponape District without first having consulted them. "The people of this district have heard a lot about sovereignty lately," he reminded the congressmen. "Usually the term is used in regard to Micronesia as a whole, but there is a kind of sovereignty that is just as important to us in Ponape District and that is the sovereignty of the district. Right now it is not entirely clear who you have been negotiating for" (*Micronitor*, 6 August 1973, p. 12). The method presently employed by the Congress for resolving the islands' future status Speaker Harris likened to an attempt of constructing a house from the top down, starting with the roof. The people of Ponape District, he explained, do not think that is the best way to build a house, for the foundation must come first and that means participation by the people at the district level. Secessionist actions already taken by legislatures in the Marianas, Marshalls, and Palau districts will be examined in the next section of this chapter.

Although Micronesian businessmen privately express their cares about the islands' political future, only rarely have entrepreneurs or chambers of commerce made public statements on the subject. Their principal interests appear to lie in continued escalation of present consumer spending, guarantees for more dependable shipping and supply procedures, and more attention to proposals generated within private enterprise for economic planning that is now programmed for the most part by political agencies, either in the Trust Territory administration or in the Congress of Micronesia.

One publisher among the independent island press recently gave front page prominence to a position paper entitled "The New Face of Micronesia." After critically examining the United Nations and the United States as two of the major forces in contemporary island affairs, the editor identified as the third and "most dangerous" force those Micronesian elitists "who no longer function as Micronesians." Some of these belong, he wrote, to the Congress of Micronesia, others are highly placed administration officials and "eminently successful" businessmen. Here, once more, is a public plea to listen to the voices of islanders themselves concerning the formulation of plans to change the political system. The following charge is aimed at this Micronesian elite:

> If these so-called Micronesians would stop for a while and listen to what the real people of Micronesia are saying they would find out that there is no cry to terminate the Trusteeship arrangement, that there is no hatred or feeling of burden being borne because of the presence of the Trust Territory Government, that the people are scared by the talk they hear of a new political status, that the people are satisfied with the way things are going now, that their children now finally have an opportunity to go to school, that no one is starving, that no one is actually oppressed. (*Micronitor*, 3 September 1973, p. 2)

Micronesians in the Congress, territorial administration, and private life were invited in June 1973 to participate in a seminar in

Kolonia, Ponape District, to consider "some of the moral issues related to the political alternatives that are presented to Micronesia today" (Micronesian Seminar 1973:2). Sponsored by the Catholic mission in the Carolines-Marshalls, the gathering attempted to view the political status question in the largest possible context. Sovereignty, principal theme of the week-long discussions, was agreed to possess three aspects: political, legal, and moral, of which the last "is a God-given, inalienable right to full control over one's own destiny in one's own territory, without being subjected to external restraints" (p. 101). The seminar strongly urged a political education program that would be universal in Micronesia with the thrust toward the unschooled, and would strive to inculcate in the Micronesians a sense of dignity, self-esteem, and responsibility. Such a program was seen as the responsibility of all, not only of government agencies, but also of private individuals and groups, including the churches. This seminar contribution to the dialogue on Micronesia's political future constitutes the first organized attempt in the Territory to examine the implications of future status beyond the political, economic, and legal outlines to which politicians so far have limited their debates.

Loosening Ties

Developments until the latter half of 1973, when the final draft of this chapter was written, suggest the strong likelihood that the packaging of Micronesia is coming undone. The possibility of ever achieving a unified Micronesia appears to depend upon prompt resolution of the varied interpretations being made by Micronesian groups and individuals about the present course and probable outcome of the status talks. The critical role of the Joint Committee on Future Status in negotiations with the United States has amplified the central importance of its sponsor, the Congress of Micronesia. Congressional deliberations, both in and out of formal sessions, have become a forum—even, at times, a battleground—for the testing of emergent views rooted in the opposing identities described above. Micronesian anticipation of a new constitutional basis of government opens up opportunities for new administrative alignments of island groups, reflecting felt needs that until now have been suppressed by the colonial governmental structure. Actions already taken to effect such changes are reviewed below.

Marianas District

As early as 1950, a majority of the Marianas District population had indicated its desire to become permanently associated with the United States. Since then, by poll and referendum, petitions to the United Nations, and resolutions from the Marianas District Legislature, the same sentiment has been voiced repeatedly. For most of this time, the popular choice was to become united with the American Territory of Guam, which is geographically part of the Mariana Islands and culturally related to the Chamorro people of the Marianas District. By 1972, however, opinion had begun to favor a commonwealth status that would relate the district to the United States independently of Guam. In April 1972, at the fourth round of talks held on Koror Island, the two Marianas members of the Joint Committee on Future Status made a formal request to the head of the United States delegation, asking for separate discussions leading to a close political relationship of the Marianas District with the United States (U.N. Visiting Mission 1973:124).

Senator Edward DLG. Pangelinan and Representative Herman Q. Guerrero, the Marianas delegates who presented the Statement of Position at Koror, provided assurance that it was fully supported and endorsed by them and by the people of their district. The Marianas position was advocated

> for the sole reason that we desire membership in the United States political family because of the demonstrated advantages of such a relationship. More than any other nation with which we have had contact, the United States has brought to our people the values which we cherish and the economic goals which we desire. Continued affiliation with the United States offers the promise of the preservation of these values and the implementation of those goals. (U.S. Office of Micronesian Status Negotiations 1972:61)

Ambassador Franklin H. Williams, after observing that official transmission of the request to him had the approval of the Joint Committee on Future Status, answered that the United States would be willing to enter promptly into separate negotiations, while moving toward termination of the trusteeship agreement simultaneously for the other five districts.

The Marianas District Legislature convened in special session during May 1972 to establish the Marianas Political Status Commission. Following a week of public hearings that produced no major opposition to the proposed legislation, a commission of fifteen members was approved to represent the legislature, the congressional delegation, municipal councils of all the principal islands, the two political parties, and the business community. Four of the commission's members appeared as petitioners before the May meeting of the Trusteeship Council in New York to argue the Marianas' case for close political union with the United States. Senator Olympio T. Borja, in his comments to the council, interpreted the Marianas' decision not as a fragmentation of the Trust Territory but rather as an acknowledgement of the different choices available for resolution of the status issue (*Marianas Variety*, 2 June 1972, p. 8). He viewed the break with the other districts as inevitable, for "the ideological schism which separates our people from the people of the other districts became all too apparent—and too pronounced to ignore any longer" (*Marianas Variety*, 26 May 1972, p. 6).

The first meeting of the Marianas Political Status Commission and the American delegation, headed by Chairman Pangelinan and Ambassador Williams respectively, took place on Saipan in December 1972. Largely ceremonial and procedural, the exchange was characterized as a "friendly and frank exploration of the questions and issues to be resolved in the course of the substantive negotiations which will follow" (*Highlights*, Special Edition, 20 December 1972, p. 8). The second round of talks, for three weeks beginning 15 May 1973, resulted in preliminary agreements where possible and identification of technical questions for further study by smaller panels of experts. The two parties reached tentative accord on a form of commonwealth arrangement with provisions for maximum self-government by the Marianas population, United States authority in defense and foreign affairs, long-range American assistance toward achieving economic self-sufficiency for the Marianas, return of public lands to the people, and availability in principle of certain lands for United States military purposes subject to negotiation. The third round of deliberations was planned for November 1973, after the implications of American military requirements for land, particularly in regard to Tinian Island, could be explored more fully by both parties (*Highlights*, Special Edition, 7 June 1973).

One indication of the possible effect the separate Marianas talks may have on the question of unity among the other five districts is contained in testimony by Senator Andon Amaraich of Truk during the 1972 session of the Trusteeship Council:

> We of course recognize the desire of the people of the Marianas; the provisions in the United Nations Charter regarding the right of self-determi-

> nation apply equally to all. . . . [However,] if the people of a single district are to enter separate negotiations, only the Congress of Micronesia has the authority to permit them to do so; any other interpretation would be a violation of the doctrine that the powers of the Congress in the legislative area are superior to those of the District Legislature. . . . The only logical conclusion is that the United States is attempting to foster disunity in the Trust Territory and to fragmentize Micronesia. (*Highlights*, Special Edition, 9 June 1972, p. 12)

Again, in the 1973 meeting of the Trusteeship Council, referring to the just-completed second round of talks between the Marianas and the United States, Senator Amaraich warned of the threat to Micronesian unity:

> Following the example of the Marianas, two districts already have taken the preliminary steps toward starting their own separate negotiations with the United States Government. The very fact that the United States started negotiations with the people of one district was enough—indeed, it was the causative factor—to initiate the disunification of Micronesia. The United States Government now has only to sit back and let time do the rest. (*Highlights*, Special Section, 1 July 1973, p. 13)

The question of the Marianas separation was investigated by the Visiting Mission of the Trusteeship Council when its members toured the Territory in February 1973. Excerpts from its recommendations to the council indicate the mission's general disapproval with the steps taken by the United States as administering authority:

> It is arguable that the separation of the Mariana Islands may have certain advantages for the Administering Authority. . . . We certainly cannot deny that a great majority of the Mariana Islanders are in favour of separation. . . . We recognize the need to be realistic. The movement in favour of separation has gone a long way. . . . [However,] it may be that a status for Micronesia as a whole will be agreed between the Congress and the United States which will be generally acceptable to the Marianas, except in regard to the provision for unilateral termination. . . . If that should be the case, it would seem to us more sensible for the Marianas to accept such a status for themselves as a continuing part of Micronesia with the proviso that, if a majority of districts should at a later stage decide to exercise the right of unilateral termination, the Marianas (or any dissenting district) should be free not to apply that decision to itself. . . . To continue the separate talks further to a definite agreement on separate status for the Marianas at this stage would destroy the prospect of achieving any compromise solutions of this kind. Accordingly, we believe that for the time being they should be stopped. (U.N. Visiting Mission 1973:128–29)

Meanwhile, Senator Pangelinan and Representative Guerrero of the Marianas continue their membership on the Joint Committee on

Future Status, their self-proclaimed role being that of insuring the recognition and protection of the interests of the Marianas in future negotiations between the joint committee and the American delegation. Only brief speculation has been heard on the question of what would be done about relocating the extensive facilities and staff of the Trust Territory administration headquarters unit from Capitol Hill on Saipan at such time as Marianas District may become independent of the rest of the Territory.

Marshalls District

Even before the Marianas move to initiate separate status talks with the United States, members of the Marshallese delegation had proposed to the Congress of Micronesia, meeting on Koror in February 1972, that each of the six districts be free to negotiate its own future with the American government. Representative Charles Domnick, author of this resolution, cited the disunity existing in Micronesia, the linguistic and cultural differences, the variety in extent of resources, and the variation among the districts in their "ambitions, initiative and rate of progress desired." He contended that "each of these clearly defined districts does have the sovereign right to determine what form of future political status would be beneficial for its citizens" (Micronesian News Service, 25 February 1972). The House failed to approve the plan. It was generally understood that a question of economics had prompted the Marshallese proposal. The delegation had already been defeated in supporting another action to have 50 percent of all tax monies collected by the Congress from the individual districts remain in the district where the revenue originated. In terms of income tax alone, the Marshall Islands yielded more than the other five districts together, by reason of the large number of salaried American and Marshallese workers at the Kwajalein Missile Range. The same revenue-sharing concept was proposed for House consideration when the Congress met on Saipan the following year. Advocates of the plan were mainly from the Marshalls and Marianas, districts which stood to gain most. However, the bill again met defeat. Representative Domnick's motion to reconsider, though successful, was overridden by a House vote to adjourn the session (*Micronitor*, 26 February 1973, pp. 9, 11).

The Marshalls District Legislature, better known by its Marshallese name *Nitijela*, approved two measures concerning the future status of the islands during its annual meeting at Majuro in April 1973. The first was a resolution that, should the Congress of Micronesia fail to pass revenue-sharing legislation at its 1974 session, the Nitijela would "promptly commence separate negotiations with the United States on the future political status of the Marshall Islands." A reminder to Micronesians that the atoll district has "borne the entire burden of the presence of the United States military in the Territory" was considered justification enough to claim a larger share of the tax revenues now collected by the Congress from the easternmost district. The second action was a bill to form an eighteen-member Political Status Commission "to assist the Nitijela and the people of the Marshall Islands in examining, considering and resolving the questions relating to the future political status of the Marshall Islands." Of the total membership, two would be appointed by the district administrator and two would be elected from each of the Marshall's four electoral districts (*Micronitor*, 23 April 1973, p. 10).

Senator Amata Kabua, interviewed regarding public criticism that he had persuaded the Nitijela to undertake the above actions, explained to a reporter that upon his return to Majuro from the Congress meetings in Saipan, "I was surprised to find a very strong sentiment for separatism in evidence, not only among the younger people but also among the leaders and the general public. When I was asked to help in the drafting of the Political Status Commission legislation I did so with the feeling that I was working for the people I represent and not myself." Well known as a strong traditional, political, and business leader in the Marshalls and Senate president in the Congress for four years, Kabua did admit to certain reservations about affiliation with the other districts. "Our fear is now greater with respect to other Micronesians," he remarked, "than with the United States." To remain with the other districts he viewed as "dangerous because it is becoming apparent we don't know what we are getting into." In his opinion, the alternative for the Marshalls is to "completely sever all connections with the other districts and get down to the business of organizing ourselves first. Then, when we are sure of ourselves, affiliate with the other districts with respect and assurance. In short, we separate, regroup, and go back" (*Micronitor*, 23 April 1973, p. 2). Marshallese opinion, it is true, continues to be divided on the relative merits of independence, free association, or retention of the status quo. For example, the cochairman of the Joint Committee on Future Status from the start has been

Representative Ekpap Silk of the Marshalls, who has consistently given his personal support to the congressional mandate to negotiate with the United States on the basis of free association.

Whether political separation of the Marshalls could survive economically might depend finally on the American intent to continue weapons-testing at Kwajalein. Even now if the Missile Range were closed down by the United States, the Marshalls would gain no more benefit from revenue-sharing legislation than the four districts in the Carolines. Island rumors in 1973 saw agreements issuing from the Strategic Arms Limitation Talks (SALT) as responsible for a shortened work week, elimination of overtime pay, and anticipated layoffs at the Kwajalein facility. Concerned about further curtailment of the local military operation, Representative John Heine of the Marshalls warned his people, "The Marshall Islands is headed for serious trouble if we fail to see the difficulties we would encounter if we were to carry through the threat to separate from the rest of the Trust Territory" (*Micronitor*, 23 September 1973, p. 1).

With the declining copra industry and uncertainty about future United States military interest in the Marshalls, the beginnings of economic cooperation with the fledgling state of Nauru just across the equator to the south appears to hold much promise for stable economic growth and, possibly, political alliance. Germany administered Nauru and the Marshall Islands as a single territory from 1888. Shortly after that, Protestant missionaries from Kusaie carried the Gospel to Nauru as they already had to the Marshalls and the neighboring Gilbert Islands. Themselves Micronesian, Nauruans by the accident of history and the resulting bonds of kinship through intermarriage became closely tied to other Micronesian peoples in the islands just named. The republic of Nauru is independent politically and self-sufficient economically, owing to its control of the vast wealth in rock phosphates, which have been mined on the island since the turn of the century. Under President Hammer DeRoburt, who in 1968 led Nauru to independence from Australian trusteeship, the 3,500 islanders have launched an ambitious program of commercial investments using funds derived from rents and royalties produced by the phosphate mining. Viewed from the Marshalls, the shipping and airline connections negotiated by Nauruan business interests within the past two years are the most significant.

Air Nauru, international flag carrier of the tiny republic, set up weekly round trips to Majuro in the southern Marshalls at the start of 1972, and thereby joined the North and South Pacific by tying in with Air Micronesia and Air Pacific, formerly Fiji Airways. Majuro has the only airport in the Trust Territory where Air Nauru is permitted to discharge and pick up passengers. The airline makes weekly flights also to Tarawa in the Gilbert Islands and, in December 1972, inaugurated regular service between Melbourne in Australia and Kagoshima in Japan. With Nauru as the implementing link, this opened up new possibilities for tourism in the Marshall and Gilbert archipelagoes, attracting potential visitors from Japan as well as from countries down under. The new airfield completed at Majuro in early 1973, 7,000 feet in length and the longest in the Trust Territory, is now capable of handling the larger types of commercial aircraft. Such developments have heightened Marshallese optimism about tapping the huge Japanese tourist market, anticipating exploratory routes by Japanese or American airlines, if not by Air Nauru, with a direct connection between Japan and Majuro via Eniwetok Atoll. Senator Amata Kabua, probably the Marshalls' most imaginative businessman, believes the Japanese citizen is "the most influential and affluent tourist in the world" (*Micronesian Reporter*, Fourth Quarter 1972, p. 6). Couple this with another of Kabua's estimates, "In Majuro here I think that the greatest thing that has ever happened is the development of the new airfield" (p. 4), and one envisions an alternative to copra and the military if these prove to be inadequate to maintain a self-sufficient Marshallese economy.

The Nauru Pacific Line, owned by the Nauruan government, was invited by businessmen and the Marshall Islands Nitijela to come to Majuro. By agreement with the Trust Territory's exclusive carrier, TransPacific Line (TransPac), Nauru shipping began to serve Majuro in January 1973. At the same time, Majuro was approved as a transshipment center, with incoming cargo to be carried by TransPac to the other five districts, Asian ports, and the West Coast. Likewise, TransPac cargo destined for Australia, New Zealand, and other South Pacific ports serviced by Nauru Pacific Line would be diverted through Majuro (*Highlights*, 15 September 1972, p. 1). Besides Nauru and Majuro, Nauruan shipping plans for 1973 were to stop at Ebeye (Kwajalein) and Kusaie in the Trust Territory, and ports in the Gilbert and Ellice islands, Western Samoa, Fiji, and the British Solomon Islands (*Micronitor*, 15 January 1973, p. 1). Majuro agent for Nauru Pacific Line is MIECO (Marshall Islands Import-Export Company), whose guiding hand for many years has been Senator Amata Kabua. Mindful of the rising cost of living and the lower prices for copra, Senator Kabua made this comment on the new shipping connection:

> We're mostly concerned with the staple items such as rice, flour, sugar and other basic food commodities that we depend on. . . . It is our hope with the inauguration of Nauru shipping lines the price of these important commodities can be reduced to the point that our people, especially those people in the outer islands whose cash income from copra is declining, can live without so much hardship as under the present circumstances (*Micronesian Reporter*, Fourth Quarter 1972, p. 5).

The Nauruan company has joined with Tonga's Pacific Navigation Company, Ltd. to operate a regional shipping line. This is a pilot project intended to provide a South Pacific passenger and cargo service to link countries like Fiji, Western Samoa, and the Cook Islands, which operate no commercial ship services to other countries. Nauru and Tonga are reported to be looking for other island groups to join in their South Pacific regional line (*Pacific Islands Monthly*, June 1973, p. 83). This may provide yet another opportunity for Marshalls District to gain a greater measure of economic independence from the American government and a greater willingness to seek political separation from the other districts of the Trust Territory.

Palau District

Micronesians had scarcely digested news of the Marshallese Nitijela's action to establish a Political Status Commission anticipating separate talks with the United States, when the Palau District Legislature adopted a resolution leading in a similar direction. The Palau group named its Select Committee on Political and Economic Development to study the desirability of a separately negotiated future status for Palau District and to report back to the lawmakers within one year (*Highlights*, 1 May 1973, p. 5). Reasons given to the public for the legislators' decision were, in part:

> The people of Palau have observed the debates in the Congress of Micronesia over the past several years, and have been discouraged by the lack of any definite decision as to when the future government of Micronesia will be achieved due to the widely diverse cultures, backgrounds, aspirations, and desires of the various people of the Trust Territory. (*Micronitor*, 30 April 1973, p. 2)

Related to the Palauan resolution was other legislation aimed at convening a 25-delegate convention to draw up a constitution for the future government of Palau. District Administrator Thomas Remengesau of Palau later vetoed the bill, which he said called for creation of a document having the effect of "organic, fundamental law." Such a step, Remengesau stated, had no sanction within either "the framework of the applicable, existing law" of the Trust Territory or "the scope of the powers of the Palau legislature." He pointed out that though no part of the Trust Territory Code prohibits the drafting of such a constitution, any new district government could achieve legal status only through a chartering process requiring the final approval of the high commissioner (*Micronitor*, 30 June 1973, pp. 1, 14).

Immediate criticism of the Palau and Marshalls legislatures came from Senator Lazarus Salii of Palau, chairman of the Joint Committee on Future Status. He viewed these separatist moves as seriously capable of disrupting the next scheduled round of talks with the United States. He pleaded with Micronesians to wait until the Draft Compact of Free Association is completed, hopefully in 1973. Then is the time, he said, to take action toward separate negotiations if terms of the compact are unacceptable to individual districts. He admitted, however, that in the light of conflicting needs and desires expressed in the districts the final solution might well be separate status agreements for all. That such a result would be not inadmissible to the United States has been suggested by Ambassador Williams' deputy, James M. Wilson. The latter in a Washington speech is reported to have said that although "it is U.S. policy to promote the unity of the Trust Territory and avoid further fragmentation if at all possible," no legal block stands in the way of negotiation with a district leading to a separate status after trusteeship is terminated. He emphasized that, regardless of progress in separate talks, trusteeship must end for all districts at the same time (*Micronitor*, 30 April 1973, pp. 1-2).

The other Palauan on the Joint Committee on Future Status, Senator Roman Tmetuchl, voiced his strong support of separatist sentiments in the following month when he submitted a statement of goals to his colleague in the latter's role as joint committee chairman. Senator Tmetuchl called for the early resumption of negotiations by the joint committee in order to terminate the Trusteeship Agreement. Meantime, each district should be free to bargain separately with the United States, continuing membership on the joint committee to maintain contact with all districts. (This is the procedure adopted by the Marianas delegation as reported above.) For the future, Tmetuchl advocated a loose political association of districts, presumably including the Marianas, too, and a central confederated government to administer such matters as communication and transportation. Each district, he contended, should be able to determine its internal government without restriction by other districts or the United States. Finally, he avowed his belief in revenue-sharing, as previously proposed to the Congress of Micronesia without success, and insisted that appropriate legislation be implemented immediately without waiting for an end to trusteeship and the present arrangement (*Micronitor*, 28 May 1973, pp. 1–2).

It will be recalled that a group of traditional chiefs and elected leaders of Palau had issued, in November 1972, a declaration expressing their "unequivocal" opposition to the use of land in Palau by the United States military forces. However, the two paramount chiefs of Palau, Ibedul and Reklai, defined a less extreme position during a personal exchange of views with Ambassador Williams on Koror in December 1972, and again in a meeting with the United Nations Visiting Mission in February 1973. In effect, they stated their willingness to consider the issue of military options in Palau, but only after the United States promises to return all "lands taken by foreign individuals and Governments" (U.N. Visiting Mission 1973:123). These are the so-called public lands, retained at present by the Trust Territory government. In Palau District, these lands amount to 83,978 acres, or 73 percent of the total land area (U.S. Department of State 1973:289). Palauans declare that this land does not now, and never did, belong to the territorial government, but to the people of Palau and their chiefs.

The impact of the Palau land controversy on the American-Micronesian status talks was discussed by the heads of the two negotiating teams in May 1973, at a conference of district administrators in Majuro. Ambassador Williams noted the prior assumption by the United States that control and disposition of public lands would be defined in the new constitution and in Micronesian official acts taken at the central and district levels after trusteeship had ended. However, he pointed out, the Congress and the joint committee had now adopted a position whereby the status talks "cannot go forward unless and until all public land in Palau is returned to the traditional chiefs in the district in trust for the people" (*Highlights*, 15 May 1973, p. 2). Senator Salii confirmed that since United States military options for Palau land use had been specified in the Draft Compact of Free Association, the Palauan leaders' declaration had in fact blocked further progress on the talks. The joint committee, he added, hoped to work out an arrangement with the American delegation by which the United States might negotiate its military needs for land independently with each district (p. 3). Simply put, the Palau people want their lands returned to them *before* they negotiate land leases with the United States, so that they may bargain from a position of strength rather than having handed back to them only those lands not required by the Americans. During the summer of 1973, fact-finding teams from Washington were in Palau, and in the other districts, exploring with local authorities and other citizens the possible early return of Trust Territory public lands to the district. In the same months, members of the joint committee held hearings in Palau, as they did also in other districts, to obtain a better sense of popular and official sentiments about land and other critical issues that had disrupted the Micronesian status deliberations.

Speaker Itelbang Luii, in his opening statement to the Palau District Legislature in October 1973, recognized the "very critical" period that Palau had entered, facing the problems of Palau's relationships with the other districts and the United States as well as suffering serious internal difficulties. The return of public lands he called "long overdue," and he deplored the fact that Palauans are "fast becoming excessively dependent" upon United States appropriations. Urging the importance of Palauan heritage and traditions, he declared that "one of our most valuable assets is our sense of pride and identity, which we should not neglect." District Administrator Thomas Remengesau seconded Luii's remarks. He warned of the need for greater cooperation among the different factions of Palau's district leadership. His final advice was: "First, let us make ourselves self-sufficient economically with the money given to us [by the United States], and then be independent as most of us seem to prefer" (*Highlights*, 15 October 1973, p. 2).

Rota Island

Steps taken in 1972 and 1973 by the Marianas, Marshalls, and Palau district legislatures toward separate status negotiations with the United States have been interpreted generally as contributing to the fragmentation of Micronesia. They are reviewed here in that same light, as centrifugal forces detracting from Micronesian attempts to maintain a territorial unity. Understandably they are the responses of opposing identities in a climate of loosening ties. At least two additional moves toward separatism, and perhaps a third, have attracted attention at a lower level of Trust Territory administration, that is, within the district itself. These concern Rota Island in Marianas District, Kasaie Island in Ponape District, and possibly the Outer Islands in Yap District. These latter expressions of a separatist nature do not deny the continued validity of the district and territorial structures. Rather they seek formal recognition of their linguistic, cultural, economic, and political identities through new alignments within the territorial organization.

When the United Nations mission visited Rota Island one day in March 1973, the Rota Municipal Council presented it with a resolution urging the island's separation from the rest of Marianas District in order to become a district in its own right within the Trust Territory. As a separate district, Rota could control its own budget, improve its development program, and have better representation. Mayor Antonio Ca. Atalig of Rota Municipality told the mission that Rotanese had not been consulted prior to formation of the Marianas Political Status Commission and did not support the current talks between the commission and the United States. Instead, he reported, the council favored the negotiations being conducted by the joint committee of the Congress of Micronesia (*Marianas Variety*, 9 March 1973, p. 12; U.N. Visiting Mission 1973:32).

Rota is the southernmost island in Marianas District. About thirty-two square miles in area and with a population of 1,727 (1971 figures), Rota lies only 30 miles north of the Territory of Guam and some 60 miles south of Saipan, administrative center of Marianas District. Toward the end of the seventeenth century, the Spanish collected together on Guam all Chamorro natives of the Marianas except Rota Island, where a few families managed to evade capture by hiding in caves. The traditional Chamorro language and culture has persisted longer on Rota because those survivors escaped much of the Spanish cultural impact. Throughout the succeeding German and Japanese periods, the governing center for the reoccupied northern Marianas, Rota Island included, was Saipan. During the American occupation from 1944, Saipan continued in that role, as it did also after 1951 when the Department of the Interior was named to replace the Navy Department as administering agency in the Trust Territory. In 1953, however, the U.S. Central Intelligence

Agency (CIA) required Saipan Island for training Nationalist Chinese as guerrilla fighters to infiltrate Mainland China; and all of the northern Marianas, except Rota, were returned to navy control. Rota was then administered under civilian authority from Trust Territory offices on Guam until 1955 when the island was elevated to the status of a separate district. In 1962, the CIA operation was closed down, and Saipan and the other northern Mariana Islands were released from security restrictions. When the Trust Territory headquarters moved from Guam to Saipan in July 1962, Rota Island was reincorporated as part of Marianas District.

In 1971, it was announced that a planning team from Hawaii Architects and Engineers, Inc. (HAE) had begun work on a master plan and harbor study for Rota Island. HAE is a consortium of Hawaii firms that had already done similar studies for nine locations in the Trust Territory, mainly district and subdistrict centers. The Rota project was reported to be part of a five-year capital improvements program being carried out by the Trust Territory government (*Micronitor*, 21 August 1971, pp. 3, 8). Given such improvements in its harbor, ship channel, airport, and road system, Rota holds much potential for maintaining economic self-sufficiency, especially through meat and vegetable production for export to nearby Guam and other Micronesian islands lacking such staples. Rota Island is regarded as one of the finest agricultural economic bases in Micronesia. The stability provided in the island community by the older generation's emphasis upon Chamorro custom, language, and values is threatened by the district administration's emphasis on English language and American orientation in school and other government areas. Under present conditions, more and more of the younger Rotanese look to Guam and Saipan for non-agricultural employment opportunities (Smith 1973:11).

When two subcommittees of the Marianas Political Status Commission staged hearings on Rota with the municipal council and general public in April 1973, to gather Rotanese views on the upcoming negotiations with the United States, the response reportedly emphasized three principal concerns. First, Rotanese wished to limit the military presence of the United States on their island. Second, they wanted their delegation on the Marianas Status Commission to have a veto power over any aspect of the negotiations that might be unsuited to Rotanese interests. Rota, like other islands in the district, had been allowed representation on the commission but its 13 percent of the total population and its opposition to the majority opinion on Saipan and Tinian gave little hope for Rotanese consideration without a veto power. Third, in anticipation of a plebiscite on any draft agreement between Marianas District and the United States, Rotanese asked for a comprehensive political education program that would put forward clearly, for example, in both Chamorro and English languages, the advantages and disadvantages of any status option proposed, in order that Rotanese voters might indicate their preference on an informed basis (*Marianas Variety*, 20 April 1973, pp. 1, 6). Although no mention of Rota's desire to separate from the rest of the Mariana Islands was reported, the statements to the commission implied continued vigor of that sentiment.

Kusaie Island

The case of Kusaie Island resembles that of Rota Island in their common cause to become separate administrative districts in any future realignment of Micronesian island groups. Kusaie and Ponape are the only high islands in Ponape District. The fourth largest island in the Trust Territory, Kusaie is 42 square miles in area, about one-third the size of Ponape Island, and supported some 4,600 inhabitants in 1972, about 28 percent of the population on Ponape. Ever since the 1880s, Ponape has dominated the easternmost portion of the Caroline archipelago as the seat of foreign government rule. Kusaie, without an airfield and dependent on shipping out of Ponape every three or four weeks, has shared the fate of most outer islands because of its geographic isolation and its tenuous transportation link with the district center on Ponape.

It was not always this way between Kusaie and Ponape. About the twelfth century after the extensive rock-built ceremonial complex of Nan Madol had been created on Ponape, the ruling line of Ponapean chiefs according to legend relinquished control of their island to a Kusaien political figure who led an invading force from the smaller island. In the mid-nineteenth century, American whaling vessels in large numbers were visiting both Ponape and Kusaie for winter provisioning. The excesses of sea-weary sailormen relaxing ashore soon prompted the establishment of an American Protestant mission in the eastern Carolines. By 1875 Kusaie had been completely Christianized. A missionary-operated school attracted Micronesian students from the Marshalls and Gilberts as well as the eastern Carolines. The church, which became autonomous under Kusaien leadership after the turn of the century, has come to dominate the island way of life. Little of the traditional Kusaien culture remains.

Early in the American period after World War II, Kusaien employees enjoyed some advantage over other Micronesians at Ponape District headquarters because of their English-language training and American mission-taught values. Today, their pride of individual accomplishment in the world of Western culture is demeaned by Kusaie's situation "at the end of the line," because Ponape Island is favored by virtue of its central role in District affairs. Kusaien efforts to gain recognition as a separate district should be viewed against this background of history.

Kusaiens first petitioned the United Nations for aid in achieving separate status as a district in 1956 and, most recently, in 1973 (U.N. Visiting Mission 1973:12). The Ponapean congressman from the Eleventh Electoral District, which comprises Kusaie and Pingelap, introduced a resolution toward the same end in 1965 during the first regular session of the Congress of Micronesia. That other attempts in subsequent sessions of the Congress were no more successful is apparently due to opposition about setting a precedent for fragmentation of the Territory and creating a problem in congressional representation in the Senate. Kusaien spokesmen have met several times with the high commissioner and his staff on the subject. Although no strong objection has been voiced, it has been suggested that the issue is more appropriately one for the congress to decide. More recently, the high commissioner is reported to have referred the matter to authorities in Washington because a change in a secretarial order will probably be required (*Micronitor*, 23 April 1973, p. 3). The territorial administration did accede to Kusaien demands for improvement in physical plant facilities on the island when in 1970 Hawaii Architects and Engineers were asked to prepare a master plan for Kusaie as a subdistrict center. That plan had begun to be implemented by early 1972 (*Highlights*, 1 January 1972, p. 6).

Kusaiens, frustrated in their fruitless quest, finally effected a breakthrough in September 1972 when their island delegation presented the subject to the Ponape District Legislature. Their request simply sought administrative separation of Kusaie Island from the rest of Ponape District at such time as the trust government was replaced by a Micronesian state. Reasons given for wanting to separate from Ponape related to differences in language, history, and custom, and the people's desire for more freedom to arrange their own affairs independent of the Ponape administration's dictation or neglect. Legislators supported the resolution unanimously (*Micronitor*, 15 January 1973, p. 7).

Kusaie formed its own Political Status Commission in January

1973, stimulated no doubt by the action taken earlier in the Marianas District to clarify its political future (*Micronitor*, 29 January 1973, p. 2). In the same month, Kusaie's Chief Magistrate Norman Skilling outlined his island's problems before a magistrates' conference on Ponape. He then went on to Saipan to renew his constituency's plea with the high commissioner and, accompanied by other members of the Kusaie Political Status Commission, made a presentation to the Fifth Congress of Micronesia. The latter body was urged to approve the principle of separate status for Kusaie before any decisions are made by the Congress or a constitutional convention on the structure of a future Micronesian state. No definitive action appears to have been taken. Skilling went on from Saipan to the Republic of Nauru to discuss with President Hammer DeRoburt matters of mutual concern in the areas of shipping and tourist development (*Micronitor*, 15 January 1973, pp. 1, 9). This last suggests that Kusaiens, also related to Nauruans by kinship ties through intermarriage over the past century, were following the model already pioneered by Marshallese for a closer economic connection with the independent Nauruan state.

Yap Outer Islands

Atoll peoples from the Outer Islands area in Yap District have for years encountered discrimination against full expression of their wants and needs by the more acculturated and dominating Yapese in the main island complex, where the district center is located. Their situation recalls the dilemma of Rotanese and Kusaiens in their respective districts. Outer island peoples in the atolls from Ulithi eastward traditionally carried tribute payments in their sea-going canoes to a paramount chief on Yap. They believed that if they failed to do so, powerful Yapese magicians would punish them by sending a destructive typhoon. Another complication from the past is that coral islands and atolls from Ulithi all the way to Namonuito in Truk District are occupied by peoples who culturally and linguistically have more in common with the Truk Islands than with the Yap Islands. These age-old ties have been depreciated by the artificial boundary separating Yap and Truk districts since Japanese times.

An Outer Islands High School got underway on Ulithi about 1965, making it no longer necessary for out-island students to board at school in Colonia on Yap for their secondary education. Five years later, in support of Ulithi's expanding role as subdistrict center, a new high school facility was projected as part of a master plan for Falalop Island on Ulithi to serve the entire eastern portion of Yap District (*Highlights*, 15 November 1971, p. 2). Until 1969, out-islanders in Yap District had no representation in any legislature. In that year, however, the Yap District Legislature was chartered to replace the exclusive Yap Islands Legislature. For the first time, delegates from the outer islands could deliberate side by side with delegates from Yap proper. Although no formal political action has been reported from this area, it would come as no surprise if the outer islands were to actively seek separate district status, and possibly to propose a merger of their islands with those in the western portion of Truk District in recognition of common traditional bonds.

Summary and Conclusions

Modern Micronesia, the Trust Territory of the Pacific Islands, is likened to a package of assorted goods held together by certain tie cords and wrappings in a semblance of political unity. The goods comprise the islands with their varied resources and the people with their contrasting traditional backgrounds and historic accommodations to foreign influences. The tie cords represent controls imposed from outside Micronesia, such as, United Nations trusteeship and the United States territorial administration; acquired wants and needs of Micronesians in education, health services, living standards, and a heightened social awareness; the indigenous Congress of Micronesia and its negotiating arm, the Joint Committee on Future Status; and the six district legislatures. Wrappings are suggested in the ambivalent significance of Micronesia's vast ocean expanse and the islands' strategic situation in the western Pacific.

Is the appearance of unity just a presumption of unity that will fade into oblivion once the tie cords and wrappings of the package begin to come undone? Anticipation of an end to trusteeship in the next three or four years threatens the package's security. United Nations supervision, American administration of the islanders' internal affairs, and Micronesian confrontation of the United States in negotiating a future status will have been eliminated. The unifying function of the Micronesian Congress, the inflated felt needs of the people, and America's denial of military access to the area by other nations will, in different ways, work to preserve the package whole. But territorial unity in the framework of Micronesian autonomy may depend finally either on continuing United States financial aid to bolster the islands' government and economy or on Micronesian capabilities to attain economic self-sufficiency by developing local resources without having drastically to reduce present levels of acquired wants and needs.

Centrifugal forces with a potential for impeding unity and encouraging fragmentation have become apparent in the Territory. They lie in the opposing identities—economic, social, and political—that are deeply rooted in the character of Micronesian peoples and cultures. These identities may be distinguished by differences in language, in sociocultural practices both traditionally based and historically imposed, in access to exploitable natural resources, and in the power, authority, and influence exercised by island publics and intramural factions. By 1972, the course of events in the Trust Territory had suggested that the climate was worsening for whatever unity Micronesians might claim. The clash of newly emerging political positions in the Congress, secessionist moves in the Marianas, Marshalls, and Palau district legislatures, and separatist actions by Rotanese and Kusaiens to be independent of their respective districts—all of these had divisive connotations that most observers were interpreting as precedents in the increasing partition of island Micronesia.

1. The principal observations and conclusions developed in this chapter began to take form in a lecture given at several American universities in late 1971 and early 1972. That lecture in turn grew out of a paper written during the summer of 1971 entitled "The Many Faces of Micronesia," intended for publication elsewhere. The principal arguments in that paper, as in this chapter, are founded on my experience of twenty-five years in field research and applied anthropology in various parts of the Trust Territory, principally in the Marshalls; my personal observations and interviews in early 1971 during a visit to all six districts of the Territory; and on my continuing review of events in 1972 and 1973 as reported in published sources or told to me personally by Micronesians and others. The final draft of this chapter includes information available to me through October 1973.

14

Micronesian Political Change in Perspective

Norman Meller

The study of change in Micronesia is normally premised upon internal phenomena selected from two or more vantage points compared along a time span of Micronesian history. It need not be so circumscribed, and the addition of external comparison can provide perspective helpful to the understanding of the Micronesian data. It is the function of this chapter to consider the Trust Territory of the Pacific Islands from the broader frame of political modifications occurring throughout the Pacific Basin.

But first a caveat. Just looking at Micronesia, as the region may be most inclusively delineated, immediately reveals in addition to the unique security trusteeship,[1] in which the American administration receives preferential treatment, an independent republic (Nauru);[2] a British colony geographically overlapping Polynesia (Gilbert and Ellice Islands Colony); and an organized, unincorporated territory of the United States (Guam). The traditional political structures of these areas did not reflect as great a diversity as do their present forms, so that cumulatively they constitute demonstration of post-contact political change. On the other hand, within the American Trust Territory alone, a differential range of conflict, cooperation, and compromise (Malinowski 1945:26) cloaks the apparent identity of introduced political institutions found within its six administrative districts. Before venturing on a comparative tour of the Pacific island polities, it is thus essential to note that the observation of similitudes and differences permits only the grossest of appraisals, neither positing nor applying any specific units of measurement. In addition, any unilineality of change encountered ought not to be confused with inexorability of movement.

Self-Determination

Today, as most everywhere in the world, a current of political self-determination is running strong throughout the entire Pacific Basin.[3] Despite its many forms, this thrust in the direction of political change remains unmistakably clear. Within the United States sphere, the admission of Hawaii in 1959 to coequal status in the Union has had a noticeable impact on the remaining American colonies. For one thing, with continental contiguity no longer a criterion, similar aspirations of Guamanians have been encouraged. Popular selection of their island's legislators and governor and recently the election of the Territory's first official delegate to the U.S. Congress symbolize that this former land battleship, for so long under temporary naval rule (Carano and Sanchez 1964:184), has moved far along the scale of internal self-government.[4] American Samoa is ambivalent in its stirrings for political change due to its peoples' desire to preserve the *matai* 'Samoan family' system. This American possession has recently copied the Guamanian ploy of holding a territory-wide election for an unofficial Washington representative, and its politicians have commenced espousing the local selection of their governor. And in the American Trust Territory, "the renewed interest of our government in the welfare of Micronesians can be traced to the grant of Statehood [to Hawaii]. . . . Akin in outlook and cultural background to the unrepresented Micronesians, Hawaii through its delegation in Congress began pressing for greater assistance for its fellow Pacific islanders. Their efforts took the form of legislative amendments to many federal aid programs which previously excluded the Trust Territory" (Mink 1971:186).

Great Britain, one of the other four metropolitan nations with possessions in the Pacific, is fully committed to the policy of divesting itself of these areas just as soon as they are capable of governing themselves as politically sovereign entities. Fiji has been granted independence, and the restrictions raised by the British treaty ties with Tonga have been terminated, so that this last of the Polynesian monarchies in the Pacific can now be regarded as truly independent. All signs point toward the severance of British administering relationships with the Gilbert and Ellice Islands Colony and the British Solomon Islands Protectorate in the not too distant future; meanwhile, the peoples of these areas continue to enjoy an ever expanding scope of participation through their newly introduced political institutions. New Zealand, for its part, has voluntarily granted full internal self-government to the Cook Islands; externally, the Cooks remain associated with New Zealand for purposes of defense, foreign affairs, and comparable other functions, but secure in the knowledge that they have the right to break all ties unilaterally. The people of Niue, as well, are opting for internal self-governance, with external ties to New Zealand; and if the Tokelaus were more viable, they probably would also be following this pattern.

France, too, administers territories in the Pacific—French Polynesia, Wallis and Futuna, and New Caledonia. Contrasting diametrically with the policy of Great Britain, they are considered departments of France, their people to be assimilated into the French nation; since their decision in the referenda of 1958 to remain within the French community, they have been incorporated ever more closely into metropolitan France.[5] Like the citizens of Hawaii, these peoples of France's overseas territories vote in presidential elections and send fully accredited representatives to seats in the French National Assembly and the French Senate. Unlike Hawaii, the political role permitted in their home Pacific areas is circumscribed, so that many of the voters consider themselves deprived of self-government. The legislation recently adopted by the French national parliament, which created a series of communes for French Polynesia, represented the metropolitan nation's counter to the Tahitian demand for a grant of greater decision-making power. Instead, it unilaterally reduced the authority of that territory's central institutions.

Bounded in different juridical and more constraining form, the trust territories of the Pacific Basin evidence much the same current of political change. Severance of Western Samoa from New Zealand's tutelage in 1962 provided the springboard by which the Nauruans obtained comparable independent status in 1968. Papua New Guinea[6] was granted internal self-government in December 1973, and is soon slated for independence.[7] And all of this is wholly consonant with the disappearance of United Nations trusteeships, for of the original eleven, none has been terminated except to become an independent nation or part of a newly formed country. It is the Trust

Territory of the Pacific Islands that stands out in sharp relief against all these other U.N. treaty–created jurisdictions, in the presently expressed opposition of the United States to severing American relations with Micronesia.

Each administering power in the Pacific has now come to face squarely the need for definitive decision on integration or independence for each of the island areas it administers. Great Britain, New Zealand, and Australia are committed to the policy of encouraging as great a degree of self-government (if not complete autonomy) as each island area is capable of sustaining. France has opted for the antipodal position.[8] In contrast, the United States has been unable to settle on a long-range policy for Guam or American Samoa, but the consistent strand running throughout its sequence of offers during the protracted negotiations with the Micronesians has been the retention of ties with Micronesia after the Trust Territory status is terminated.

Factors for Change

Contributing to the current of political change in the Pacific have been a number of mutually reinforcing factors, in character some external and others internal to the course of events within the various island areas. On the world scene, overseas possessions are denigrated as continuations of white man's colonialism, tolerable at best only to the extent that "natives" are facilitated to their self-determined ends. The United Nations has served both as the stage for voicing this position as well as the instrument to muster cooperative effort aimed at elimination of all territorial possessions. Representatives of some of the newly emergent nations reject as incredible the possibility that political independence may not be the goal of every dependent people. The East-West cleavage, with communism's attribution of the continuation of capitalism to the exploitation of colonies by their imperialistic masters, provides an ideological imperative for severing territories from their mother country. Probably as widespread a rationale for the status change of so many former dependent areas, although not necessarily as publicized, has been the factor that colonial costs can no longer be justified in economic or other beneficial terms to the metropolitan power. Rather, as it comes to be accepted that it is the moral burden of the wealthier nations the world round to assist the less-developed portions of the globe, renewed linkages of aid devoid of suzerainty are being forged within the newer rubric.

Nascent nationalism with all its symbolic trappings has emerged in all the dependent areas of the Pacific Basin, in some encouraged by their administering authorities, in others suppressed.[9] The sponsored competition for a design of the American Trust Territory flag has had its repetition in Papua New Guinea, and contrasts with government officers tearing down the red and white Pomare standard of the old Tahitian monarchy when it was recently raised as a token of anti-administration opposition in Tahiti. Citizens of the American Trust Territory now experience a sense of symbolic community when they identify themselves as "Micronesians,"[10] whereas not so long ago they were hard put to recognize commonalities of interest extending beyond the boundaries of their small home island and encompassing even the rest of the archipelago with which they are geographically and culturally grouped.

Not all agitation of a nationalistic nature in the Pacific is occurring as advocacy for the creation of a polity coterminous with the colony it will replace. Along with the rise of political expectations, there has also been a growth of centrifugal separatism. The Mataungan Association among the Tolai of the Gazelle Peninsula of New Britain (Gunther 1970) and the Napidakoe Navitu in the Kieta area of Bougainville, both ethnically based mass movements, are explainable as nationalistically motivated, with the latter committed to its island's secession from Papua New Guinea (Wolfers 1971:144). There is in this a degree of parallelism with the position of the Northern Marianas in their apparent desire to break off from the rest of the American Trust Territory. However, the separate independence sought for Bougainville contrasts with the integral ties with the ministering nation that the Marianas desire to establish, irrespective of what befalls the rest of the American Trust Territory.[11]

Integral to the self-determination movement has been the emergence of a Western-educated elite, outward-looking, competent in the language of modern realpolitik.[12] It has learned to adapt to its cause the leverage afforded by pertinent developments occurring around the world. Protests to atomic tests by the French may be voiced by Cook Islanders troubled over Southern Hemisphere atmospheric pollution, but opposition to the same testing may also be used to advantage by the leaders of the French Polynesians seeking political autonomy. It appears obvious to the members of the Joint Committee on Future Status of the Congress of Micronesia that as

United States armed forces are withdrawn from forward bases in Japan, Okinawa, the Philippines, Viet Nam, and Thailand, military strategy turns upon Micronesia remaining as "America's frontier in the Far East" (O'Conner 1970). In return, Micronesians count on receiving the financing necessary to support a self-governing Micronesia.[13] The greater familiarity of the average indigene with the political forms introduced by the administering nations, even when not accompanied by the sophistication necessary to master the associated processes,[14] has eased the tasks of this elite leadership in mustering popular support in aid of its position. Although external events undoubtedly do have a transference effect—thus, imminent political change in Papua New Guinea is bound to have some influence on the outlawed independence movement of neighboring West Irian (Hastings 1970:67)—their input must be treated with that of internal factors in contributing to the emergence of the Pacific's mini-states and to influencing the many other ways in which demand for self-government is expressing itself in the islands.

Ignoring of Traditional Forms and Processes

The "very conspicuous tendency for metropolitan countries to offer their smaller dependencies a constitutional framework based on their own experience and preconceptions . . . is perhaps more evident among the small possessions of the United States than in other places, and it is far from being an unmixed blessing" (DeSmith 1970: 5). The separation of government into the three major branches so familiar to American practice has been transferred holus-bolus to Micronesia. In part, this has meant that in Micronesia there has been relatively less initiative taken by the United States than by some other metropolitan countries to shape the political institutions introduced elsewhere in the Pacific so as to make them more compatible with traditional forms and processes.[15] There is no parallel with the integral weaving of the Samoan family system into the political warp and woof of Western Samoa (Davidson 1967).[16] Or consider the recent deliberate reconstruction of the Legislative Council and Executive Council in the British Solomon Islands Protectorate, varying the structures so common to British practice by creating a Governing Council, which represents an experiment in the use of subject-matter committees alleged to be more compatible with Melanesian consensus practices (Russell 1970). A parallel innovative effort in the Gilbert and Ellice Islands Colony with a Governing Council exercising both executive and legislative powers had previously been abandoned.

To approach this from another tack, the traditional leadership has been afforded little role in the introduced political institutions of the Micronesian sector. In only two of the six district legislatures of the Trust Territory do the traditional leaders enjoy a differentiated position: full participation with voting power has been retained by the four *iroij* 'paramount chiefs' in the Marshalls; in the Palau District legislative body, the chiefs sit by right but their formal participation has been reduced to one of debate (Meller 1969:chap. 9).[17] This sharply differs from the South Pacific Polynesian possession under United States jurisdiction, where normally chosen by consensus procedures for seats in the senate of American Samoa are the persons with the highest titles among those eligible for holding office. In neighboring Western Samoa, it was no happenstance that after independence two of the holders of that area's three paramount titles[18] emerged as joint heads of state for life, and the third as prime minister. The efforts made by the British in Fiji to preserve the indigenous system of local government, much as that may have been misunderstood (France 1969), runs counter to the American introduction of municipalities into Micronesia. One of the first decisions the Cook Islanders made after their islands became an associated state of New Zealand was to give formal, even if only nominal, recognition to their *ariki* 'chiefs'. They amended the Cook Islands constitution so as to set up a House of Ariki empowered to make recommendations on matters affecting *maori* 'indigenous Cook' customs and traditions.

There will always be a degree of looking enviously over territorial boundaries to the seemingly more attractive political institutions established somewhere else—as the Speaker of the Papua New Guinea legislative assembly favoring substitution of the presidential for that Australian-administered area's parliamentary system of government,[19] just as in the American Trust Territory the reverse sentiment has been expressed. Although this may both stem from, and constitute, legitimate criticism of the administering nation's procrustean fitting of the respective territory within its own constitutional concepts, there is no necessary relationship between any such indigenous leaders' decision to borrow exogenous political institutions and subsequent support forthcoming from endogenous political forms and practices.[20] It might be added that, in the instances cited, experience and education of the members of these two legislative bodies suggests that the legislators of Micronesia may have been more qualified to operate a parliamentary system than were their indigenous counterparts in Melanesia, whereas for the latter a presidential system might have more adequately accommodated the role then being played by the Australian administration (Meller 1968:57).

Keesing early noted that when provision was made for the selection of political representatives in the South Seas, it was governmental employees who appeared in the new role (Keesing 1945:165). Micronesia proved no exception. As in the other American areas of the Pacific when legislative institutions were first introduced, their members retained their posts in the executive agencies (see Meller 1969:211–12). Now with the legislature becoming institutionalized both in the American zones and elsewhere in the Pacific, governmental employees are required to elect between civil service or legislator status in charting the course of their future personal advancement. Functionally, this dichotomization between administration and politics has had greater impact than merely to serve as a rote adoption of the political concepts observed by the metropolitan nations, or even to reflect an accommodation of their expatriate administrators' pique arising out of the desire to have indigenous leaders identified as either supportive of the "government" or aligned with those making demands upon it. Rather, it represents a development probably essential to the growth of government competent to deal with the complexities of the modern world, namely, functional specialization and the emergence of the professional politician. There is no question but that, as a consequence, the interface between the Micronesian Congress and executive departments in the American Trust Territory has grown more abrasive, and the respective contributions of indigene and state-sider sharpened in the shaping of public policy.

Political Parties

Whether the "politicizing" of modern self-government will be followed by the emergence of one or more area-wide political parties remains problematical in the Trust Territory. To date, they exist in only two of the six administrative districts (Meller 1969:262 ff.), and have been in no position to "organize" either house of the Congress. This contrasts with many parts of Oceania where political parties function on the central level of government. Even in Papua New Guinea, where parties are similarly novel, a majority coalition of several parties in the unicameral House of Assembly now directs the area's administration. Nationwide parties have a communal base in Fiji and owe strong ties to the charisma of single leaders in the Cooks and French Polynesia.

Guam illustrates the emergence of parties along American lines, but attempts to follow suit in American Samoa have been unsuccessful. The explanation may lie in the relative distance of the two areas from fully embracing American philosophy and practices of government. However, Western Samoa also has not institutionalized political parties, even though it has adopted a parliamentary form of government. Thus, the explanation for American Samoa may lie in a basic antipathy between Samoan consensus processes and the confrontation fostered by political parties. Correlatively, the ill fit of political haranguing and self-promotion to parts of Micronesia does not bode well for the institutionalizing of more than localized parties in the Trust Territory.

Language Usage

Choice of language to be used in governance and the particular forms employed have immediate as well as long-range relevancy for political change. The American Trust Territory is not unique in the Pacific as being a multilingual area that adopted the language of its ministering nation as its legal *lingua franca* and as the medium of instruction for public schools but continued the use of indigenous languages for a variety of other public purposes. Although the usage of English is recognized as having had political significance in Micronesia, so too has the indigenous tongue. When the nobles' language appropriate to the position of chiefs in Ponape was not observed on their assuming roles in the introduced legislative institutions (Meller 1969:127), this carried potential for undermining their status. As another illustration, the dominance of one ethnic group over another when in contact is reinforced by such indicia as the former's language being adopted for informal communication in carrying on district government or becoming the medium for debate and record-keeping in the new legislature that brings together representatives from both groups.

The justification for using only English in the Congress of Micronesia, where members are all indigenes, is not incontrovertible.[21] The House of Assembly in Papua New Guinea provides simultaneous translation of floor debate in Melanesian Pidgin, Police Motu, and English. Western Samoa utilizes both English and Samoan in its parliament, irrespective of the English-speaking competence of its people. Rather, the directed use of English by the Congress of Micronesia had the effect of opening only one of a number of conceptual vistas to political phenomena, evidencing a general course of development envisioned by the administering authority. It may have been the most efficient of solutions to a difficult, multilingual problem, but it was not ineluctable.

Viewed from the perspective of the Micronesian voters, who know that the introduced government of the Americans is conducted in English, there are obvious advantages in choosing a representative fluent in English. This realism has made a noticeable impact on Micronesian politics. English-language skill has come to be regarded as almost a sina qua non for candidacy for the Congress of Micronesia (see Meller 1969:276–77). Although the Trust Territory's regional legislatures conduct their proceedings in the dominant indigenous language of the district, and later publish summary English records of proceedings and product, longitudinal observations seem to indicate that the English-language abilities of these district legislators, too have been steadily increasing. Communications expressed in English constitute an ever-expanding input into the totality of district decision-making.

Undoubtedly, the use of a common language throughout the American Trust Territory has facilitated Micronesian integration and provided verbal symbols necessary for the growth of a national identity.[22] In the other remaining trust territory, Melanesian Pidgin is the fastest-spreading political language in both that area and jointly administered Papua, and may prove to be a major element continuing to bind New Guinea to Papua when Australian tutelage ceases. Caution is required, however, in generalizing on the weight of the contribution made by a widely used language. Almost universal bilingualism—Samoan and English—has not stemmed the evergrowing rift between the two Samoas. The divisive pulls that promise to cleave the Northern Marianas from the Caroline and Marshall islands will not be offset by their joint leadership carrying on debates in English, or, notwithstanding the Chamorros of all of the Marianas using the same two languages, possibly keeping the Northern Marianas separated from Guam. To the extent that there is utility in focusing attention on the relation of language usage to change, probably it does not lie in causation of political specifics. Instead, just as the language of Pacific legislators may serve to point the direction of modifications under way in the broader society (Meller 1959), so may the language adopted for political discourse reveal the conceptual underpinnings of its users, and thus broadly adumbrate the general nature of the future polity.

Foreign Affairs

A final dimension against which to appraise Micronesian political change is from the perspective of external relations. The "revolt" of the indigenous members in the South Pacific Conference that transformed the conference "from a subsidiary organ of general gossip . . . into a forum . . . [that] has moved toward domination of the Commission structure" (Forsyth 1970:40) was sparked jointly by a Fijian (present Prime Minister Mara) and a Chamorro (former Speaker Carlos Taitano).[23] Although this marked one of the rare instances in which a Micronesian has played a major role in a bi- or multi-polity Pacific organization, in this case he was from Guam. In many of the Pacific conferences currently being held, there is no American Trust Territory presence. The Territory entered no athletes in the recent South Pacific Games, in which teams from fourteen Pacific countries competed in Tahiti, or entertainers in the first (1972) South Pacific Festival of Arts in Fiji. True, in the spring of 1971 the Trust Territory did participate in a regional coconut conference with Western Samoa, Fiji, Tonga, the Cooks, Niue, and the Gilbert and Ellice Islands Colony. The following week, however, its representatives were absent from the meeting of the same group of Pacific polities that convened as the Pacific Islands Producers Association, and consulted not only on banana marketing but the forming of a regional transportation system.

Befitting its character as an American-administered area, the Trust Territory's involvement in the Pacific Islands Development Commission[24] may in some minuscule way parallel the membership of Fiji, Tonga, and Western Samoa in the British Commonwealth.[25] But completely out of the orbit of Trust Territory international involvement would be the recent action taken by the Cooks, Fiji, Tonga, and Western Samoa, joined by Australia and New Zealand, in establishing a regional forum outside of the South Pacific Commission for political consultation and economic cooperation. So, too, would be Fiji's entry into the United Nations as a full member. In short, the external role of the American Trust Territory has been relatively low-key.

Future Status

Although the pace of political change has noticeably quickened during the last decade in the American Trust Territory, in a number of island areas of the Pacific it has proceeded at a faster tempo, so that to them—in either relative or absolute terms—the Trust Territory may be regarded as just catching up. This generalization holds whether it be premised upon the political independence achieved by Fiji, Nauru, Tonga, and Western Samoa; the internal self-government of the Cooks and (qualifiedly) Guam; or even the volte-face of Australia with respect to Papua New Guinea. Further differentiating the American Trust Territory from some of the Pacific areas is the fact that no unifying political party or charismatic leader with following throughout Micronesia has emerged to provide the guidance necessary to manage or to resolve the conflict caused by the centrifugal forces of regionalism and custom serving as countervailing pressures against the growth of territory-wide, integrative political institutions.

It is at a crucial stage of political advancement that the Trust Territory now faces the uncertainties attendant on the assertion of its people's right to full political self-determination. Offers by the United States of, first territorial, and next, commonwealth status have been rejected by the Micronesian representatives. The free association now in negotiation appears stalled over basic issues, such as the situs of sovereignty or "that free association should be in the form of a revocable compact, terminable unilaterally by either party" (Congress of Micronesia 1970:11). Pacific island experience indicates that this type of problem is not unique; Western Samoa (Davidson 1967:325) and Nauru (Viviani 1970:170–71) faced comparable issues of control over defense and foreign affairs. By the time each of these trusteeships was terminated, Nauru had rejected all such ties to Australia, and Western Samoa had reached a contrary position.

At present, it remains uncertain whether the Micronesian talks will end with the voicing of a Micronesian demand for complete independence or the reaching of a compromise recognizing internal autonomy for the Marshalls and the Carolines under a single, overarching government. It is not that the Territory's leaders lack the individual capacity to bargain successfully with the representatives of the United States over the details of the future status, always holding in reserve as threat an appeal to the United Nations and world opinion.[26] Rather, it is a question of whether this leadership can maintain the solidarity necessary for such collective bargaining, or if the mounting divisive pressures arising internally can be accommodated only by a Micronesian agreement to disagree. Already the Marianas have commenced their own negotiations. Any further district defection from Micronesian solidarity may well see the arranging of varying relationships with the United States, reflective of district and subdistrict differences. Paradoxically, then, even in disagreement there may still lie a solution, unsatisfactory as that would be to the advocates of a united Micronesia. Given the present state of the status talks, it appears appropriate to echo the words of Professor Robbins, used at an earlier period in a somewhat different context: "Fortunately all doors appear to have been left ajar for further negotiations" (Congress of Micronesia 1971:19).

1. This very uniqueness of the Trust Territory of the Pacific Islands has led one author to refer to it as a "somewhat bastard and contradictory" conception (McDonald 1949:54).

2. It is recognized that because Nauru geographically lies below the equator, and because of certain cultural reasons, objection may be raised to the inclusion of the republic within the area identified as Micronesia.

3. The commonalities of the islands of the Pacific Basin are such to warrant this chapter's use of the entire (as well as limitation to only the single) region as a referrent: "Throughout the region the dominant physical disadvantages are isolation from large metropolitan centres, the highly dispersed nature of many individual groups, smallness of population and, with a few notable exceptions, lack of basic mineral and industrial raw materials. On the economic side one is confronted with generally low levels of incomes and rates of savings, indigenous populations lacking in all but the most rudimentary managerial and technical skills, and methods of land tenure and social organizations that have their roots in traditional systems. In addition, heavy dependence on one or two agricultural export products renders them vulnerable to fluctuations in world markets for primary commodities as well as to the hazards of adverse weather. The combination of rapidly growing populations and rising expectations for the goods and services of the modern economy poses further challenges" (Fairbairn 1971:75). Although as written this statement was specifically applicable only to the central South Pacific, so that such areas as French Polynesia or Micronesia were not encompassed, it has obvious fit for most of Oceania. It should be added by way of discounting its economic implications that

established practice, if not policy, does not condition political change upon the existence of economic capacity to support it.

4. Despite this course of political change on Guam, the U.N. Special Committee on Colonialism apparently does not consider it an acceptable alternative to independence.

5. Wallis and Futuna elected a year later, in 1959, to become an Overseas Territory.

6. New Guinea is a trusteeship, Papua a territory, of Australia. They are now administered as a single unit, and Australia contemplates that they will continue so bound as future political events take shape. As one of the symbolic acts contributing to this union, the hyphen that previously served as the umbilical cord tieing the names of the two areas together has now been removed from the official designation of "Papua New Guinea."

7. See "Constitutional Development" 1971.

8. Similarly, Japanese policy apparently contemplated ultimate integration of Micronesia into the Japanese Empire. See chapter 15 below.

9. For American Trust Territory, see Meller 1969:355–56.

10. Presciently, the working committee of the Council of Micronesia recommended the new congress it was planning be named the "Congress of Micronesia." See Meller 1969:1, n. 1; 374.

11. Perhaps a more apt parallel would be the Modekngei Movement with its advocacy of Palau for the Palauans (Vidich 1952:chap. 10).

12. Not necessarily an elite devoid of ascriptive criteria, as, *inter alia*, King Taufa'ahau of Tonga, Prime Ministers Ratu Sir Kamisese Mara of Fiji and Tupua Tamasese Lealofi III of Western Samoa, and President Hammer DeRoburt of Nauru. For the new elite in the American Trust Territory, see Meller 1970:308.

13. The October 1971 negotiations in Hawaii between joint committee and U.S. delegation revealed smaller specific land aspirations on the part of the American military than Micronesians had anticipated (and feared). However, the American need remains to secure the neutrality of those island areas where no U.S. military presence is sought. Here see chapter 16 below, proposing neutralization of all Pacific Islands, including Micronesia.

14. As voters no longer approaching the ballot box in ritual fashion (Meller and Anthony 1968:99; Meller 1969:269).

15. The early proposal by Barnett to limit district legislatures to matters foreign to Micronesian custom, so as to recognize two parallel patterns of authority, would have represented such a modification (Meller 1969:68).

16. Or even with the structuring of the American Samoa Fono so as to bridge neatly the gap between Samoan customary methods for consensus selection of representatives and the universal adult suffrage that is common to American practices (Meller 1961:114).

17. This is not to underestimate the influence of the chiefs in Yap, or for that matter in Palau or Ponape, on decision-making within the district legislatures. Here see chapters 3 and 4.

18. The fourth paramount title has been temporarily eclipsed. Even so, the Council of Deputies, which would act in the absence of the head of state once the office was reduced to a single holder, could have a membership of up to three, and eligibility was so phrased as to accommodate the holder of the fourth title (Davidson 1967:372).

19. As reported in *Pacific Island Monthly*, February 1972, p. 33.

20. This in no way denies that the inappropriateness of borrowed political institutions, due to their lack of fit with traditional practices, may adversely affect political development, as see Niue (Parsons, 1968).

21. Non-English-speaking congressmen are assured interpreters by the secretarial order establishing the Congress of Micronesia.

22. For language as an identity trait, also see chapter 13.

23. Previously, the South Pacific Conference, comprised of island representatives from the various areas of the Pacific, met only triennially, and primarily for communication exchange. Starting in 1965, the conference demanded the right to make recommendations on the commission's proposed work budget. By 1967, annual sessions of the conference were being held, and the conference formulating the SPC work budget. Correlatively, the territories have commenced contributing funds as both a matter of right and obligation.

24. Membership includes American Samoa, American Trust Territory, Guam, and Hawaii.

25. Nauru, as an associate member of the British Commonwealth, participates in non-governmental commonwealth organizations.

26. The U.N. Special Committee on Colonialism has been requested to send an observer team to the Trust Territory if no satisfactory agreement on future status is reached.

15

The Old and the New: Japan and the United States in the Pacific

Felix Moos

> Time is running out for the United States in the Western Pacific. The seeds of discontent have been sown among the people because of inadequate money, lack of interest and often inept administration. At the same time the new Japanese are moving into the islands in increasing numbers, dollar bills sticking out of their pockets.—Joe Murphy, *Guam Daily News*

The political development in Micronesia will depend ultimately on the relationship of the six districts with the United States and with other Pacific nations, particularly Japan. Japan has had in the past a major interest in Micronesia. This interest has shifted from a military one to a primarily economic one. However, whatever happens in Micronesia in the future will depend very much on any agreements reached between Micronesia, the United States, and Japan.

When one strolls on Marine Drive in Agana, or walks along Guam's Ipao Beach, there exists little doubt that the Japanese are back in force—at least in Guam. The same is undoubtedly true for Saipan. And even though arguments may be made that Japan is not really knocking on the door of the U.S. Trust Territory of the Pacific Islands, just as good an argument could be advanced to the contrary. Japan's presence is felt most strongly in terms of Japanese goods. Foodstuffs on the shelves of stores in Ponape, Yap, Koror, and even Babelthaup are Japanese. Cars in the district centers are

Datsuns and Toyotas. And if one had any great doubt about the reemergence of Japan in Micronesia, then the toy salesman from Osaka discussing next year's line with NECO, a major wholesale outlet in Koror (Palau), is but another symbol that Japan is back. There are not yet the great number of Japanese tourists in Palau and Yap that one is getting used to in Saipan and Guam, but one does encounter them. The concrete pillar with *Palua Koen* inscribed on it, or the memorial stone tablet commemorating Japan's coming to the islands in Koror, are slowly succumbing to age, but the memories of Japan and the Japanese linger on. One could well ask why it is that Micronesians feel this strong nostalgia for the Japanese and things Japanese. Is it that the past masters are easier to deal with or to admire than the present ones?

Micronesian Patterns: The Past

Japan's early presence in the southwest Pacific began auspiciously with *ronin* (masterless *samurai*) seeking new lands and new ventures.[1] In 1890, the governor of Tokyo and his colleagues decided to interest some displaced and disinherited *samurai* in a fund established by the Meiji regime to assist such individuals and to encourage them to use their energies on other activities than those disrupting the rapid modernization of Japan at the time. One Taguchi Ukichi received 44,000 yen under this legislation, and although he apparently did not have a great desire to make his living as a fisherman, he did take the money and proceeded to outfit a 91-ton boat, the *Tenyū maru*, and created this enterprise the *Nantō Shokai*. He assembled a crew and sailed shortly thereafter to Guam, Ponape, and Palau, and on to other islands in the western Pacific. He returned to Ponape and established a store. Ponape, at the time under Spanish rule, was restless; and warfare among and between all groups—natives, Spaniards, and other Europeans—was rampant. From the very beginning, Taguchi experienced financial difficulties; he returned to Japan in December 1890 and failed in efforts to interest the Japanese government in providing additional funds to him. A second *ronin*, Komida Kiji, borrowing 12,000 yen from the governmental *samurai* fund, did not fare much better. He made two trading voyages into the western Pacific and then abandoned the project, leaving his employees on Ponape (Nanyō Boeki Kaisha, 1942:12-13). In 1891, Enomoto Takeaki and some associates established a firm on Ponape and later transferred the operation to Palau. In 1892, Mizutani Shinmu established a store on Truk. In 1893, three Japanese founded the *Nanyō Bōeki Hioki Gōshi Kaisha*, initiating flourishing business activities that would become the foundations of Japan's almost total economic domination of the area from then to the end of World War II. Not surprisingly, only some ten years later, Japanese commercial interests became political interests as well. Nanyō Boeki in 1900 was forced by the German authorities to cease operations on Truk because it had sold weapons to natives, and by 1901, "other Japanese traders in the Eastern Carolines had been barred for similar reasons from the islands."[2]

In short, beginning in the 1890s, the Japanese rapidly began to recognize, and to seize, opportunities for initial commercial expansion into the southwestern Pacific. These same commercial footholds gradually became strategic interests as well. In the pre–World War I period, the influence of the Japanese in the Pacific islands was much greater than their numbers might suggest. By mid-1913, there were fifty-six Japanese in Palau and the Western Carolines and about fifty-one in the Marianas. However, "from the time of their commercial establishment in the Marianas in the late 1890's, the Japanese practically monopolized the foreign trade of the region. . . . The Japanese control of the Marianas trade declined somewhat in later years; nevertheless, it was so nearly complete that the Pagan-Gesellschaft, (a German trading firm), under German government sponsorship had no choice but to ship all of its copra to Yokohama. . . . " So wrote the American governor general to his superiors in Washington (U.S., Dept. of Navy, Office of Chief of Naval Operations 1944b:29). What became rapidly true for the Marianas became even more true for Guam. In June 1905, the American governor general noted that there only forty Japanese on Guam, but at the same time he reported to Washington:

> The absence of a line of freight-carrying craft between San Francisco, Guam and Manila throws all the trade with this island into the hands of the Japanese. They have established stores, regular lines of schooners, practically monopolize trade and fix prices. Under these conditions, living expenses for natives are cruelly high. (U.S., Dept. of Navy 1905:7)

In 1908, the governor general wrote to his superiors: "Practically all the trade of Guam is in the hands of the Japanese, who are generally, gradually, acquiring commercial mastery by buying up all the choice lands of the island" (U.S. Dept. of Navy 1908:23).

It was only to be expected that a negative U.S. reaction was to follow. By 1915, the United States had succeeded in almost completely freezing out Japan from her territory of Guam. Japan, in turn, began to recognize that she would have to protect her commercial interests by political and military means.

By 1914, evidence points to the fact that Japan's leaders had definite plans for Japan's expansion into the Pacific. Japan's government took immediate advantage of the unique and immense opportunity offered by World War I, which permitted Japan to launch a diplomatic and military offensive that would extend and consolidate Japan's interests in East Asia and the Pacific.

Japan saw from the beginning of the twentieth century that she would have to command a dominant influence in the western Pacific if she were to become the dominant power in East Asia, a role to which she clearly aspired from 1895 onward. In World War I, the German Western Pacific Islands were occupied by Japan rapidly and with no resistance. Between 9 and 14 October 1914, Japanese naval forces occupied Kusaie, Ponape, Truk, Palau, and Angaur. On 14 October, a Japanese battleship seized Saipan. From that moment on, all vessels either entering or leaving the islands were under the jurisdiction of the Japanese Ministry of the Navy or its designated representative. From that moment on, nothing could be done without the permission of the Japanese military. The rapid occupation of these islands came as somewhat of a shock to the United States and, even more, to Britain. England had become apprehensive about what the Japanese might do in that area, and thus tried to place restraints on Japan. For example, on 12 September 1914, the British ambassador in Tokyo informed the Japanese government that before long Australian forces would be dispatched to occupy Yap and Nauru, and he hoped that the activities of the Australians would not conflict with those of the Japanese (Shikishima Mamokusuke 1957:404). Although the Japanese government did discuss a joint occupation with other Allied nations, nothing came of it. On 1 December 1914, the Japanese government informed the Allied powers that Japan had made a considerable contribution to the war effort and that the Japanese people felt that they should be duly rewarded. Needless to say, the reward that Japan had in mind was the permanent acquisition of the former German islands in the Pacific. It is clear that the Japanese leaders in 1914 used World War I to take control of areas in the Pacific for economic and population-pressure reasons. As far as the islands are concerned, the Japanese efforts can be viewed as two interrelated stages. The first was during August and September 1914, and led eventually to Japan's military intervention in the islands. The second stage, which developed after November 1914, took place under different circumstances because hostilities ceased after that date in East Asia. Japan was under no military pressure at the time, and her policies were designed to secure by written agreement what she had been unable to gain in the first few months of the war. This second stage lasted essentially until 1922 when a treaty was signed with the United States over German islands north of the equator.

In 1914, the headquarters of the Japanese military government was established on Summer Island (Natsu Shima). In December of that year, Saipan, Palau, Truk, and Ponape were designated as civil government districts. The Japanese government appointed advisers who would assist the commanding officers of the temporary defense garrisons and who would have jurisdiction over all civil affairs. Detachments of defense troops were stationed on these four islands as well as on Yap, Jaluit, and Angaur. Each of these civil government districts was under the control of Japanese naval officers who had ultimate authority; the adviser appointed by the civil government was nothing more than a secretary. From 1914 to 1922, the development was one in which the character of the Japanese administration in the islands changed from a predominately military one to a civilian one. This development culminated in the establishment in March 1922 of the South Seas Bureau. In general, one can conclude that between 1914 and 1922 the Japanese maintained as much as possible the German system of administration that existed when Japan took over the islands. It was not until 1922 that the administration of the islands began to show a distinctively Japanese flavor. But even then, the Japanese initially were rather careful not to introduce too many changes that they thought to be harmful to the various island cultures. However, the primary change that they eventually did introduce was one of taxes.

It is clear that the administrative and financial measures that the Japanese enacted, such as the appointment of native officials and the collection of a poll tax, are of critical importance. Both acts meant that the Japanese had in fact arrived to govern these islands and to derive the maximum benefits from them for the empire. The poll tax levy affected the livelihood of the islanders, particularly because the levy was in coconuts, which were a staple food on many islands. The appointment of indigenous officials struck at the very heart of traditional patterns of leadership and political power in the islands. The Japanese intent in their mandated islands seems to have been to administer them with a minimum of expense and a maximum of benefit for Japan. There supposedly existed an international control of these Japanese activities, and the League of Nations did act as a guardian, if a remote one, until 1932. However, after that the Japanese regarded any outside interference and pressure as an affront to the integrity of the Japanese empire.

As now, when the difficulties of the Trust Territory political status focus on the letter and spirit of the United Nations Strategic Trust agreement with the United States, then the problems with Japan arose from the spirit implied in Article 257, paragraph 2, of the Treaty of Versailles, whereby all property and possessions belonging to Germany in what is now the U.S. Trust Territory were ceded to Japan. Article II specified that the mandated islands were to be governed as "an integral portion of the Empire of Japan," and that the Japanese government could "apply the laws of the Empire of Japan to the territory, subject to such local modifications as circumstances may require." And circumstances soon did require Japanese measures.

The Japanese government placed all lands and possessions in the islands under the jurisdiction of a National Resources Law (Kokuyūzaisanhō). With the exception of the land and possessions to which the German government had formal title in the islands, neither the Treaty of Versailles nor the mandate from the council of the League of Nations conferred the right of ownership of either land or possessions in the islands; and the government of Japan was supposed to acquire ownership through purchase, donation, or application of legal principles that conveyed ownership without the necessary purchase. Nevertheless, the Japanese government started with the principle that the land transferred to Japan in its capacity of mandatory was "land which *ipso facto* belongs to the state by virtue of the principle that all real property without owner belongs to a state." This concept was as meaningless in the traditional Micronesian social ethic as was the Japanese "legal" approach to the question of private and public property. In 1914, it was virtually impossible to determine land ownership rights by any modern Japanese or Western practice because the Germans had conducted land surveys only on Saipan and Ponape. The records were incomplete, and due to the war many had been lost or had vanished. In addition, indigenous land was owned on both a communal and an individual basis. Then, as in instances now, this situation was aggravated by the fact that the islanders maintained no written records of land ownership; claims to land were based on oral testimony or tribal customs, or both.

If today's cries in the Trust Territory as to land ownership and land-leasing to the United States government for civil or military use are heard, the Japanese administration provided a shining example of how a colonial government operates. The South Seas Bureau followed a policy of leasing land to private interests with the overt understanding that the land would be developed in keeping with the overall economic planning of the Japanese administration. Most of the land was leased to the Nanyō Bōeki Kaisha and the Nanyō Kōhatsu Kaisha. If Yanaihara is correct, the land leased to these two companies totaled 52,740 acres (Yanaihara Tadao 1935:422). Not only does this amount to about one-third of all the land that the Japanese government claimed to own in March 1932, but it also comes to a little less than one-third of the total surface area of arable land in the islands, which the Japanese government estimated as about 172,900 acres (p. 281). In fairness, it must be noted that from all indications it is reasonable to assume that the South Seas Bureau did not pursue general land ownership policies in the mandated islands that were detrimental to the interests of the indigenous population. Both land surveys and land sales and leasing were carefully supervised. It is to the credit of the Japanese administration that laws were passed and observed protecting natives from being exploited in private land sales. But perhaps even more important is the fact that, from all indications, land development was carefully nurtured by the Japanese with the result that by 1932 about two-thirds of all arable land in the islands was under some cultivation.

The Japanese did not intend, or attempt, to introduce the islands and their peoples into the mainstream of modern economic development. Nevertheless, the fact remains that the extent to which a cash-currency economy developed and the amount of investment capital that found its way into the islands were much greater in proportion than had been the case under either the Spanish or the Germans. This was true in both a quantitative and qualitative sense; qualitatively because the Japanese government financed a program of agricultural and commercial subsidies, land surveys, welfare programs, and agricultural research to name but a few. In short, in contrast to the Spanish and the Germans, the Japanese introduced programs of economic development similar to those that are sponsored today by the "have" nations in the developing nations around the world.

What effect did a cash economy and investment capital and the military build-up efforts have in the islands? Did Japanese economic and military development disrupt native social, political and economic institutions? The answer obviously is a definite yes. Perhaps initially, the effects were not cataclysmic or traumatic. Islanders had little demand for cash to satisfy either their daily needs or the demands placed on them by the Japanese administration. At first, when the Japanese did introduce stores, entertainment establishments and other cash-consuming facilities, it seems unlikely that there existed a great desire or need on the part of the islanders to acquire either these goods or services. Nevertheless, as time went on the aspirations, tastes, and thus needs of the population increased substantially. Barter for a considerable period of time was the system of exchange of goods and services that the Japanese relied on. Yanaihara has described this system to us by observing that so prevalent was the use of a barter system between different islanders, and between islanders and Japanese, that the Japanese administration maintained figures on the purchasing power of the indigenous population in terms of coconuts.

However, regardless of all these Japanese commercial and administrative measures, it can be said that neither was the Japanese political system in the islands truly oppressive, nor was the commercial value of the Pacific mandate to Japan ever very great. And yet—the Japanese did grow most fond of their possessions in the Pacific. Some have argued that, with few exceptions, no administrative policies implemented by the Japanese caused fundamental changes in native political or social patterns. And though it cannot be denied that the Japanese did have an economic impact on the indigenous economy, some persist in saying that there is no evidence to indicate that this impact was profound or detrimental to the interests of the islanders. Yet, indigenous currency was gradually replaced by Japanese currency, although it is true that the consuming power of the local population remained very limited and their purchasing power was never very great. Nevertheless, the presence of Japanese goods, now as then, has and had an adverse effect on native production. It is probably somewhat of an understatement when we say that, in all matters related to economics and politics in the islands, the Japanese administration was characterized by caution, careful planning, and a considerable degree of thoroughness.

Since education eventually came to play such a great role in binding the islanders to Japan, it is worthwhile to consider how some Japanese saw the islanders.

> How about the life of black men and barbarian women who are glaring at each other under the trees in the hot equatorial sun? Eating natural fruit with great relish, sleeping when bored, eating whenever hungry, dancing wildly in the moonlight on the white beach, dreaming of pleasures under the coconut tree—this is all they do. . . . Human nature of the natives throughout the islands is very lazy and only a few engage in productive work. (Nanyō Kenkyū Kai 1934)

Or, to cite from this same source:

> They have a tendency to go wild when drinking, although officially drinking is prohibited. Nevertheless, drinking is their favorite thing, and even women drink large amounts without getting drunk. Because their life is extremely simple and primitive, it is needless to say that their thought is also childish. They do not possess any desire or spirit for self improvement nor any thought for diligence. Their pleasures are eating, dancing, and satisfying their sexual desires. . . . (Nanyō Kenkyū Kai 1934)

Another Japanese source seems to indicate that acculturation did make an impact:

> Recently (1939) the islanders realize the value of Japanese policies and they contribute money for the national defense. Some Chamorros enjoy a high style of living, some of them even have a piano at home. On the other hand the *kanakas* are still poor, but even though in their poverty they still contribute money for the national defense effort having saved a few yen from their income. They visit the shrine to pray for good luck and long life to the [Japanese] military. They hoist the Japanese flag on holidays and sing marching songs. They realize that they are governed in the name of the Emperor, and some request to join the Japanese military forces. This allows us to think that we have made friends. (Domoto Teiichi 1940:47)

In terms of the lingering Japanese influence on thought, and the overt use of the Japanese language by the older generation in districts like Palau, Yap, Saipan, and Ponape, one must necessarily turn to the system of education the Japanese administration introduced and then efficiently implemented. This effort by the Japanese represented a drastic departure from what the Germans had done in their administration. As the Japanese navy occupied the islands, the German missionaries, who had been almost exclusively responsible for education, were gradually expelled. At first, to compensate for the resulting void in education, the officials of the navy and the few administrators of the Nanyō Boeki Kaisha residing in the islands, assumed the responsibility of educating the natives and the

Japanese children. The native children were given instruction in the Japanese language, singing, and arithmetic. This situation continued until December 1915, when regulations were established for an islands-wide elementary school system. Six *shogakkō* (elementary schools) were established, one each on Truk, Saipan, Yap, Palau, Ponape, and Jaluit. Island children between the ages of eight and twelve were permitted to enroll and were then given four years of education. They were taught Japanese, ethics, and skills or handicrafts useful in everyday life.

The Japanese understood from a very early point in their mandate that the necessity of superimposing a *lingua franca* upon all islanders was one of the most important single steps of their administration and was absolutely crucial to the development of an overall sound system of education. The Japanese in doing so offered essentially the same type of education as the Germans (traditional academic subjects as well as vocational training) but on a much larger and more efficient scale. However, it is obvious that the impact of Japan's educational policies was far greater than that of the Germans.

As these educational efforts developed indigenous human resources in the islands, so for Japan the islands of the western Pacific soon became more than "additional territories for surplus population" from the four home islands: they became an important part of the strategic power nucleus from which Japan was able, by 1941, to challenge the two Pacific superpowers—Britain and the United States.

Strategies of World War II

In East Asia, World War II lasted for three years and eight months, from December 1941 when Pearl Harbor was air-attacked to August 1945 when Japan was atom-bombed. There were four principal contestants, the United States, Japan, China, and Britain. Britain was eliminated fairly early, her rapid defeat in the Pacific proving how well and effectively Japan had created her strategic area interests in conjunction with her economic policies. China remained, for all practical purposes a dependant of the Allies, and the Chinese theater of operations—for the Japanese—remained static from 1940 to 1945. Thus, the main contestants were Japan and the United States.

World War II was perhaps the last large-scale conflict not restricted or inhibited by any consideration, and was a straight contest for victory or defeat. Two general phases are clear: one, the period of ascendency of Japan, and two, the period of decline from this superiority and the rise (and rebounding) of the United States after Pearl Harbor. Japanese essential strategy was something like this: to retain Korea and parts of China already conquered; to conquer the chain of islands from Japan to the East Indies and occupy Burma and Indo-China, the latter seized from France; to occupy the Malay Peninsula and neutralize Thailand; to establish inner and outer defense lines in the Pacific; to cut off the United States from her Western allies by controlling communications between the Indian and Pacific oceans. Pearl Harbor was bombed, and the American naval and air fleets there were immobilized. From the Kurile islands to Wake to the Gilberts stretched an outer defense line nearly 4,000 miles east of Japan. Simultaneously, a multi-pronged *Blitzkrieg* followed southward by land, sea, and air forces. Hongkong, Singapore, and Malaya fell by February 1942, the Philippines and parts of Burma by May 1942, and the East Indies by June 1942; along with them also fell a number of small islands necessary to secure communication with the home islands of Japan. Thus was established a Japanese inner defense line through the Marianas, Guam, Yap, Palau, and down to the East Indies.

Ironically enough, precisely when Japan appeared invincible, at the height of her conquests, she headed for decline. The battles of the Coral Sea and Midway were to become the prelude to the American offensive eventually leading to the defeat of Japan.

The American strategy was as follows: to break the outer Japanese defense line (1) through the Central Pacific by a three-pronged attack across Wake, the Gilberts, and the Marshalls, and (2) through a flank across the Coral Islands and the Solomons. New Guinea was retaken in 1943, the Philippines in 1944, and with the simultaneous fall of the adjacent chain of islands, the Japanese inner defense line also was broken up.

Pacific Patterns

It has been suggested, and most likely correctly so, that one of the most significant changes brought about by World War II is the emergence of what may be called the Pacific era of world politics just as the preceeding era has been described as the European era.

For something like 400 years, beginning about 1498, it was the nations of Western Europe bordering on the Atlantic who set the course of world history. Their wars, their ambitions, and their decisions constituted world politics and world history. Now, however, the center of political gravity may well have shifted to the Pacific. In the Pacific region, there is, for the first time in human history, a spectacular meeting of the current superpowers of the world. Four of the world's six continents—or five, if one regards Europe as a geographical extension of Asia—rim the Pacific and make up in political numbers three-fourths of the world population. The two superpowers, the United States and the Soviet Union, come capriciously close to one another in the Pacific across the Bering Strait. In fact, during winter, even the narrow strait vanishes. The Pacific is now also becoming the birthplace of yet two other potential superpowers, Japan and the People's Republic of China. And then, if we can believe Herman Kahn, the twenty-first century will be the Japanese century (Kahn 1970).

This impressive assemblage of nations, most of them young and dynamic, are each rediscovering their inherent strength. Thus, dramatic and momentous confrontations can easily be expected during the remaining years of this century. Potentialities for disastrous conflicts in the Pacific—or for a hopeful reshaping of the world from the Pacific—now open. In a tradition-bound way, three of the four continents—Australia, North America, and South America—are extensions of Europe. But these extensions are those of an essentially exhausted Europe, even though the recovery rate and the developments within the Common Market nations may belie this fact. It is in the Pacific where we find today the greatest potential concentration of industrial and military power. If the errors and miscalculations of past European power politics are repeated in the "Era of the Pacific," then it could well mean the end of all superpowers.

The Pacific is larger than the whole land surface of the globe. Its immensity creates special problems of strategy. Distance gives protection but it also creates surprises, as Pearl Harbor amply illustrated. The United States Navy in the 1940s with mobility and flexibility created a clear revolution in naval strategy if we compare this strategy with the British traditions of fixed bases and fighting always relatively close to land. In missile terms, the Pacific makes the nuclear, as well as the traditional, submarine a much smaller needle in a much bigger haystack. In military terms—as well as in commerce—it calls for larger and faster ships.

Political Development in Micronesia

The east coast of Asia is screened by three large island nations—Japan, the Philippines, and Indonesia—in whose history the sea has continued to play a major part and whose national interests have a definite maritime dimension. In contrast, the scattered islands of Micronesia, Melanesia, and Polynesia assume significance primarily because of their communications facilities and for the strategic opportunities they afford to other powers for distant defense (as for Japan in World War II), or for threats of distant offensives. Micronesia, now a Strategic Trust Territory administered by the United States, is spread over an area of 300,000 square miles, which is an area as large as that of the United States. Within this vastness, the some 2,140 islands have a combined population of about 100,000 settled in the 100 or so largest islands. These islands for the United States represent a projection of Asia into the Pacific and conversely, as American strategy in the Pacific during World War II illustrated, an island line of approach to Asia as well. Most important today is the fact that except between the Aleutian and the Hawaiian islands—the area through which the Japanese Navy moved in 1941-42—and between the Hawaiian Islands and Marquesas to the west and the coast of the Americas to the east, there is no channel of unobserved and unobstructed water between Asia and America.

Pacific Strategies and the Future

The United States, it is clear today, is geographically a Pacific power. Unfortunately, however, especially after Vietnam, we are perhaps not ready psychologically to accept this fact. Although the width of the Pacific between the U.S. West Coast and Japan or China may suggest that the Pacific separates America from Asia, it is not so. From Alaska, the Soviet Union in Asia is visible at the peak of the Pacific arch, as we have pointed out, across the Bering Strait. The top of the chain of Aleutian islands, which reaches as far west as New Zealand does, is but 600 miles from Soviet Kamchatka and 1,500 miles from Japan, and the fiftieth state, Hawaii, extends the United States some 2,900 miles into the Pacific. By including the territory of Guam, surely America is now more than ever a Pacific rather than an Atlantic or Mediterranean power. The Atlantic equivalent to Hawaii would be the Azores, and the closest the United States comes to Europe, at best, is 1,800 miles. The past dies slowly, and many American eyes and minds remain turned to Europe.

South America's interest in, and impact on, the Pacific in strategy, in commerce, and in fishing is still growing and is still, usually, vastly underestimated. So is Central America an essential element of the emerging Pacific pattern. But it is the Soviet Union, the People's Republic of China, and Japan that loom largest as Pacific superpowers just over the horizon. Russia is in essence an Asian state with more Asian real estate than any other Asian country. The Soviet Union has the longest Pacific coastline of any nation, stretching some 12,000 miles. Vladivostok today is one of the largest and most important Soviet naval bases and ports. It is the growing and expanding center of a large industrial area adjacent to industrial Japan and industrial Manchuria and similar to the Ruhr in Europe. Although most recently Vietnam has proved to overshadow most of our other Asia-oriented decisions, it should be clear that the American strategic interest remains basically in the safety and physical presence in her territories and her trade. This holds even more true in the 1970s, when the Pacific is no longer pacific, and the Far East is no longer far. The question today again emerges, How far beyond California and Hawaii should the United States extend herself? The problem of Micronesia and demilitarization of that vast territory is psychologically as important for the United States as it is politically important to the six districts of Micronesia. These islands will continue, as in the past, to reflect the changing winds of power. We would do well to remember, for example, that the Marshall Islands were explored by the British, mapped by the Russians, influenced by the Spanish, annexed by the Germans, seized by the Japanese, and conquered by the Americans. Beyond Guam, today, there remain American forces in the Philippines, Taiwan, Vietnam, Korea, and Japan, reflecting American assumption of responsibilities based on concepts of ideological and strategic necessity as a world power.

With shifting power patterns in the Pacific, the question as to the past unchallengable U.S. worldwide naval power is becoming important. The United States has deployed still two of its fleets in the area: the First in the eastern Pacific, and the Seventh in the western Pacific. Three of its air forces, with a total strength of over 100,000 men, are stationed in the Pacific area: the Fifth with bases in Japan, Korea, and Okinawa; the Twelfth in the Philippines, with responsibility for Thailand and Taiwan; and the Seventh operating in Vietnam.

Whereas up to 1945 the great challenge to American security in the Pacific came primarily from Japan, the problem now along the

Asian coastline of the Pacific stems as well from the growing power of the Soviet Union and the People's Republic of China, both seeking their fulfillment of interest in the Pacific–Indian Ocean area.

President Nixon's Guam doctrine has made it clear that the United States intends to withdraw the range and dimensions of her power. While America, her homeland intact, was expansive after World War II in a surge of power and idealism, Russia, her homeland battered, was defensive. She was defensive in both the re-creation of her power and the reassertion of her ideology. She has recovered, as have Japan and China, from the ravages of war, and all four powers are now competing for an area where hitherto only Japan and the United States had any possible conflicts that might result in confrontation. As the United States withdraws and an increasingly Asian pattern of power emerges in the western Pacific, a crucial new role falls to Japan. Across the Yellow and the East China seas, Japan faces industrial North China and Manchuria and the industrial Soviet Far East. We should remember that Shanghai is only 600 miles from Kagoshina; and easy access to Vladivostok is had through the 200-mile-wide Straits of Korea.

Japan today is the one Asian state that is economically a fully developed country. She is the one Asian example of having been a great power in her own modern history. With a 100 million–plus population, she is the world's seventh largest nation, the third largest power by GNP, and the fourth greatest exporter. She possesses today a nuclear missile potential that could quickly be mobilized. Her GNP of $43 billion in the early 1970s is estimated to reach $418 billion by 1975 (Kahn 1970:4). However, to maintain that past dazzling pace of development, she must maintain an uninterrupted trade in the Pacific and keep her sea lanes open through the Pacific and the Indian Ocean. Hence, Japan has remained compulsively maritime in her thinking; and although her population is less than 3 percent of the world's, her imports in the late 1960s were 6.2 percent of the world's total and are still rising, and her exports are 5.8 percent of the world's and still rising. Lacking raw materials, fuels, and food, she must continue to search for them overseas. Sixty percent–plus of her energy requirements are supplied by petroleum fuels, and the figures are estimated to grow to 75 percent by 1975. Ninety per cent of her crude oil comes from West Asia. Japan's iron ore comes from the United States, Canada, Australia, and India, and she is the largest buyer of Australian wool. In fishing, Japan's catch is second to none, and fishing remains a major concern for both internal consumption and for export. Japan took the lead from

Britain in 1955 in shipbuilding, and her production in the early 1970s is six times greater. As a shipowner, she is third to the United Kingdom and Liberia, and she originates over 15 percent of all ocean-going traffic of the world. For a United States concerned with threats from the sea, and China and Russia expanding toward and across the sea, Japan already plays, and will continue increasingly to play, a unique strategic role. Her strategic and economic strengths in friendship or hostility, in cooperation or competition, cannot and certainly should not be ignored.

By the early 1970s, Japan's self-defense forces no longer uniquely point merely to self-defense. Her third Five Year Plan (1967–71) provided for the non-nuclear missile defense of her whole territory—under the nuclear umbrella provided by the United States. Her armed forces now number about 250,000 men, including twelve infantry and one armored divisions, a navy with eight submarines and 23 destroyers, and an air force of some 570 combat aircraft. The recent cruise by four Japanese destroyers from Australia to India was but a fair reminder of Japan's new Pacific naval presence.

On 9 October 1972, Prime Minister Tanaka ended two years' of debate within the Japanese government and won his cabinet's approval for a five-year, $16.558 billion plan to more than double Japan's defense spending. The $16.558 billion plan, which provides pay boosts over the period through fiscal year 1976, is 2.2 times as much as the amount allocated in the last five-year buildup that ended 31 March 1972. It will add two new Nike antiaircraft battalions, 280 tanks, 154 heliocopters, 54 warships with a total tonnage of 69,600 tons, 92 naval planes, and 211 air force craft. Under the new plan, Japan will domestically build revised versions of the FTS-2 aircraft as well as other naval and ground support planes hitherto imported from the United States.

Japan's growing political independence from the United States, and its growing independence of policy generally, invites comparison with her prewar policies but with one great difference: the Soviet Union and the People's Republic are vastly stronger nations than they were in the late 1930s. The question that emerges clearly is coupled to the Japanese potential to dominate the Pacific in order to ensure her national interests.

Micronesia, the United States, and the Future

Paul Burlin, a member of the Committee of Concerned Asian Scholars, wrote in November 1971:

> During the second week in October, in secrecy, the United States made another strategic move in support of its Pacific Rim policy. The move came during the third round of political status negotiations between the United States and Micronesia. During the talks, the United States presented, for the first time, specific plans for the military use of the Micronesian islands. Although these plans came as no surprise to the Micronesians, or to anyone else familiar with the situation there, this late U.S. move represents the culmination of a long series of actions, all of which have violated the rights of the Micronesian people, and all serve the ends of the U.S. imperialism. (Burlin 1971:6-7)

Although the question of Micronesian independence and political status has not generated a burst of headlines around the world, the problem remains one of the United States' essential security commitments in the Pacific. If the United States is to respond to any eventual challenges from the Soviet Union, the People's Republic, or Japan, she can not do otherwise than to maintain her physical and strategic presence in the western Pacific. Furthermore, if she is to honor her nuclear umbrella commitments to Japan, likewise, she must maintain her strategic presence in this area. The tragedy of Micronesia—and this writer would challenge that at the present time there exists an entity that can truly be called Micronesia—then and now, is the fact that none of the six districts can possibly hope to become a viable, self-sustaining, independent entity. The location across the world's Pacific shipping, communication, and aviation lanes means that the islands continue to preserve their strategic importance. Whereas for the past 27 years the doctrine of "strategic denial" served the interests of the United States, the reemergence of Japan as a Pacific superpower, and as the dominant economic power of the area, brought about an end to the essentially passive occupation of Micronesia by the United States. It is thus not only the momentum of Micronesian independence feelings that is pushing toward a change in Micronesian political status, but it is also the reemergence of Japan's economic domination of Micronesia that is providing momentum to changed political status aspirations.

The policy of the United States over the years has been to release and return land to the Trust Territory government.

All Department of Defense land, in fact, has been returned in the Palau, Truk, and Yap districts. In the Marshall Islands, the United States government, through the Department of Defense, holds 3,031.08 acres. In the Marianas, the United States holds 8,881.95 acres of "military retention" land on Tinian and 4,943.31

acres on Saipan, for a total of 13,825.26 acres. The total land in use or reserved by the United States military represents 3.8 of the total land in the Trust Territory (President's Personal Representative for Micronesian Status Negotiations 1971:25–26).

In the Hana (Hawaii) meetings of 4–12 October 1971, the United States proposed to forgo the exercise of eminent domain. This means that henceforth any strategic land requirements in Micronesia would be negotiated for on a quite different basis than has hitherto been the case. Furthermore, the Hana meetings established that the United States would have no defense needs for land in the Yap, Ponape, or Truk districts (President's Personal Representative for Micronesian Status Negotiations 1971:31–39). The primary new strategic planning seems to be focused on the island of Tinian in the Marianas and on the District of Palau.

Micronesian Patterns: The Present

The nostalgia for the Japanese in most of the six districts has meant in the past that economic development has been tied to the return of Japanese economic presence and the non-economic developmental spirit of the Trust Territory governmental machinery.

Today's Japanese presence is one that is felt primarily through Japanese things. Much of Micronesia's staple diet, other than foods like taro, coconuts, yams, and cassava (manioc), is tied invariably to the dietary preferences of Japan. One has only to look at the inventory of a grocery store, where Japanese canned goods, Japanese cookies, and Japanese beer abound. What would Micronesian feet be like without the "zori"? And what would Palauan music sound like without the heavy Japanese influence? And although Micronesian roads are not made either for Japanese-style traffic or Japanese cars, nevertheless it is the Japanese automobile industry that furnishes the means of transport for most of Micronesia. In Ngerchelong (Palau), there may not be any electricity, and there may be no roads, but nevertheless, the village (1972) does have three Hondas. Wherever there is electricity, rice is being cooked in Japanese rice cookers; and wherever pots and pans are being sold, the majority of these kitchen implements come from Japan. The outboard engines may be Evinrudes and Johnsons, but the fiberglass boat itself, more often than not, comes from Japan. The list of Japan-made material goods is indeed vast. But perhaps more important is the influence that Japan still holds on the life style of much of Micronesia. Japanese today, twenty-seven years after World War II, is still the *lingua franca* among Micronesians over thirty-five or forty years old. Japanese *kana* is still used by some for written communication. And in terms of the American presence, the Japanese impact through their educational system, as was pointed out previously, is still extensive. One has the feeling that a great number of Micronesians think of the Japanese era as one in which Micronesia was being developed and modernized. In Palau, for example, Japanese times meant more than a municipality of Koror with some 30,000 people, with a streetcar, paved roads, a geisha house, restaurants, and a public park. We must necessarily presume that most of these facilities were primarily for the Japanese rather than the Micronesians, and yet, these developments apparently represented progress with which the Micronesians could identify and that served as a model for their own achievements and aspirations. In the minds of many Micronesians, the Japanese period represented one in which they were slowly pulled into the modern world. When speaking with them, one easily gains the impression that Micronesians, perhaps, intentionally overlook that the Japanese made use of their land for Japanese purposes and used their labor essentially for Japanese objectives. They fortified the islands for the defense of Japan, and they exploited the natural resources for the improvement of the Japanese standard of living. And yet when one has said all this, one still feels that in many ways the Japanese occupation "succeeded" where the American presence has not caught the imagination of the people in a similar way, and thus has not "succeeded."

To anyone who has recently lived in Micronesia, the problem of "success" in administration becomes a fascinating comparison between the accomplishments of Germany, Japan, and the United States. America has, indeed, attempted to introduce a reasonably sophisticated system of education, the impact of which has not been felt in terms of true economic development. It has introduced a system of public health that, even at worst, still favorably compares with what the Japanese had done. It is in the use of land and large-scale agricultural entrepreneurship that Americans have not even approached the Japanese after nearly three decades. But then, such agricultural undertakings are negated by the newfound sense of land ownership among Micronesians. If one compares the effectiveness of colonial powers, one rapidly comes to the conclusion that the United States is not a very effective colonial power. We have created in Micronesia, and especially among the young Micronesians, individuals who are politically more sophisticated and more opportunistic than their elders. The United States has introduced a more equitable system of law and political participation than anything the Japanese did. The Germans ruled, the Japanese governed and ruled. Americans administer. This point was made clear when a Micronesian spoke of the three periods, i.e., the German, Japanese, and the American, by saying that the Micronesians feared the Germans, but they worked for them; respected and feared the Japanese, and did not like them, but worked for them; and that they liked the Americans, but neither feared nor respected them, and no longer necessarily want to work for them. One could, perhaps, make a very good case with the fact that current political unrest and dissatisfaction with the American administration is but a sign that America has been successful in teaching the Micronesians to think and act for themselves, has raised their aspirations, and has unfulfilled many of their wants. Japan's ghost will not disappear, and Japan's presence in Micronesia will depend very much on the unwillingness of the United States to remain a power in the Pacific, as much as on the nostalgic memories of Micronesians for their past masters.

A Reminder for the Future

When the cry is raised that only an independent Micronesia can hope for an even modest economic takeoff, the cry usually has been based on a somewhat wishful thought that if the United States was not ready to do something, then Japan's new economic presence would surely compensate for the American inactivity. On the other hand, it would be untrue to state unequivocally that all Micronesians reject a renewed United States military presence. For example, the *Micronesian Star* in December 1971 headlined an article with "Tinian People Favor Military One Hundred Per Cent."

The controversies regarding Micronesian independence, Micronesian future political status, and Micronesian strategic importance will continue to occupy our minds. Nevertheless, it remains clear that future Micronesian strategic considerations will influence the results of future United States–Japanese relations and future U.S. security policies with regard to the Soviet Union and the People's Republic of China. We may argue as to a specific instance of a specific U.S. presence on a specific island. But we can probably argue much less successfully for any non-U.S. presence, military or otherwise, or for any neutralization of Micronesia. Recognition of the strategic importance of Micronesia was, after all, the primary reason for the creation of the U.N. Strategic Trusteeship under U.S. administration. That trust was, in effect, confirmation—positive or negative—by all U.N. members of the military importance of these islands to the United States.

Joe Murphy and others have suggested that the time is late. But despite the neglect and the mistakes of the past, and despite the utopian, wishful thinking by some, and despite the nostalgia for Japan and Japanese goods by many Micronesians, a solution satisfying to both Micronesians and Americans must—and still can—be found.

1. An excellent historical account of the Japanese in the Pacific is contained in D. C. Purcell, Jr.'s *Japanese Expansion in the South Pacific, 1890-1935.*

2. Yoshino Sakuzo, *Nanyō*, p. 23 (East Caroline Islands). All quotations from Japanese sources have been translated by the author.

16

Neutralization of Pacific Island States: A Proposal

Eugene B. Mihaly

Admiral Mahan would have been pleased.[1] More than three-quarters of a century have lapsed since the peak of the admiral's influence on the strategic practices of nations. Two major wars and a host of small ones are memories. Air power and a plethora of new military technologies have transfigured the conduct of war. Notwithstanding all that, and the equally profound changes in the relations between nations, today's principal military powers are currently engaged in a naval arms race, in one ocean, worthy of Mahan and the Edwardians. They are initiating a similar race in a second ocean and are inexorably moving toward such a race in a third.

This chapter focuses on the third area, the Pacific. It proposes a policy of neutralization to minimize the adverse effects of a competition for naval superiority there on those likely to pay the most dearly for it—the small independent and semi-independent states (existing and nascent) of the South and western Pacific. The proposal, thus, is inherently modest. It attempts to treat symptoms, not the malady itself. The assumption here is that a new naval competition in the Pacific almost certainly will not be stopped, not that that competition cannot or should not be stopped.

The Malaise

A few thoughts on the malaise itself may serve to justify the assumption and sketch in the background for the use of neutralization as treatment.

Naval arms (the term here refers to surface units only) races are triggered by largely the same fears, suspicions, and hopes for advantage that actuate arms races in general. There are, though, some elements that are particularly characteristic of naval arms races. The demonstration effect seems to play an especially large role: if they have it (a type of ship, a magnitude of fleet), it must be useful, so we should have it too. This sort of logic certainly underlies the Soviet-American naval competition in the Mediterranean. Granted, other factors come into play there: a desire on both parts to give muscle to diplomatic positions, to maximize influence on smaller powers' behavior, and to balance or neutralize the other's influence. When all that is entered in the ledger, however, the fact remains that surface forces have little credibility in a body of water that is small and can be easily bottled up at the only exit points, in which all vessels are easy to locate, and in which those vessels are sitting ducks for submarine, air, and missile attack. The Soviet Union built up its fleet because, in the last analysis, the United States was there. The United States and other NATO countries are now trying to counter because the Soviets are there.

The demonstration effect looks like it will have its day in the Indian Ocean soon. The once dominant Royal Navy is more or less gone. The Soviet Navy has a minimum of 14 vessels there. The United States, so far, has only two destroyers and a seaplane tender on permanent station. The British, with their vestigial presence and substantial oil interests in the Persian Gulf, have been, until recently, the most openly worried about this. This imbalance of forces is central to the official British rationale for the importance of the Simonstown base in South Africa (and as a reason why Britain cannot afford to offend the South Africans too much). Washington has made periodic statements that the growing Soviet fleet in the Indian Ocean is a problem. The admirals usually add in a stage whisper that they do not have the resources to do anything about it as long as Vietnam ties down the ships. This is probably so. The excursion of the U.S.S. *Enterprise* and escorts into the Indian Ocean during the Indo-Pakistan War, however, is a clear sign of things to come. As the small task force sailed back to the Pacific, the White House asserted that the Indian Ocean was strategically important and that therefore American units would be back in twelve to eighteen months. Simultaneously, there was a flap over the nature of the arrangement the United States had made with Bahrein for use of a naval facility (apparently we are tenants, but without commitments) and renewed publicity for the new U.S. "communications" facility in Diego Garcia, an island under the British flag to the south of India.[2] Again, the contenders will have a complex rationale for the race that all this portends. One wonders, though, how the various parties have managed so far. And what the ships will do to keep busy.

A Race in the Pacific

The picture in the Pacific is at once more inchoate and more complex. More is already going on; more complex political roles, it appears, will be assigned to the ships. But who is going to do what is unclear. The potential cast is large. The United States heads the list by dint of its current superiority in surface vessels, in support facilities, and probably in submarines. The Soviet Union is reputed to have a large submarine force and is building up its force of surface naval ships, scientific ships, and the ubiquitous trawlers. Japan has a small but growing navy. So, apparently, does China. In addition, Taiwan, Australia, New Zealand, and Canada have small but not insignificant fleets. Britain and France retain a few units in the Pacific.

To date, despite, and probably because of, the warfare in Vietnam, the Pacific has been strikingly quiet. The Seventh Fleet no longer patrols the Formosa Straits. The Royal Navy has sailed away, with appropriate pomp, from Singapore, leaving behind a few units to join the Australians and New Zealanders in a tripartite defense arrangement for a onetime linchpin of empire.

Recognition that the Chinese emperor exists, and that he is quite well clothed, has given formal standing to the long-obvious reality that there are more than two major powers in the Pacific and that the pattern of future international relations in the area is highly uncertain. One of the few outcomes that can be confidently expected is a naval arms race. The ingredients are there in abundance: uncertainty on a regional scale; uncertainty in the political futures of most of the littoral states; several major and a host of minor island nations in the area; substantial commercial links extant and more likely. The usual arguments for building up naval capacities will have more than the usual amount of supporting circumstantial evidence.

The buildup has, in fact, begun. Thus, Soviet maritime activity is on the increase: more submarine patrols, more commercial and scientific ships in Pacific waters; a stepped-up diplomatic campaign in the islands. Thus, the apparent expansion of the Chinese fleet. Thus, the increasingly voiciferous demand in Japan for a fleet adequate to the task of protecting Japan's foreign commerce (Mahan again). In the United States, the navy has been making the unsurprising case that surface fleets should be the backbone and a good part of the body of the American military presence in the western and South Pacific. The admirals argue that self-contained fleets will permit the United States to retain an adequate degree of influence in Asia, even if she has very limited land-based facilities in the area. The navy, in short, sees fleets serving as the basis for implementation of the Nixon Doctrine. Vietnam does not seem to have offered convincing evidence that naval units cannot do the job in limited war (or wars of liberation).

The future, in sum, has a boring inevitability about it. It can be summed up in one word: *more*—more ships, more predictions of doom by defense ministries, followed by more ships. Resource constraints may slow things down, but almost certainly will not halt or reverse the process. That will require some form of agreement. Given the number of actors on stage and the uncertainty they share about how to cope with each other; given the pace of progress in strategic arms limitation and the virtually total silence on the question of limiting naval forces in the one place where things are getting out of hand, the Mediterranean, it seems eminently reasonable to assume that we shall not see such an agreement for some time.

The Impact

The question then arises: Is a naval arms race in the Pacific necessarily disastrous? I doubt it—not, at least, for the participants. Arms races are always absurd, but, as Samuel Huntington has observed, they do not necessarily increase the likelihood of conflict and may, in some instances, reduce it. At a minimum, large quantities of resources will be expended by states that have other pressing requirements. The multiplication of weapons and targets in the area will increase the probability (though not by much) that a weapon will go off and a target hit. The diplomacy of the region will be complicated for the major powers by the introduction of an instrument that they must handle gingerly. But that could be the worst.

What about the spectators? How will they fare? The onlookers fall into two rough categories: states that are likely candidates for wars of liberation or limited wars; and states fortunate enough not to be in that bracket but likely to be asked to offer facilities to one or another of the competitors.

My focus is on the latter group. Of the former, it should suffice here to say that the government or the opposition in any country is likely to welcome naval superiority by that major power most likely to accord it assistance when the going gets rough. Governments may offer facilities to the naval powers or support the maintenance of existing ones; oppositions will dangle facilities as an inducement to likely supporters and organize against existing facilities of the regime's backers. The small states of the South and western Pacific are another story, for they have almost nothing to gain by all this, and a great deal to lose.

Naval task forces, their proponents tell us, can be self-sufficient these days. The quest for naval bases and access to harbors for naval vessels in the Mediterranean, the Indian Ocean, and the Pacific, however, illustrates that self-sufficiency is still severely limited. The further from a support facility a fleet operates, the greater the cost. The number of ships required to do any task rises: more ammunition ships to keep the guns loaded, more refrigerator ships to feed the fleet, more oilers, and so on; more warships to protect these unarmed vessels as they move back and forth from the home port to the fleet; more warships to keep the fleet up to strength while units are cycled back for routine maintenance and repairs. The greater the distance from a safe haven, moreover, the greater the vulnerability and the greater the need to expand the fleet to compensate for that vulnerability.

The Pacific islands are the logical locus for facilities that would serve to cut these costs. And the beginnings of the competition for naval supremacy have been paralleled by moves to acquire the facilities. Here again the United States starts off with a considerable lead. Even if the naval stations in the Philippines, Taiwan, and Japan are written off as ultimately unreliable, the United States is in a comfortable position by dint of a large facility in Guam, access to the fine harbor in American Samoa, and facilities in Australia that, it is safe to assume, can be expanded on request.

The Nixon administration proposed in 1971 that the United States retain an option to use several islands in the western Caroline Islands to support naval operations. The proposal is part of a larger package offered to the Congress of Micronesia in the course of negotiations on that Trust Territory's political future. These facilities in the Palau group, which lies 600 miles east of the Philippines, would be small but significant—at least in the calculus of the other naval powers.

The Soviet Union has been shopping for facilities in the Pacific. Its most prominent move so far has been an overture to the independent state of Western Samoa. The proposal—for access to the harbor at Apia with unspecified formal arrangements—was rejected by the Samoans, who have a healthy skepticism about close ties with any foreign powers other than New Zealand, which acts as their diplomatic agent abroad.

The independence rush in the Pacific, however, is just beginning. Today, only Western Samoa, Fiji, and Nauru are fully independent. New Guinea is scheduled for independence in late 1974 or early 1975. The future of Micronesia, the French territories (primarily Tahiti and New Caledonia), and a number of groups controlled by the United Kingdom, are yet to be resolved. It does appear certain, however, that there will shortly be a sizable number of independent states in the Pacific. With the exception of Nauru, all will be poor and will have very small populations and limited prospects for changing their economic situation without massive—in relative terms—external assistance. Per capita incomes are analogous to middle-income African states: in Western Samoa, it is roughly $120; in Fiji, a relatively prosperous state, $319 (1967); compare with Kenya at $208 (1968).[3] Resource development prospects are dim, at least until expensive exploration efforts give reason to think otherwise. For the moment, tourism is the best, nonmilitary, bet. Tourism, however, is a limited economic instrument and, if not planned well, can pose a serious threat to orderly social and cultural change.

The island states will not have much to offer in return for assistance. Political support from, say, Western Samoa will have marginal value to any major state. These small states will have only one commodity of value to offer to the great powers; that is, access to their land and harbors.

Is that prospect worth getting excited about? Military facilities are hardly ever a blessing, even on home territory, but they are not necessarily a notable problem. West Germany manages. So do Britain, Australia, and, perhaps, Egypt. But these are large states, and economically developed—with the exception of Egypt, where the impact of Russian facilities is still to be measured. The states of the Pacific on the other hand are incapable of absorbing a sizable foreign presence without severe economic and social—not to speak of political—dislocation. The Pacific islands have still not recovered entirely from the first foreign invasion of Bibles, syphilis, smallpox, and booze. A second invasion comprised of high wages their own economies could not match, payments for which they could find no substitute, and young men in sufficiently large numbers to raise hell with rather enviable patterns of social relations would make a shambles of a magnitude comparable to the nineteenth-century wave and a mockery of their independence.

Probable U. S. Reaction

Among the present and future great naval powers in the Pacific, the United States has the most to lose if events move in this direction. As the dominant power, it will undoubtedly feel compelled to take compensatory steps to offset any advantage gained by others through access to island facilities. Those steps could take a variety of forms—more aircraft carriers, more nuclear-powered vessels, floating bases—all of them expensive. As a longtime Pacific power, the United States will also feel called upon to use its diplomatic and financial resources to slow or reverse the process (post facto; the problem will probably go unnoticed at high-enough levels for preventive action in advance). This means we would be back in the business of trying to outbid the Soviets and others for allegiance, friendship, and the various other mirages pursued by the Soviets and the United States in Africa and Asia for more than twenty years.

This scenario assumes that the United States will, at a minimum, strive to retain parity in naval armaments in the Pacific. There are two sets of issues here: the first is determination of the posture that the United States will take in the Pacific; how much influence over events in Asia will the United States seek to retain? I shall not attempt to address myself to these questions. Suffice it to say here that any administration in Washington will have little choice but to play a major role; and that the United States is thus not likely to settle for naval parity, but will attempt to retain superiority.

Neutralization

The second set of issues is how to deal with the islands. In this case, there is a clear option open that, if picked up now, could retard the development of a naval arms race in the Pacific. That option is neutralization of the islands. The proximate aim is deceptively simple. The independent and quasi-independent states of the South and western Pacific would deny the use of their lands, airfields, and harbors to the military forces of any other states. At such time as other territories attained independence or a status close to independence, they too would adhere to the same policy. The means to attain this end are complex, but not extraordinarily so.

The United States could take the initiative and do the diplomatic groundwork to achieve the objective. Preferably, it would encourage one of the now independent states to carry the ball. The first step would be an agreement between Fiji, Western Samoa, Nauru, and the Cook Islands (which are in "Free Association" with New Zealand, a status that permits New Zealand to conduct the Cooks' defense but allows the Cooks to declare their independence at any time). The second step would be an effort to commit the colonial powers in the area—Britain, France, and the United States—to urge adherence to the agreement on their wards at the time of transfer of power. The third step would be to seek the support, preferably in the form of a guarantee, of the great powers. If the first and second steps are successfully carried out, a failure in this third area—which is quite likely—may not be critical.

It will be obvious that neutralization has the effect of freezing the status quo; and this favors the United States. If, therefore, the approach is to have any chance of success, the United States will necessarily have to make a gesture of more than a symbolic nature. The logical place to make it is in Micronesia. As noted earlier, the United States is now in the process of negotiating the political future of the Trust Territory. It has proposed that a self-governing Micronesia grant or lease the United States lands for military use in three of Micronesia's six districts. Specifically, the United States wants to retain the existing ABM test facility on Kwajalein in the Marshall Islands, to rebuild the large air complex on Tinian (from which the atomic bomb flights originated) in the Mariana Islands, and to reserve lands for navy and Marine Corps use in the Palau group. The neutralization approach will have a decent chance only if the United States withdraws this proposal and agrees to have Micronesia incorporated within the neutralized area.

The hardship this will impose on the United States is minimal. The ABM site exists, the other facilities are only gleams in the Pentagon's eyes. Because the former is a research and development installation, and because the economy of the Marshall Islands is heavily dependent on employment there, it might be prudent to work out a formula to phase Kwajalein out gradually over a period of, for example, five years—with the explicit understanding that no fighting units would be stationed on the atoll during that period. The ABM element of the 1972 Strategic Arms Limitation agreement with the USSR effectively eliminated a long-term role for Kwajalein as a research facility in any case. Kwajalein is quite far east, moreover, and the base has limited use for any other military purposes. The air base in Tinian would undoubtedly be a useful insurance policy against the possibility of attack upon the air complex on Guam, and—more to the point—against the closure of bases elsewhere in the western Pacific area; but the marginal risk is well worth running for the gain that neutralization offers. Finally, the naval facilities can easily be forgone. The navy has made it clear that it may never pick up the options it has asked for. Moreover, the navy for obvious bureaucratic reasons is taking the line that bases are inherently inessential.

A possible split-off of the Marianas could be seen as simplifying the proposal. That is, if the Marianas become a separate U.S. territory, or are merged with Guam, Tinian would no longer fall under this proposal. This point is elaborated below. The merits of another expensive facility on Tinian notwithstanding, this outcome would make the U.S. sacrifice still easier to bear. The total loss would then be a small naval base that, given the proximity of Guam, is frosting on the cake and a research facility on the way out anyway.

If Neutralization Fails

An attempt to achieve a neutralized South and western Pacific may fail. Thus, it would not seem unreasonable for the United States to arrange with the Micronesians that the door be kept open. One approach would be to set a time limit of, say, four years. If the policy was clearly not working by that time, the United States could go ahead with its original plans.

Other states have something to lose by neutralization of the type suggested here. Australia would lose landing rights in Fiji for its military aircraft. The United States could alleviate the problem by turning over a few in-flight refueling aircraft to the Australian air force. France would lose its capacity to play any military role in the Pacific independent of the United States. For this reason, France will undoubtedly not cooperate in the short run. If public statements are to be given any credence, France still considers Tahiti valuable as an atomic weapons test site.

Ideally, territories would be included in the neutralized area, in order to give the maximum incentive to those powers with no possessions in the Pacific to cooperate. However, this just will not happen—not for some time. Guam is the only secure site for U.S. military installations in the western Pacific; and its economy is heavily dependent on the large facilities there. The United States cannot and should not make any change in its posture on Guam now. For psychological reasons, it might consider offering to forgo the use of American Samoa for military purposes. At present, an occasional navy vessel calls at Pago Pago, and a few air force cargo aircraft land at the civil airfield; no more.

The biggest losers from neutralization in the short term will be the small states, who will be giving up a source of foreign exchange earnings. The United States and as many great powers who go along can deal with this at little cost. Small amounts of economic assistance in the form of direct grants, rather than loans, would be sufficient.

What if the other major powers in the Pacific do not go along? I would argue that the scheme can survive under these conditions if the small states are determined to hold the line. And as long as they have the resources to resist temptation—that is, if they are not desperate—they should be able to do so. Political leaders in some of the states are already quite aware of the risks that getting involved with the great powers entails. Micronesia paid heavily for its Japanese connection during World War II. So did New Guinea and a number of the other islands that were caught in the cross fire. Memories are still sharp.

Conclusion

Neutralization is a modest innovation. It is insurance against future difficulties, not a wrench from present arrangements. The costs are miniscule compared with the costs of the alternatives. The future imbroglio it is intended to avert, however, is not far off. If the approach is to be attempted with any reasonable hope for success, a beginning must be made now.

Neutralization of the Pacific Islands, moreover, would have a global significance. This could be the first in a series of disarmament steps by geographic zones. It could, in short, be a geographic analogue to the incremental approach to weaponry implicit in the SALT agreements.

There is a fine opportunity here. It should not be lost.

1. Rear Admiral Alfred Thayer Mahan, 1840–1914, the preeminent American naval strategist and geopolitical thinker of his time. Mahan shaped thought on the role of seapower throughout the then Western world. His primary works include *The Influence of Sea Power upon History, 1660–1783* and *The Influence of Sea Power upon the French Revolution and Empire, 1793–1812.*

2. *New York Times,* 7 January 1972, p. 1.

3. Figures for Fiji and Kenya are from *Statistical Yearbook, 1969* (New York: United Nations, 1970), p. 564. Figure for Western Samoa is an estimate given the author by officials of Western Samoa in interviews in January 1971.

Notes on the Contributors

Paul A. Dahlquist is assistant professor of anthropology at Ohio Wesleyan University, Delaware.

John L. Fischer is professor and chairman of the Department of Anthropology at Tulane University, New Orleans, a member of the executive board of the American Anthropological Association, and coauthor, with Anne Fischer, of *The Eastern Carolines.*

Daniel T. Hughes is associate professor and director of graduate studies in the Department of Anthropology, Ohio State University, Columbus, and the author of *Political Conflict and Harmony on Ponape.*

Sherwood G. Lingenfelter is assistant professor of anthropology at SUNY-College at Brockport, Brockport, New York, and the author of *Political Leadership and Culture Change in Yap.*

Leonard Mason is professor emeritus, University of Hawaii, Honolulu, and the author of *The Laura Report.*

Robert K. McKnight is professor and chairman of the Department of Anthropology at California State University, Hayward.

Norman Meller is professor of political science and director of the Pacific Islands Studies Program, University of Hawaii, Honolulu, and the author of *The Congress of Micronesia* and, with James Anthony, *Fiji Goes to the Polls.*

Eugene B. Mihaly is director of Mihaly Associates, the consulting firm on international economic and political relations, Berkeley, California, and was formerly associate director of the Institute of International Studies, University of California, Berkeley. He is the author of *Foreign Aid and Politics in Nepal.*

Felix Moos is professor of anthropology and director of the Center for East Asian Studies, University of Kansas, Lawrence.

James D. Nason is assistant professor of anthropology at the University of Washington and chairman of the Anthropology Division and Curator of Ethnology at the T. Burke Memorial Washington State Museum, Seattle.

Michael A. Rynkiewich is assistant professor of anthropology at Macalester College, Saint Paul, Minnesota.

John Singleton is professor of education and anthropology in the International and Development Education Program, University of Pittsburgh, and past president of the Council on Anthropology and Education.

References

General

Adam, Thomas R.

1967 *Western interests in the Pacific realm.* Studies in Political Science, No. PS 61. New York: Random House.

AERA (American Education Research Association)

1968 *International development education.* Special issue of the *Review of Educational Research* prepared by Seth Spaulding and John Singleton.

Apter, D. E., and S. S. Mushi

1970 The role of political science in development. Paper presented to the UNESCO Symposium on the Role of the Social Sciences in Development.

Brookfield, H. C.

1972 *Colonialism, development, and independence: The case of Melanesian islands in the South Pacific.* Cambridge: At the University Press.

Cohen, Ronald, and John Middleton

1970 *From tribe to nation in Africa.* Scranton, Pa.: Chandler Publishing Co.

Coleman, James

1965 Introduction. In *Education and political development,* ed. James Coleman. Princeton, N.J.: Princeton University Press.

Constitutional development in Papua-New Guinea

1971 *Current Notes* 42 (June): 314, 328.

Davidson, J. W.

1967 *Samoa mo Samoa.* Melbourne: Oxford University Press.

Easton, David

1959 Political anthropology. In *Biennial review of anthropology,* ed. B. Siegel. Stanford, Calif.: Stanford University Press. Pp. 210-62.

1957 An approach to the analysis of Political systems. *World Politics* 9:383-400.

1953 *The political system: An inquiry into the state of political science.* New York: Alfred A. Knopf.

Fairbairn, I. J.
1971 Pacific island economies. *Journal of the Polynesian Society* 80 (March): 74-118.

Forsyth, W. D.
1970 France and the S.P.C. *New Guinea* 5 (September-October): 38.

France, Peter
1969 *The charter of the land.* Melbourne: Oxford University Press.

Fried, Morton H.
1967 *The evolution of political society.* New York: Random House.

Gladwin, Thomas
1971a Micronesian Independence: The essential elements, part two. *Met Poraus* (Trukese weekly newspaper) 3:32.
1971b Modernization and Anthropology. *AAA Newsletter* 12 (8): 9-10.

Gluckman, Max
1963 *Politics, law, and ritual in tribal society.* Chicago: Aldine Publishing Co.

Goodenough, Ward Hunt
1963 *Cooperation in change.* New York: Russell Sage Foundation.

Goldman, Irving
1970 *Ancient Polynesian society.* Chicago: University of Chicago Press.

Goody, Jack
1966 *Succession to high office.* Cambridge: At the University Press.

Goulet, Denis
1971 An ethical model for the study of values. *Harvard Education Review* 41:205-27.

Gunther, J. T.
1970 Trouble in Tolailand. *New Guinea* 5 (September-October): 25.

Hastings, Peter
1970 West Irian—Papua-New Guinea. *New Guinea* 5 (June-July): 64.

Hiatt, Robert W., and Donald W. Strasburg
1950 *Marine zoology study of Arno Atoll, Marshall Islands.* Scientific Investigation of Micronesia 4.

Hunt, Robert, and Eva Hunt
1967 Education as an interface institution in rural Mexico and the American inner city. *Midway* 8 (2): 99-109.

Illich, Ivan
1968 The futility of schooling in Latin America. *Saturday Review*, April, pp. 20, 57-59, 74-75.

Kahn, Herman
1970 *The emerging Japanese superstate, challenge and response.* Englewood Cliffs, N.J.: Prentice-Hall.

Keesing, Felix M.
1945 *The South Seas in the modern world.* New York: John Day.

Lambert, Berndt
1966 The economic activities of a Gilbertese chief. In *Political Anthropology*, ed. Swartz, Turner, and Tuden. Chicago: Aldine Publishing Co.

Malinowski, Bronislaw
1945 *Dynamics of culture change.* New Haven, Conn.: Yale University Press.

Mead, Margaret
1946 Problems of education in dependent territories. *Journal of Negro Education* 15:346-57.

Meller, Norman
1961 Political development in American Samoa. In *Study Mission to Eastern (American) Samoa.* Report to the Committee on Interior and Insular Affairs, U.S. Senate, 87th Congress, 1st Session.
1959 Bilingualism in island legislatures of the Pacific as an index of acculturation: A hypothesis. *Sociology and Social Research* 43 (July-August): 408.

Meller, Norman, and James Anthony
1968 *Fiji goes to the polls.* Honolulu: East-West Center Press.

Michael, Franz, and Gaston J. Sigur
1972 *The Asian alliance: Japan and United States policy.* New York: National Strategy Information Center.

Micronesian Star. Newspaper. Saipan, Mariana Islands.

Murdock, George P.
1949 *Social structure.* New York: Macmillan Co.

New Guinea House of Assembly
1968 *Papers of the Papua-New Guinea House of Assembly.* New Guinea Research Bulletin No. 22. Canberra: Australian National University.

Pacific Islands Monthly. Sydney, Australia: Pacific Publications.

Parsons, Roger
1968 Self determination and political development in Niue. *Journal of the Polynesian Society* 77 (September): 252.

Russell, Tom
1970 The 1970 constitution for the British Solomon Islands. In *The Politics of Melanesia,* ed. Marian W. Ward. Canberra: Australian National University.

Sahlins, Marshall D.
1963 Poor man, rich man, big-man, chief: Political types in Melanesia and Polynesia. *Comparative Studies in Society and History* 5:285-303.

Scheffler, H. W.
1966 Ancestor worship in anthropology: Or, observations on descent and descent groups. *Current Anthropology,* 7:541-43.

Schnee, H.
1920 *Deutsches Kolonial-Lexicon.* Vol. 1. Leipzig: Quelle & Meyer.

Sharp, Andrew
1962 *The Discovery of the Pacific Islands.* London: Oxford University Press.

Shikishima Mamokusuke.
1957 *Nichi-Ei Gaikoshi* (A history of diplomatic relations between Japan and England). Tokoyo: Sanshusha.

Staley, Eugene
1961 *The Future of Underdeveloped Countries: Political Implications of Economic Development.* New York: Harper & Bros.

Statistical Yearbook. New York: United Nations.

Steward, Julian
1955 *Theory of culture change.* Urbana: University of Illinois Press.

Swartz, Marc, Victor Turner, and Arthur Tuden (eds.)
1966 *Political anthropology.* Chicago: Aldine Publishing Co.

Thomson, George G.
1970 *Problems of strategy in the Pacific and Indian Oceans.* New York: National Strategy Center.

U.S., Department of the Navy
1905 *Annual report of the Naval Station, Island of Guam.*
1908 *Annual report of the Naval Station, Island of Guam.*

Viviani, Nancy
1970 *Nauru.* Honolulu: University of Hawaii Press.

Westwood, John
1905 *Island Stories.* Shanghai: Printed at the *North-China Herald* office.

Wolfers, Edward P.
1971 Papua New Guinea . . . and self-government. *Current Affairs Bulletin* 48 (October): 131.

Traditional and Changing Political Organization
U.S. Trust Territory of the Pacific Islands

GENERAL

Alkire, William H.
1972 *An introduction to the peoples and cultures of Micronesia.* Addison-Wesley Modular Publications, No. 18, pp. 1-56.

Bliss, Theodora C.
1906 *Micronesay: Fifty years in the island world; a history of the American Board.* Boston: American Board of Commission for Foreign Missions.

Burlin, Paul
1971 Imperialism in Micronesia. *Phoenix,* 17 November 1971, pp. 6-7.

Clements, James W.
1954 A survey of United States administration of the Trust Territory of the Pacific Islands. Paper presented to the faculty of the American University and to Birmingham Southern College.

Clyde, Paul H.
1935 *Japan's Pacific mandate.* New York: Macmillan Co.

Comptroller General of the United States
1956 *Audit report to the Congress of the United States, Trust Territory of the Pacific Islands, Department of the Interior, for the Fiscal Years Ended June 30, 1955 and 1956.*

Congress of Micronesia
1971 *Journal of the House of Representatives of the Congress of Micronesia.* Fourth Congress, First Regular Session (January-February), 19.
1970 *Report of the Political Status Delegation of the Congress of Micronesia.* Saipan.
1969a *The Congress of Micronesia: Background Material.*
1969b *Biographical Sketches.*
1969c *Report of the Committee on the Government Organization*
1969d *Report: The Future Political Status Commission.*
1968a *Interim Report from the Future Political Status Commission, Saipan.*
1968b *Verbatim record of the meeting between the U.S. Senate Subcommittee on Interior and Insular Affairs and the Future Political Status Commission, Congress of Micronesia.*

Congress of Micronesia (Office of Legislative Counsel)
1968 *The Congress of Micronesia after 1969: Arguments for and against unicameralism and bicameralism.*

DeSmith, Stanley A.
1970 *Microstates and Micronesia.* New York: New York University Press.

Domoto, Teiichi.
1940 *Minzoku Nanshin No Tame Ni* (For our nation's advance to the south). Nanyō Bunka Kenkyukai (Association for the Study of South Sea Islands Culture), Tokyo.

Embree, John F.
1946 Micronesia: The navy and democracy. *Far Eastern Survey* 15 (June): 164.

Friends of Micronesia Newsletter
n.d. Published quarterly. 2325 McKinley Avenue, Berkeley, Calif. 97403.

Force, R. W., and M. Force
1965 Political change in Micronesia. In *Induced political change in the Pacific,* ed. R. W. Force. Honolulu: Bishop Museum Press.

Force, Roland W. (ed.)
1965 *Induced political change in the Pacific.* Honolulu: Bishop Museum Press.

Gilchrist, Huntington
1944 *Dependent peoples and mandates.* (Reprinted from *Pioneers in world order: An American appraisal of the League of Nations.*) New York: Columbia University Press.

HAE (Hawaii Architects and Engineers, Inc.)
1967 *Goals and objectives: Trust Territory of the Pacific Islands Physical Planning Program.* Honolulu.

Hardy, Osgood, and Glen S. Dumke
1934 *A history of the Pacific area in modern times.* Cambridge, Mass.: Houghton Mifflin.

Heine, Carl
1970 Micronesia: Unification and the coming of self-government. In *The politics of Melanesia,* ed. Marian W. Ward. Canberra: Australian National University.
1967 *Constitutional development of Micronesia since 1500 A.D.* Report to the Congress of Micronesia.
1965 *A historical study of political development and the prospect for self-government in the United States Pacific Trust Territories.* Reproduced for the Library of the Congress of Micronesia.

Hezel, Francis X., S.J.
1970 *Spanish Capuchins in the Caroline Islands.* Micronesia Seminar Bulletin. Truk, Caroline Islands.

Highlights
n.d. Published semimonthly. Public Information Office, Trust Territory of the Pacific Islands, Saipan, Mariana Islands.

Irie, Toraji
1943 *Hojin Kaigai Hatten Shi* (A history of the development of the Japanese Overseas). 2 vols. Tokyo: Ida Shoten.

James, Roy E.
1949 The Trust Territory of the Pacific Islands. In Rupert Emerson et

al., *America's Pacific dependencies.* New York: American Institute of Pacific Relations.

Japanese Government, Takushokukyoku (Colonial Bureau)
1922 *Nanyō Guntō Jijō Gaiyō* (A summary of conditions in the South Sea Islands). Tokyo.

Kanost, R. F.
1970 Localization in the Trust Territory of the Pacific Islands. In *The politics of Melanesia,* ed. Marian W. Ward. Canberra: Australian National University.

McKnight, R. K.
1971 Past and future culture change: A quest for variant explanations. In *Human futuristics,* ed. M. Maruyama and J. A. Dator. Honolulu: University of Hawaii Press.

McQuarrie, Alan M.
1969 The effects of political modernization in Micronesia: The job of nation-building. Paper presented to the South Pacific Symposium, University of California at Santa Cruz, March.

Marianas Variety News and Views
n.d. Published weekly. P.O. Box 231, Saipan, Mariana Islands.

Mason, Leonard
1971 *The many faces of Micronesia.* Mimeo. In press.
1968 The ethnology of Micronesia, In *Peoples and cultures of the Pacific,* ed. A. P. Vayda. New York: Natural History Press. Pp. 275-98.
1959 Suprafamilial authority and economic process in Micronesian atolls. In *Humanités: Cahiers de l'Institut de Science Economique Appliquée,* 5:87-118. (Reprinted in *Peoples and cultures of the Pacific,* ed. A. P. Vayda. New York: Doubleday, Natural History Press. Pp. 200-329.)
1948 Micronesia: Isolation or assimilation? In *Hawaii IPR Notes,* 3:1-7.

Mason, Leonard, with T. W. Taylor et al.
1951 *Management survey of the government of the Trust Territory.* Washington: U.S. Depart. of the Interior, Office of Territories, 161 pp.

Matsue, Shunji
1932 *Nanyo Kaitaku Ju Nen Shi* (A record of ten years of developing the South Seas). Tokyo: South Seas Development Company.

Matsumura, Akira
1918 Contributions to the ethnography of Micronesia. Tokyo: Imperial University College of Science Journal, 40, art. 7:1-174.

Maurier, Michael David
1968 *Maurier Report on political education in Micronesia.* Report to the Congress of Micronesia.

McDonald, Hugh
1949 *Trusteeship in the Pacific.* Sydney: Angus & Robertson.

Melniker, Harvey David
1968 Questionnaire concerning the future political status of the Trust Territory of the Pacific Islands. Seminar, Trust Territory of the Pacific Islands, Department of Political Science, Tufts University, Medford, Mass. June.

Meller, Norman
1972 The Congress of Micronesia: A unifying and modernizing force. *Micronesica* 8 (December): 1-2.
1970 Indigenous leadership in the Trust Territory of the Pacific Islands.

In *Development administration in Asia,* ed. Edward W. Weldner. Durham, N.C.: Duke University Press.

1969 *The Congress of Micronesia: Development of the legislative process in the Trust Territory of the Pacific Islands.* Honolulu: University of Hawaii Press.

1967a Representational role types: A research note. *American Political Science Review* 61 (June): 474

1967b Districting a new legislature in Micronesia. *Asian Survey* 7, No. 7, Political Science and Public Administration Series, No. 5.

1966 The identification and classification of legislatures. *Philippine Journal of Public Administration* 10 (October).

MH (Missionary Herald)

1908 Vol. 104 (June)
1904 Vol. 100 (June)
1879 Vol. 75 (June)
1877 Vol. 73 (April)
1876 Vol. 72 (July)
Boston: American Board of Commissioners for Foreign Missions.

Micronesian Reporter

n.d. Published quarterly. Public Information Office, Trust Territory of the Pacific Islands, Saipan, Mariana Islands.

Micronesian Seminar

1973 Seminar on moral issues related to choice of political status. Held in Kolonia, Ponape, June 3-9, under auspices of the Catholic Mission. Truk, Caroline Islands 96942.

Micronesian News Service

n.d. Press wire service. Public Information Division, Department of Public Affairs, Trust Territory of the Pacific Islands, Saipan, Mariana Islands.

The Micronitor

n.d. Published weekly. Majuro, Marshall Islands: Micronitor News and Printing Co.

Milner, George

1965 Political process in Micronesia. Ph.D. thesis, Princeton University.

Mink, Patsy T.

1971 Micronesia: Our Bungled Trust. *Texas International Law Forum* 6 (Winter): 181-207.

Murdock, G. P.

1949 *Social organization and government in Micronesia.* CIMA Final Report, No. 19. Washington: Office of Naval Research.

Nanyō Boeki Kaisha (South Seas Trading Company)

1942 *Nanyō Boeki Go Ju Nen Shi* (A history of fifty years of commerce in the South Seas). Tokyo.

Nanyō Guntō Kyōiku Kai (South Seas Education Association)

1938 *Nanyō Guntō Kyoikū Shi Kyoklu Shi* (A history of education in the South Seas). Tokyo: South Seas Education Association.

Nanyō Kyokai (South Seas Association)

1935 *Nihon no Nanyō Guntō* (Japan's South Sea islands). Tokyo: South Seas Association.

Nanyō Kenkyū Kai (Association for the Study of South Sea Islands)

1934 *Shin Nantō Daikan* (General survey of new southern islands). Tokyo.

Nanyō chō (South Seas Bureau)
1927 *Nanyō Guntō Chosa Shiryō* (South Sea islands research report). Tokyo.

Nathan Associates
1966 *Economic development plan for Micronesia.* Washington: Robert R. Nathan Associates.

O'Connor, Edward C.
1970 Micronesia: America's frontier in the Far East. *National War College Forum* (Spring), p. 57.

Pompey, Sherman Lee
1968 *Micronesia.* Report to the Congress of Micronesia.

Pearse, Richard, and Keith A. Bezanson
1970 *Education and modernization in Micronesia: A case study in development and development planning.* Stanford, Calif.: Stanford International Development Education Center.

Platt, William J., and Philip H. Sorensen
1967 *Planning for education and manpower in Micronesia.* Menlo Park, Calif.: Stanford Research Institute.

President's Personal Representative for Micronesian Status Negotiations
1971 *The future political status of the Trust Territory of the Pacific Islands. Status talks held at Hana, Maui Island, Hawaii, October 4-12, 1971.* Pp. 25-26.

Purcell, David C.
1967 *Japanese expansion in the South Pacific, 1880-1935.* Ann Arbor, Mich.: University Microfilms.

Richard, Dorothy E.
1957 *United States naval administration of the Trust Territory of the Pacific Islands.* 3 vols. Washington, D.C.: Office of Chief of Naval Operations.

Robbins, Robert R.
1969 Political future of Micronesia and the timing of self-determination. Paper presented to a seminar at the University of Santa Cruz, Calif., March 26.

Sandelman, John
1953 *Some observations on the problems of "self-government" in the Trust Territory of the Pacific Islands.* Honolulu:

Skinner, Carlton
1963 Self-government in the South Pacific. Xerox extract from *Foreign Affairs* 42 (October).

Stackpole, Edouard A.
1953 The sea hunters. New York: J. B. Lippincott Co.

Strong, W. E.
1910 *The story of the American Board.* Boston: Pilgrim Press.

T. T. Public Information Office
1969 *Briefing materials.* Saipan: Trust Territory of the Pacific Islands.

T. T. Political Affairs Office
1968 *Significant events in the development of government in the Trust Territory of the Pacific Islands.* Saipan.

Townsend, Mary E.
1930 *The rise and fall of Germany's colonial empire, 1884-1918.* New York: Macmillan Co.

Uludong, Francisco T.
1969 Whither Micronesia? Paper presented to Symposium on Political Modernization of Micronesia, University of California, Santa Cruz, March.

UNITAR
1971 Small states and territories: status and problems. New York: Arno Press.

United Nations Trusteeship Council
1973 Report of the United Nations Visiting Mission to the Trust Territory of the Pacific Islands, 1973. T/1741 English. 16 May. Mimeo.

U.S. Department of Commerce
1969 Local climatological data. Asheville, N.C.

U.S. Department of the Navy, Office of the Chief of Naval Operations
1944a *Civil affairs handbook, west Caroline Islands.*
1944b *Civil affairs handbook, Marshall Islands.*
1944c *Civil affairs handbook, mandated Marianas.*
1944d *Civil affairs handbook, east Caroline Islands.*
Washington: Office of Chief of Naval Operations.

U.S. Department of State
1973 *25th annual report to the United Nations on the administration of the Trust Territory of the Pacific Islands, July 1, 1971, to June 30, 1972.* Washington, D.C. Government Printing Office.
1972 *24th annual report to the United Nations on the administration of the Trust Territory of the Pacific Islands, July 1, 1970, to June 30, 1971.* Washington, D.C.: Government Printing Office.

U.S. Government Survey Mission
1963 *Report by the U.S. Government Survey Mission to the Trust Territory of the Pacific Islands.* (Solomon Mission Report, Vol. 2.)

U.S. Office of Micronesian Status Negotiations
1972 *The future political status of the Trust Territory of the Pacific Islands: Official records on the fourth round of Micronesian future political status talks, Koror, Palau, April 2-13.* Washington, D.C.:

Vidich, Arthur J.
1952 The political impact of colonial administration. Ph.D. thesis, Harvard University.

Weins, Herold J.
1962 Atoll environment and ecology. New Haven, Conn.: Yale University Press.

[Williams, Franklin Haydn]
1971 *Future political status, Trust Territory of the Pacific Islands: Report by the president's personal representative for Micronesian status negotiations on the Hana, Maui, Hawaii talks, October 4-12, 1971.* Washington, D.C.:

Yamazaki, Tadao
1916 *Waga Nanyō* (Our South Seas). Tokyo: Kobundo.

Yanaihara, Tadao
1939 *Japanese islands under Pacific mandate.* Shanghai: Kelly & Walsh.
1935 *Nanyō Guntō no Kenkyū* (A study of the South Seas islands). Tokyo: Iwanami Shoten.

Yoshino, Sakuzo
1915 *Nanyō* (The South Seas). Tokyo: Minyusha.

MARSHALLS DISTRICT

de Brum, Oscar, and Henry Rutz
1967 Political succession and intra-group organizations in Laura Village. In *The Laura Report*, ed. Leonard Mason. Honolulu: University of Hawaii Press.

Finsch, Otto
1962 *Bilder aus dem Stillen Ozean: 1. Kriegsführung auf den Marshall-Inseln* (Sketches from the Pacific Ocean: 1. Warfare on the Marshall Islands). *Gartenlaube* 29 (1881): 700-703.

Kiste, Robert C.
1968 *Kili Islands: A study of the relocation of the ex-Bikini Marshallese.* Eugene, Ore.: Department of Anthropology, University of Oregon.

Kiste, Robert C., and Michael A. Rynkiewich
n.d. Incest and exogamy: A comparative study of two Marshall Islands populations. In *Incest prohibitions in eastern Oceania*, ed. Vern Carroll. Honolulu: University Press of Hawaii.

Kramer, Augustin, and Hans Nevermann
1938 *Ralik-Ratak (Marshall-Inseln): Ergebnisse der Sudsee-Expedition, 1903-1910* (Ralik-Ratak [Marshall Islands]: Results of the South Sea expedition, 1903-1910), ed. G. Thilenius. Hamburg: Friederischsen, de Gruyter & Co.

Mason, Leonard (ed.)
1967 *The Laura Report: A field report of training and research in Majuro Atoll, Marshall Islands.* (Papers by P. Kabua and N. Pollock, C. Cominick and M. Seelye, O. de Brum and H. Rutz, and C. Milne and M. Steward.) Honolulu: Department of Anthropology, University of Hawaii.

Mason, Leonard
1958 Kili Community in transition, In *South Pacific Commission Quarterly Bulletin* 18:32-35+.
1957 Ecologic change and culture pattern in the resettlement of Bikini Marshallese. In *Cultural stability and cultural change*, ed. V. F. Ray. American Ethnological Society Proceedings, pp. 1-6.
1955 The characterization of American culture in studies of acculturation. *American Anthropologist* 57:1264-79. (Portion reprinted in *Intellectual foundations of American education: Readings and commentary*, ed. Harold J. Carter. New York: Pitman Publishing. Pp. 333-40).
1954 Relocation of the Bikini Marshallese: A study in group migration. Ph.D. diss., Yale University.
1950 The Bikinians: A transplanted population. *Human Organization* 9:5–15.
1950 *Anthropology-geography study of Arno Atoll, Marshall Islands.* Scientific Investigations of Micronesia, No. 7, Pacific Science Board. 20 pp.
1947 The economic organization of the Marshall Islanders. In U. S. Commercial Co., *An economic survey of Micronesia.* Mimeo. U.S. Novy.
1946 *Economic and human resources, Marshall Islands.* Vol. 8, U.S. Commercial Co., *An Economic survey of Micronesia.*

Rynkiewich, Michael A.
1972 Land tenure among Arno Marshallese. Ph.D. diss., University of Minnesota.

Senfit, Arno
1962 Die Marshall-Insulaner (The Marshall Islanders). In *Rechtsverhält-*

nisse von eingeborenen Völkern in Afrika und Ozeanien, ed. S. R. Steinmetz. Berlin: Julius Springer, 1903: 425-55.

Silk, Ekpap, Henry Moses, and William Allen (Marshall Islands Political Development Team):

1961 Political development for municipal councils, Marshall Islands District.

Spoehr, Alexander

1949 *Majuro: A village in the Marshall Islands.* Chicago: Field Museum of Natural History.

Tobin, Jack A.

1967 *The resettlement of the Enewetak people: A study of a displaced community in the Marshall Islands.* Ann Arbor, Mich.: University Microfilms.

1958 Land tenure in the Marshall Islands. In *Land tenure patterns, Trust Territory of the Pacific Islands,* ed. John E. de Young. Guam: Office of the High Commissioner, Trust Territory of the Pacific Islands.

1954 *Ebeye Village: An atypical Marshallese community.* Majuro: Mimeo.

1953 An investigation of the socio-political schism on Majuro Atoll. Majuro: Mimeo.

PONAPE DISTRICT

Bascom, William R.

1965 *Ponape: A Pacific economy in transition.* Berkeley: University of California Anthropological Records 22.

1950a Ponape: The tradition of retaliation. *Far Eastern Quarterly* 10:56-62.

1950b Ponape: The cycle of empire. *Scientific Monthly* 70:141-50.

1949 Subsistence farming on Ponape. *New Zealand Geographer* 5:115-29.

1948 Ponapean prestige economy. *Southwestern Journal of Anthropology* 4:211-21.

Brandt, John H.

1962 Nan Matol: Ancient Venice of Micronesia. *Archaeology* 15 (2): 99-107.

Dahlquist, Paul A.

1972 *Khodo Mwenge: The food complex in a changing Ponapean community.* Ann Arbor, Mich.: University Microfilms.

Emerick, Richard

1960 *Homesteading on Ponape.* Ann Arbor, Mich.: University Microfilms.

Fischer, J. L.

1966a A Ponapean Oedipus tale: Stuctural and socio-psychological analysis. *Journal of American Folklore* 79:109-29.

1966b Respect language and social structure: A comparison of Japanese and Ponapean. Abstracts of Papers Related with Social Sciences and Anthropology, Proc. Vol. 9, *Linguistics.* 11th Pac. Sci. Congr., Tokyo.

1964 The abandonment of Nan Matol, ancient capital of Ponape. *Micronesica* 1:49-54.

1957 Totemism on Truk and Ponape. *American Anthropologist* 59:250-65.

1956 The position of men and women in Truk and Ponape: A comparative analysis of kinship terminology and folktales. *Journal of American Folklore* 69:55-62.

1955 Avunculocal residence on Losap. *American Anthropologist* 57:1025-32.

Fischer, John L., and Anne Fischer

1957 *The Eastern Carolines.* New Haven, Conn.: HRAF.

Garvin, Paul A., and Saul H. Riesenberg
1952 Respect behavior on Ponape: An ethnolinguistic study. *American Anthropologist* 54:201-20.

Hambruch, Paul
1932-36 *Ponape. Ergebnisse de Sudsee-Expedition 1908-1910*, ed. G. Thilenius. 3 vols. Hamburg: Friederichsen & Co.

Hughes, Daniel T.
1973 Democracy in the Philippines and on Ponape: a comparison of two political systems structured on the U.S. model. *Micronesica* 9:1-10.

1972 Integration of the role of territorial congressman into Ponapean society. *Oceania* 53:140-52.

1970 *Political conflict and harmony on Ponape*. New Haven, Conn.: HRAF.

1969a Conflict and harmony: Roles of councilman and section chief on Ponape. *Oceania* 50:32-41.

1969b Reciprocal influence of traditional and democratic leadership roles on Ponape. *Ethnology* 8:278-91.

1969c Democracy in a traditional society: Two hypotheses on role. *American Anthropologist* 71:36-45.

Lewis, J. L.
1967 *Kusaiean acculturation 1824-1948, Kusaie Island, E. Caroline Islands, Micronesia*. Saipan: Reprinted for Division of Land Management.

Leiber, Michael D.
1967 *Porakiet: A Kapingamarangi colony on Ponape*. Eugene, Ore.: Department of Anthropology, University of Oregon.

Riesenberg, Saul H.
1968 *The native polity of Ponape*. Washington, D.C.: Smithsonian Contributions to Anthropology, No. 10.

1966 The Ngatik Massacre. *Micronesian Reporter* 14 (5): 9-12, 29-30.

1952 Ponapean Omens. *Journal of American Folklore* 65:351-52.

1948 Magic and medicine in Ponape. *Southwestern Journal of Anthropology* 4:406:29.

Riesenberg, Saul H., and J. L. Fischer
1955 Some Ponapean proverbs. *Journal of American Folklore* 68:9-18.

Sugiura, Kenichi
1940 Respect words on Ponape. *Journal of the Anthropoligical Society of Tokyo* 55:479-88.

Wilson, Walter Scott
1968 *Land, activity and social organization of Lelu, Kusaie*. Ann Arbor, Mich.: University Microfilms.

TRUK DISTRICT

Caughey, John
1970 *Cultural values in a Micronesian society*. Ann Arbor, Mich.: University Microfilms.

Clifton, James A.
1964 The acceptance of external political controls on Truk & Ponape. *International Journal of Comparative Sociology* 5 (1): 91-103.

Fischer, John
1961 The Japanese schools for the natives of Truk, Caroline Islands. *Human Organization* 20:83-88.

Gladwin, Thomas
1960 Petrus Mailo, chief of Moen (Truk). In *In the company of man*, ed. J. B. Casagrande. New York: Harper and Row.
1958 Canoe travel in the Truk area: Technology and its psychological correlations. *American Anthropologist* 60:893-99.
1956 Anthropology and administration in the Trust Territory of the Pacific Islands. In *Some uses of anthropology: Theoretical and applied.* Washington, D.C.: Anthropoligical Society of Washington.
1970 *East is a big bird: Navigation and logic on Puluwat Atoll.* Cambridge, Mass.: Harvard University Press.

Gladwin, Thomas, and Seymour B. Sarason
1954 *Truk: Man in paradise.* New York: Wenner-Gren Foundation for Anthropological Research

Goodenough, Ward H.
1951 *Property, kin and community on Truk.* Foreword by G. P. Murdock. New Haven, Conn.: Yale University Press.

Hall, Edward T., and Karl J. Pelzer
1946 *The economy of the Truk Islands: An anthropological and economic survey.* Honolulu: U.S. Commercial Company, Economic Survey.

Kramer, Augustin
1932 Truk. Hamburg: Friederichsen, de Gruyter.

Kubary, Jan S.
1880 *Die Bewohner der Mortlock-Inseln.* Mitteilungen der Geographischen Gesellschaft in Hamburg (1878-79).

Mahony, Frank J.
1960 The innovation of a savings system in Truk. *American Anthropologist* 62:465-82.

Murdock, G. P., and Ward Goodenough
1947 Social organization of Truk. *Southwestern Journal of Anthropology* 3:331-43.

Nagao, Clarence M., and Masao Nakayama
1969 A study of school-community relations in Truk. In *The Truk report*, ed. Stephen Boggs. Honolulu: Department of Anthropology, University of Hawaii.

Pramuanradhakarn, Thiravetya
1969 Current influence of traditional leaders and their attitudes and expectations toward modern leaders on Truk. In *The Truk report*, ed. Stephen Boggs. Honolulu: Department of Anthropology, University of Hawaii.

Raken, Yokitaro, and Robert Edmondson
1969 Representative democracy in Truk District: The development and operation of a new political form. In *The Truk report*, ed. Stephen Boggs. Honolulu: Department of Anthropology, University of Hawaii.

Swartz, Marc J.
1965 Political acquiesence in Truk In *Induced political change in the Pacific*, ed. R. Force. Honolulu: Bishop Museum pp. 17-39.
1962 Recruiting labor for fissionary descent lines on Romonom, Truk. *Southwestern Journal of Anthropology* 18:351-64.
1961 Negative ethnocentrism. *Journal of Conflict Resolution* 5 (1):75-81.
1960 Situational determinants of kinship terminology. *Southwestern Journal of Anthropology* 16:393-97.

1959 Leadership and status conflict on Romonom, Truk. *Southwestern Journal of Anthropology* 15:213-18.

1958 Sexuality and aggression on Romonom, Truk. *American Anthropologist* 60:467-86.

Tolerton, Burt, and Jerome Rauch

n.d. *Social organization, land tenure, and subsistence economy of Kukunor, Nomoi Islands.* Coordinated Investigations of Micronesian Anthropology, report 26. Washington, D.C.: Pacific Science Board.

MARIANAS DISTRICT

Carano, Paul, and Pedro C. Sanchez

1964 A complete history of Guam. Tokyo: Charles E. Tuttle Co.

Emerick, R. G.

1958 Land tenure in the Marianas. In *Land tenure patterns, Trust Territory of the Pacific Islands,* ed. John de Young. Guam: Trust Territory Government. Pp. 217-50.

Joseph, Alice, and Veronica Murray

1951 *Chamorros and Carolineans of Saipan.* Cambridge, Mass.: Harvard University Press.

Smith, J. Jerome

1973 Land tenure on Rota: Yesterday, today, and tomorrow. *Association for Anthropology in Micronesia Newsletter* 2(2):9-12.

Solenberger, R. R.

1967 The changing role of rice in the Marianas Is. *Micronesica* 3 (2): 97-103.

1964 Continuity of local political institutions in the Marianas. *Human Organization* 23 (1): 53-60.

1962 The social meaning of language choice in the Marianas. *Anthropological Linguistics* 4 (1962): 59-64.

Spoehr, A.

1957 *Marianas prehistory: Archaeological survey and excavations on Saipan, Tinian and Rota.* Fieldiana: Anthrop. 48. Chicago: Chicago Natural History Museum.

1954 *Saipan, the ethnology of a war-devastated island.* Fieldiana: Anthrop. 41. Chicago: Chicago Natural History Museum.

1951 The Tinian Chamorros. *Human Organization* 10(4): 16-20.

Thompson, Laura

1947 *Guam and its people.* 3d ed. Princeton, N.J.: Princeton University Press.

1945 *The native culture of the Mariana Islands.* Bulletin No. 185. Honolulu: Bishop Museum.

YAP DISTRICT: YAP ISLANDS

de Beauclair, Inez

1967 On religion and mythology of Yap Island, Micronesia. *Bulletin of the Institute of Ethnology,* Academia Sinica no. 23, pp. 23-36.

Defingin, Francis

1966 The nature and scope of customary land rights of the Yapese community. Land Management Conference, Saipan. Mimeo.

Hunt, Edward E. Jr., et al.

1949 *The Micronesians of Yap and their depopulation. Report of the Peabody Museum Expedition to Yap Island, Micronesia 1947-1948.* Coordinated Investigation of Micronesian Anthropology, 1947-1949, No. 24. Washington: Pacific Science Board, National Research Council.

Labby, David
1972 *The anthropology of others: An analysis of the traditional ideology of Yap, Western Caroline Islands.* Ann Arbor, Mich.: University Microfilms.

Lingenfelter, Sherwood G.
1971 *Political leadership and culture change in Yap.* Ann Arbor, Mich.: University Microfilms (forthcoming, University Press of Hawaii).

Mahoney, Francis
1958 Land tenure patterns on Yap. In *Land tenure patterns in the Trust Territory of the Pacific Islands,* ed. J. E. de Young. Saipan. pp. 251-87.

Muller, W.
1918 *Yap. Ergebnisse der Sudsee-expedition, 1908-1910,* ed. G. Thilenius, 3 vols. Hamburg: Friederichsen & Co.

Schneider, David M.
1967 Depopulation and the Yap Tabinau. Mimeo.
1962 Double descent on Yap. *Journal of the Polynesian Society* 71:1-22.
1957 Typhoons on Yap. *Human Organization* 16:10-15.
1957 Political organization, supernatural sanctions and the punishment of incest on Yap. *American Anthropologist* 59:791-800.
1953 Yap kinship terminology and kin groups. *American Anthropologist* 55:215-36.
1949 The kinship system and village organization of Yap, West Caroline Islands, Micronesia: A structural and functional account. Ph.D. thesis, Harvard University.

Tetens, Alfred, and Johann Kubary
1873 Die Carolineninsel Yap oder Guap nach den Mitteilungen von Alf. *Journal des Museum Goddeffroy.* f. 84-130. Hamburg.

Yap District, Office of Political Affairs
1952-68 Political and social development file
1951-68 Public affairs file
1945-47 Yap district chief's file.

Yap Islands Legislature
1968 Minutes, Municipal Government Study Commission. Municipal Government Study Commission File.
1967-68 Laws and Resolutions. Sessions 17, 18, 19

YAP DISTRICT: CENTRAL CAROLINIAN ATOLLS

Alkire, William H.
1965 *Lamotrek Atoll and interisland socioeconomic ties.* Urbana: University of Illinois Press.

Burrows, E. G.
1963 *Flower in my ear.* Seattle: University of Washington Press.

Burrows, E. G., and M. E. Spiro
1953 *An atoll culture: Ethnography of Ifaluk in the Central Carolines.* New Haven, Conn.: HRAF.

Lessa, William A.
1966 *Ulithi: a Micronesian design for living.* New York: Holt, Rinehart & Winston.

1950 Ulithi and the outer native world. *American Anthropologist* 52:27-52.

1950 The place of Ulithi in the Yap empire. *Human Organization* 9:16-18.

PALAU DISTRICT

Barnett, H. G.

1960 *Being a Palauan.* New York: Henry Holt.

1956 *Anthropology in administration.* New York: Row, Peterson.

1949 *Palauan society: A study of contemporary native life in the Palau Islands.* Eugene: University of Oregon Press.

Force, Roland W., and Maryanne Force

1972 *Just one house: A description and analysis of kinship in the Palau Islands.* Honolulu: Bishop Museum, Bulletin No. 235.

Force, Roland W.

1960 *Leadership and cultural change in Palau.* Fieldiana: Anthrop. 50. Chicago Museum of Natural History.

Kaneshiro, Shigeru

1958 Land tenure in the Palau Islands. In *Land tenure patterns, Trust Territory of the Pacific Islands,* ed. John de Young. Guam: Trust Territory Government. Pp. 289-336.

McKnight, R. K.

1969 *Orachl's drawings, Palauan rock paintings.* Micronesian Research Working Papers, No. 1. Saipan: Literature Production Center.

1968a Proverbs of Palau. *Journal of American Folklore* 81, No. 319: 3-33.

1968b Palauan culture heroes as agents of change. Paper presented at the Oceania Symposium, Southwestern Anthropological Association Annual Meeting, San Diego, April 12. Mimeo.

1962 *The mouth that explains: Mesaod Ngerel, an allegory in Palauan lore.* Special Edition for the United Nations. Koror, WCI: Palau Museum Publication No. 2.

1961 *Mnemonics in pre-literate Palau.* Anthropological Working Papers, Office of the Staff Anthropologist, TTPI. Guam, M.I. August.

1960 *Competition in Palau.* Ann Arbor, Mich.: University Microfilms.

Ritzenthaler, R. E.

1954 *Native money of Palau.* Publ. in Anthrop. No. 1. Milwaukee: Milwaukee Public Museum.

Useem, John

1955 Palau. In *Culture patterns and technical change,* ed. M. Mead. New York: New American Library.

1952a South Sea island strike: Labor management relations in the Caroline Islands, Micronesia. In *Human problems in technological change,* ed. Edward H. Spiro. New York: John Wiley & Sons. Pp. 149-64 (1967 ed.).

1952b Democracy in process: The development of democratic leadership in the Micronesian Islands. In *Human problems in technological change,* ed. Edward H. Spiro. New York: John Wiley & Sons, Pp. 261-80 (1967 ed.).

1950 Structure of power in Palau. *Social Forces* 29:141-48.

1949 *Report on Palau.* Coordinated Investigation of Micronesian Anthropology, No. 21. Washington, D.C.: Pacific Science Board.

1945 Changing structure of a Micronesian society. *American Anthropologist* 47:567-88.

Vidich, Arthur J.

1949 Political factionalism in Palau. Coordinated Investigation of Micronesian Anthropology, No. 23. Washington, D.C.: Pacific Science Board.

Index

Index

Index